'Ioris' theoretically and empirically informed analysis of neoliberal agri-food in Brazil highlights the power, folly and injustice of contemporary capitalism. The book presents the socio-ecological implications – both local and global – of bringing central Amazonia into the core of the global economy with disturbing clarity and urgency.'

– *Steven Wolf, Professor of Environmental Social Science,*
Cornell University, USA

'Back from a reporting trip in the Brazilian Amazon, where agribusiness is expanding at a savage pace, I was delighted to discover this book. Ioris is one of the few voices to be analysing from a radical perspective the horrendous social and environmental costs of the commodification of our food.'

– *Sue Branford, former Latin America analyst at*
the BBC World Service, UK

'This is a book of immense importance to anyone seeking to understand the influence, the rationale and the limitations of agribusiness in the word today. It is a powerful and insightful text that should be read by anyone interested in the neoliberal turn of the agri-food systems and the related agrarian, environmental and socio-ecological problems which particularly characterise the new agricultural frontiers of Brazil.'

– *Bernardo M. Fernandes, chairholder of the UNESCO Chair*
in Territorial Development and Education for the Countryside and
geography professor at São Paulo State University (UNESP), Brazil

T0372535

Agribusiness and the Neoliberal Food System in Brazil

Due to new production areas and persistent productivity gains, Brazil has consolidated its position as a global leader and even as a 'model' of commercial, integrated crop production. The country is now seen as an agricultural powerhouse that has a lot to offer in terms of reducing the prospect of a looming, increasingly global, food crisis.

Agribusiness and the Neoliberal Food System in Brazil focuses on the intensification of Brazilian agribusiness as a privileged entry point into the politicised geography of globalised agri-food. Drawing on rich empirical analysis based around three fieldwork campaigns in the state of Mato Grosso, the book examines the connections between farming, markets and the apparatus of the state. The importance of agribusiness expansion within the wider politico-economic context of Brazilian neoliberalism is demonstrated, thus drawing broader conclusions about the main trends of agribusiness in the world today and providing recommendations for future research.

This book will be of great interest to students and scholars of agribusiness, neoliberalism and global food production, as well as those interested in Brazil and Latin America more generally.

Antonio Augusto Rossotto Ioris is a Senior Lecturer at the School of Geography and Planning at Cardiff University, UK.

Other books in the Earthscan Food and Agriculture Series

For further details please visit the series page on the Routledge website:
www.routledge.com/books/series/ECEFA/

Agribusiness and the Neoliberal Food System in Brazil

Frontiers and Fissures of Agro-neoliberalism

Antonio Augusto Rossotto Ioris

Routledge
Taylor & Francis Group

LONDON AND NEW YORK

from Routledge

First published 2018
by Routledge

2 Park Square, Milton Park, Abingdon, Oxfordshire OX14 4RN
52 Vanderbilt Avenue, New York, NY 10017

Routledge is an imprint of the Taylor & Francis Group, an informa business

First issued in paperback 2019

British Library Cataloguing-in-Publication Data
A catalogue record for this book is available from the British Library

Library of Congress Cataloging-in-Publication Data
Names: Ioris, Antonio Augusto Rossotto, author.
Title: Agribusiness and the neoliberal food system in Brazil: frontiers and
fissures of agro-neoliberalism / Antonio A.R. Ioris.
Description: Abingdon, Oxon; New York, NY: Routledge, 2017. |
Series: Earthscan food and agriculture
Identifiers: LCCN 2017010974 | ISBN 9781138744660 (hbk) |
ISBN 9781315180878 (ebook)
Subjects: LCSH: Agriculture--Economic aspects--Research--Brazil. |
Agricultural industries--Brazil. | Food industry and trade. |
Neoliberalism.
Classification: LCC HD1410.6. B6 I57 2017 | DDC 338.10981—dc23
LC record available at https://lccn.loc.gov/2017010974

ISBN: 978-1-138-74466-0 (hbk)
ISBN: 978-0-367-24876-5 (pbk)

Typeset in Goudy
by Florence Production Ltd, Stoodleigh, Devon, UK.

To my father and my mother, Ernani and Nádia, who in the 1970s also took part, with many other relatives, in the dream of the new agricultural frontier.

My most profound admiration and respect for the inspirational work, the wisdom and the poetry of Pedro Casaldáliga, Emeritus Bishop of São Félix do Araguaia, Mato Grosso.

Dedicated to the memory of the individuals, indigenous tribes, squatters and subsistence farmers, as well as their ecosystems and cultural landscapes, who perished or will still suffer under the power and arrogance of agribusiness in the Amazon and in the Centre-West of Brazil.

Contents

Figures

Tables

Abbreviations

ABAG	Brazilian Agribusiness Association
Aprosoja-MT	Mato Grosso's Association of Soybean and Maize Producers
BM&F Bovespa	São Paulo Stock Exchange
BNDES	National Bank for Economic and Social Development
CAP	Common Agricultural Policy
CEPEA	Centre for Advanced Studies on Applied Economics (São Paulo University)
CNA	National Confederation of Agriculture and Livestock
CONAB	National Food Supply Company
CPT	Pastoral Land Commission
CRA	Agribusiness Receivables Certificate
CTG	Gaúcho Tradition Centre
Embrapa	Brazilian Agricultural Research Corporation
FAMATO	Mato Grosso Agricultural and Livestock Federation
FAO	Food and Agriculture Organisation of the United Nations
FIESP	Federation of Industries of the State of São Paulo
FPA	*Frente Parlamentar da Agropecuária* – Parliamentary Farming and Cattle Raising Front
GDP	Gross domestic product
GMO	genetically modified organism
IBGE	Brazilian Institute of Geography and Statistics
IFAD	International Fund for Agricultural Development
IMEA	Mato Grosso Institute of Agribusiness Economy
INCRA	National Institute of Colonisation and Agrarian Reform
MAPA	Brazilian Ministry of Agriculture
MDA	Ministry of Agrarian Development
MDIC	Ministry of Development, Industry and Foreign Trade
MST	*Movimento Sem Terra* – Brazil's Landless Workers Movement
MT	Mato Grosso
NGO	non-governmental organisation
PDP	Productive Development Policy
R$	real (Brazilian currency since 1994; plural is 'reais')

REDD	Reducing Emissions from Deforestation and Forest Degradation
RESEX	extractive reserve (a Brazilian conservation unit category)
SUDAM	Superintendence for the Development of the Amazon
SUDECO	Superintendence for the Development of the Centre-West
TNCs	transnational corporations (in Brazil, these are commonly called 'tradings' or 'trading companies')
UFMT	Federal University of Mato Grosso
WFP	World Food Programme
WTO	World Trade Organization

Introduction
Titanic agriculture or agriculture-titanic?

There is no doubt that we live in a strange world. That is even more true for those of us who live in urbanised and Westernised parts of the planet, where food and agriculture are so often taken for granted and what we eat seems to appear by magic from faraway places. Food is so readily available in our many local supermarkets, restaurants and takeaways that we tend not to think twice about how and where it was produced. There are so many other urgent and apparently more important issues to worry about, such as the demands of our jobs, workplace interactions, housing constraints, parking spaces, national security, digital gadgets, that food does not seem to deserve the same level of attention. Eating is, of course, unavoidable, as without food we feel hungry and weak; sometimes it can even be a source of pleasure, an excuse for social gatherings and celebrations. However, in practice food is often just a question of paying and eating – not a big deal. We have all heard or read about health problems associated with some forms of food, the dangers of high levels of sugar, fat and salt, the need to be healthy, and so on, but the typical reaction is to ignore the warnings, or maybe put them aside for the next new year's resolution – after all, there will be time later to do something about it. And life goes on: we eat and shop every day without thinking too much, while trying to save money and time. In the end, reflecting on food and agriculture seems to be at odds with the intensity, vibrancy and enjoyment of modern lifestyles.

But is it? The above narrative, though a caricature, illustrates how many of us are seriously detached, or even alienated, from the organic, social and political dimensions of the mechanisms by which food is produced, processed and distributed. In this sense, it is incredible what global capitalist society has done to two of the most essential elements of human existence: food and agriculture. And the same has happened in relation to water, land, schools, universities and even to air (remember that climate change is basically the result of the pollution and industrial waste that have accumulated in the atmosphere). This strange situation is the final chapter in a long process that began about 150 years ago, when agriculture became intertwined with the money-making machinery of imperialism and industrialising capitalism. Sophisticated and highly profitable technologies were developed in the northern countries and gradually transferred to most farming regions in the world to increase production and productivity.

The process accelerated significantly in the second half of the 20th century. The results were mixed, and the socio-ecological impacts were immense, but that did not stop scientists and corporations from accelerating their investigations into the genetic constitution of animals, plants and microorganisms, searching for new opportunities for manipulation and business. At the same time, agriculture started to move beyond its traditional connections to food and rural community life, as farming land increasingly attracted investments and speculation in both production and non-production (as in the case of market-based environmental conservation).

Agriculture has been dramatically resignified and food is now perceived by many people as something merely found on supermarket shelves, with a price tag and some vague description, to be purchased and mechanically consumed. Most food is now tasteless and phantasmagorical, empty of any important signifier, void of nourishment, culture and politics. Quite often, it is reduced to its mere commercial expression, subject to advertising and market competition just like any other commodity. All of this has deeply disturbing echoes of the first line of Adam Curtis's 2015 movie *Bitter Lake*: 'Increasingly, we live in a world where nothing makes any sense.' Agriculture systems and rural development programmes have become sources of food with questionable nutritional value and contradictory socioeconomic contributions, while consumers are increasingly disinterested and separated from farmers and fields of production. The most tangible achievement of these developments is that millions and millions of pounds, euros and dollars are made from food every day by powerful supermarkets and corporations, with or without the approval of farmers and consumers, but largely tolerated by sympathetic governments and endorsed by associated (corrupt? short-sighted?) academics.

Despite the conspicuous silence about the controversies of food and agriculture, it is hard to find another topic that is more central to social life, critical to human survival and fraught with incongruities. There is nothing new in the fact that food is purchased and sold, given that agricultural markets have existed for many centuries. The novelty is that the operational and commercial apparatus of the large agri-food companies has come to be so accepted that it is seen as natural, and is constantly renaturalised and legitimised, while other fundamental properties of food and agriculture – such as nutrition, the well-being of farmers and their families, the preservation of local knowledge and cultural practices, the biological equilibrium necessary for sustained harvests – are all being lost due to the imperatives of profit, low costs and so-called (and very narrowly defined) consumer satisfaction. The focus on food's life-supporting properties has been diluted or negated by the money-making priorities of the contemporary agri-food economy. (Note that the expression 'agri-food' refers to any agriculturally produced food.) Agriculture mutated into agribusiness and encapsulated the dilemmas of capitalist society, particularly the imperative to convert labour and nature into commodities and pull them into the realms of commodity relations. Imagine a modern supermarket, which is now the main source of food for populations in both large and small settlements. Most food is now sold in plastic bags and paper boxes, prepared by agro-industrial companies that rely on numerous, anonymous farmers and intermediary traders. This means that contact between the vast numbers of consumers and producers is largely mediated by a handful of corporations, subject to often biased state intervention.

We are then led to ask whether agriculture is a titanic sector, or whether, alternatively, the world is counting on a *Titanic*-like agri-food industry sailing towards the iceberg. Great production and productivity records or short-term gains, ostentation and imminent shocks? How to change the course of events and take the ship to a safe port? These are monumental questions that are impossible to answer in the pages of a single book. Nonetheless, they deserve to be and must be asked, at least to provoke some consideration of the accumulating problems and the short-sightedness of many of the suggested solutions. The work of critical scholars engaged in agri-food studies has focused on the spatial politics of food deserts, food security and food justice movements, as well as on the socialities of food identities and the embodiments of food (Del Casino Jr, 2015), but less attention has been given to the institutional and spatial frontiers of capitalised agri-food and to the reconfiguration of the scales of interaction affected by the pressures of agribusiness. This is one of the central premises of this text, which aims to go beyond regular and simplistic accounts of the problems, and scrutinise some of the underlying chaos that pervades the modernisation and expansion of capitalist agriculture. Our starting point is the need to review the main trends and fundamental contradictions of mainstream agri-food structures and, more importantly, their enactment at local level in farms and regions. Two important themes merit special attention and will be revisited throughout this book: first, the incorporation of neoliberalising approaches into all aspects of techno-economic and politico-ideological strategies, which has helped to direct agriculture and food markets along the lines of agro-neoliberalism. Second, the highly significant and emblematic enlargement of agribusiness throughout Brazil following the adoption of agro-neoliberalism as public policy and a pillar of the macroeconomic environment. In anticipation of the following chapters, it is worth introducing the concept of agro-neoliberalism and also presenting an overview of the Brazilian context.

Agro-neoliberalism as a dynamic and unfinished process

The quantitative problems of food and agriculture may have been widely discussed by the mass media and in academic papers, but, as advised by Karl Marx in his 'Theses on Feuerbach', interpretation is not sufficient; the point is to change the world. At the same time, effective change requires a proper interrogation and critical understanding of the mounting capitalisation of agriculture and, in particular, the perverse impacts of the hegemony of agribusiness. These became relatively well known during the 20th century, but over the last three decades the concept of agribusiness, which was originally introduced in the 1950s at the time of Fordist agriculture in the United States, has mutated in such a way as to transform agri-food production along the lines of the neoliberal tenets of flexible accumulation and business-friendly state regulation. It has meant a partial and uneven replacement of state-led development strategies in favour of agri-food liberalisation and the consolidation of an economic landscape largely dominated by transnational corporations, mega-supermarkets, global financial organisations and trade-focused (utilitarian) diplomacy. Although neoliberalised capitalism maintains many of the disruptive and transformative attributes of Fordism and Keynesianism, it has also embraced novel value exchange mechanisms, flexible labour relations and market-based responses to environmental and social problems. It is in this context that the transformation of traditional agriculture (a spatially and culturally specific subsistence and socioeconomic activity) into global agribusiness (intense production for the market through reorganised property and labour relations) has emerged as a significant element of the more general transition to neoliberalism.

Agriculture, in the form of agribusiness since the turn of the 20th century, has constituted a fertile ground for the advance of neoliberal ideologies and associated practices over social and socionatural relations. Neoliberalising pressures are an attempt to amend state–market relations in order to maximise the accumulation of capital for a tiny group of people at the expense of the vast majority of the population and their socionatural conditions (Ioris, 2015). Since the 1990s, when agro-neoliberalism became widespread, there has been growing speculation in land properties and agricultural commodities (sugar, coffee, soybean, etc.), which are increasingly treated like any other form of investment, such as gold, housing or petroleum. In general, most of today's agriculture activities can actually be described as the encroachment of neoliberal capitalism into rural areas, and upon the production, processing and distribution of agri-food goods and associated services. Examples include a number of techno-economic innovations introduced by neoliberalised agribusiness sectors – e.g. GMOs, digital farming technologies and satellite guided machinery – as well as new dynamics of production – e.g. land and gene grabs, dispossession of common land and the decisive role of global corporations. The creation of the World Trade Organization in 1995 (despite its failure to significantly reduce protectionism and achieve market freedom as expected by more orthodox neoliberal ideologues) has served to mediate and further legitimise agribusiness neoliberalisation strategies and to minimise socio-ecological and political obstacles to flexible capital accumulation.

It is useful here to pause and note that neoliberalism, and agro-neoliberalism in particular (this concept will be defined later), are difficult, slippery concepts, which are easy to perceive and suffer from, but difficult to describe and define in terms of boundaries. The constituting elements of neoliberalism – essentially, free-market libertarianism and neoconservative moral authoritarianism that are ideologically planned, opportunistically constructed and repeatedly reconstructed (Peck, 2008) – seem highly teleological and apparently inadequate for dealing with agri-food demands in a world under climatic and socio-cultural change. That is why it is necessary to consider agro-neoliberalism as simultaneously an economic and technological project and a politico-ecological phenomenon that relies on the ideology of market-based solutions to old and new production and commercialisation problems. Because of the particularities of agriculture, agro-neoliberalism is predominantly manifested in idiosyncratic connections between national protectionism and globalised markets, which have also deepened and intensified multiple mechanisms of labour exploitation and the exploitation of nature, employed to maximise exchange values. Although some scholars consider neoliberalism an unhelpful concept, as it seems to incorporate too many ideas and to limit the perception of internal complexities and spatial specificities, it nonetheless retains an analytical role if considered as a political–economic–cultural phenomenon and an explanatory framework to appreciate contemporary regulatory transformations (Peck, 2013). Despite all the criticism, and clear evidence of its negative impacts, neoliberalism remains a dominant ideology, quite often disguised as improvements to public policies and solutions to alleged state-led mismanagement. Yet agriculture endures a paradoxical situation in which neoliberal goals and neoclassical economic beliefs continue to be a determining influence on policies and socioeconomic relations, but also show increasing signs of failure and exhaustion.

The complex association between neoliberal policies and agri-food management is evident in the reconfiguration of state interventions concerned with the adoption of capital-intensive technologies, access to new markets and use of natural resources and the protection of ecosystems. Agricultural policy-making has been profoundly reformulated in the last decades as a choreographed transition from government to governance, which comprises a range of flexible mechanisms that have redrawn the public–private divide by compelling the state apparatus to collaborate with non-state actors, such as businesses, NGOs and think tanks. Instead of the state stepping back, new agricultural production patterns are supposed to be achieved through the re-regulation of markets and food consumption. Governance entails coordinated responses between different socio-political sectors that gradually turn the responsibility back on to civil society, although in a way that typically maintains long-established forms of political control, as in the case of public health and nutrition standards. It has been promoted as something neutral and universal, whereas in practice it utilises business models that involve a universe of atomised stakeholders and generate profound asymmetries of gains and beneficiaries. There is a growing literature today on such politico-ecological dynamics of state power and on the class-based disputes that help to shape, and are affected by, the state apparatus (examined, *inter alia*, in Ioris, 2014). More research is, no doubt, required to understand the commitments and responsibilities of the state. Never before has so much food been produced and so much space been used by farmers, but at the same time record amounts of food are wasted every day, and a significant proportion of the global population struggles to maintain minimum levels of nutrition, while a comparable percentage suffers from the consequences of obesity (Rocha *et al.*, 2013).

To summarise this section, the hegemonic neoliberalisation of agribusiness has been less about food, nutrition and well-being – the alleged objectives of the rural development policies promoted during most of the 20th century – and more about capital accumulation strategies and removing obstacles to the spread of market-based globalisation. One one hand, neoliberal agribusiness has achieved significant results over the last three decades, both in terms of additional areas under cultivation, intensification of production and complex market integration. The aim of neoliberalised agriculture has been to increase money-making opportunities and eliminate alternative, traditional forms of agriculture more directly associated with the politico-economic priorities of the labouring classes and the majority of the population. On the other hand, however, these are also activities characterised by contradictions, failures and protests at the local, national and global scales. Brazil encapsulates many aspects of this controversial trend.

Brazilian agro-neoliberalism and its disputed frontiers

The history of existing neoliberal experiences is fraught with struggles between the affirmation of capitalist values and multiple forms of popular resistance against the perverse consequences of neoliberalising strategies. In Latin America in particular, while most national governments in the region have tried to maintain a constant flow of foreign capital, the neoliberal agenda has also led to the disorganisation of various economic sectors and high rates of unemployment (Saad-Filho, 2005), as a destructive phenomenon that exacerbates, rather than reduces, the uneven geographies of development (Ioris, 2012). The result is that, whereas the shortcomings of neoliberal responses may be criticised by some, there are others who persistently argue in favour of additional doses of neoliberalism as the best available medicine for government inefficiencies. Neoliberalism has remained 'the dominant paradigm [in Latin America], albeit in crisis, and constitutes the most obvious sign of the contradictory advance of capitalist globalization' (Lara and López, 2007: 21). It is central to the purposes of this book to observe that the socio-ecological contradictions of neoliberalised agribusiness are highly evident in the case of contemporary Brazil and its burgeoning agribusiness-based economy. The country is increasingly perceived as an agricultural powerhouse that, in principle, has a lot to offer in terms of reducing the potential for global food crises. Due to sustained promotion campaigns, and its frequent use in public policy-making, the term 'agribusiness' has a particularly positive meaning in Brazil, and it is more widely used in common public debates here than in most other parts of the world. Governments and business associations portray the advance of agribusiness in the country as the embodiment of the most progressive elements of an emerging economy.

The acclaimed success of the agribusiness sector in Brazil since the late 1990s, after a brief and painful transition period, therefore represents an intriguing balance of the achievements of agro-neoliberalism and the aspects of the phenomenon that can cause unease. The conversion of agri-food activities and different farming approaches into industrial-type agricultural production and commercialisation have been important elements of the hegemonic response to the multiple crises of capitalist accumulation and to the fatigue of a model of development largely based on direct state support. In this neoliberalising process, the apparatus of the state moved from a position of defender and main financer to become the manager of extensive production chains and of the incorporation of Brazilian agribusiness into globalised markets. The aggressive defence of neoliberal agribusiness by both the private and public sectors is the result of a synergy between local scales of interaction, national politics and transnational flows of capital. The performance of the agribusiness sector is now eulogised daily through various mechanisms of self-justification, together with the condemnation of other rural activities, considered archaic or misplaced in time and space. In recent years, even populist-developmentalist governments (managed by presidents representing the Workers' Party [PT] between 2003 and 2016) actively promoted neoliberalised agribusiness in partnership with the highly organised agribusiness sector, whose best and most symbolic products are soybeans, sugar and animal protein. This has entailed ambivalent combinations of tradition and (conservative) modernity, and of a new social order and old political structures, which are vividly present in the discourse and practices of representative organisations and the most influential landowners. Nonetheless, the advance of agro-neoliberalism in Brazil has sparked huge contention about its actual benefits, uncertain prospects and mounting socio-ecological impacts. Neoliberal agribusiness essentially constitutes a late, already obsolete, type of modernity that replicates and magnifies old, unresolved problems from national history.

Starting from the fact that Brazil is one of the most important theatres for the neoliberalisation of agribusiness, this book serves as an invitation, or perhaps a provocation, to critical research. The intensification of Brazilian agriculture certainly constitutes a privileged feature of the geography of contemporary global agribusiness. The current importance of agribusiness to the country's economy is undeniable and, particularly with the economic slowdown since 2014, neo-liberalised agribusiness has been seen as an island of prosperity and economic dynamism in a national context of job losses, falling revenues and lack of investment. The sector has played a particular role in terms of foreign currency reserves and macroeconomic stability. Agribusiness has been a decisive economic sector, able to respond more quickly than industry and mining to new market opportunities and, as a result, able to help provide the trade surplus that the country desperately needs vis-à-vis its widening current account deficits. A related phenomenon has been the rapid formation of large Brazilian transnational corporations, which are among the largest and most aggressive agri-food players in the world. Not unexpectedly, Brazil has been a strong advocate of free market globalisation and has pushed for further liberalisation of agricultural trade. Some authors have identified the interference of Brazil and other emerging economies as reaction to the pressures of neoliberalism (e.g. Hopewell, 2016), but in effect state-led flexibilising interventions are an integral element of neoliberalism-in-practice, which have always combined market and state forces. As Brazilian agribusiness has developed, it has demonstrated the intricacy and strength of agro-neoliberalism rather than challenging it, a national model of production that has been exported to other parts of South America, Africa and beyond.

Neoliberalised agribusiness certainly has many new attributes when compared with Brazil's previous, nationalistic period of agriculture modernisation in the 1960s and 1970s, but it is also characterised by the strong elements of social exclusion, authoritarianism and corruption that have governed economic development in the country. Although the sector makes use of the appealing symbolism of triumph and modernisation, the evolution of agribusiness according to neo-liberalising pressures has actually served to unify the interests of rural groups, renovate processes of political hegemony and class domination and conceal the system's inherent contradictions. A deeper interpretation of those processes is still needed, and this should focus on the idiosyncratic, apparently paradoxical, combination of small innovations, or transgressions, that take place in the context of capitalist relations of production and reproduction. The rapid advance of agribusiness towards the central and northern states of Brazil in particular has been associated with severe environmental, cultural and socioeconomic impacts, including deforestation, violence against peasants and Indians, and marked cases of state capture and corruption. One of the main areas for the expansion of agribusiness in the world has been the Centre-West region of Brazil, particularly the state of Mato Grosso, where more than half of the local economy and GDP are based on agribusiness-related activities. In Mato Grosso, which lies on the boundary between the Centre-West and the Amazon geographical regions, plantation fields have replaced millions of hectares previously covered by savannah [*cerrado*] and forest ecosystems.

From being a marginal, almost forgotten area in the middle of South America, Mato Grosso is now at the core of national economic life and plays a key role in Brazilian exports and global markets (it is responsible for around 10 per cent of global soybean production, for example). The continuing growth of the agribusiness sector in the state is occurring in tandem with the construction of new roads and towns, the creation or renovation of fluvial ports, and the introduction of large, medium and small hydropower schemes. At the interpersonal level, intensive agribusiness dominates the landscape in large areas of Mato Grosso, but it depends on the perpetual re-enactment of fantasies related to the promises of rapid wealth accumulation and social prestige (merged with novel forms of violence and frustration). The result is that the state has been extensively transformed by the exponential growth of agribusiness, while at the same time problems associated with the concentration of rural property, social discrimination and environmental injustice persist. Nonetheless, although Mato Grosso has been modernised by the expansion and gradual consolidation of agribusiness in recent decades, it remains a material and symbolic agricultural frontier. The rapidly increasing agribusiness activities in the state of Mato Grosso have been at the forefront of the neoliberal renovation of capitalist institutions (e.g. globalised transactions, maximised use of territorial resources, novel forms of political legitimisation), but also of the reintroduction or reinforcement of old practices from the pre-industrial or early industrial phase of capitalism (e.g. the brutal appropriation of the commons, the commodification of features previously considered to be beyond market transactions, and even cases of slavery and forced labour). These tensions are notably present in comparable agricultural frontiers currently opening in other Brazilian states and beyond, and are likely to trigger new rounds of socio-spatial contestation.

Interestingly, despite the intense rate of transformations that are currently reshaping its geography, Mato Grosso is still largely understudied and under-represented in the international academic literature. This book is, in effect, the first initiative to move towards establishing a new field of research on the Amazon, its environment and development. To achieve this, it was important to refine existing theoretical and methodological approaches to allow a critical reinter-pretation of the complex status and uncertain direction of neoliberalised agri-business in the region. Agribusiness in Mato Grosso is a truly kaleidoscopic phenomenon that mirrors, combines and recreates the best and worst materialities and subjectivities of different times and locations in Brazil. It is highly advanced in terms of the rhetoric of efficiency and membership of the group of BRICS countries, but at the same time it reproduces demagogic strategies adopted by the military when their national security project started to fail in the mid-1970s (Schmink and Wood, 1992). In that context, Mato Grosso is at the frontier of the advance of neoliberalised agribusiness, and it is an area where contemporary capitalism is showing its most profound contradictions, abilities and, ultimately, failures. The peculiar dialectics of globalisation taking place at the frontier, including processes of transnationalisation, socio-ecological change and politico-economic mystification, are firmly mediated by structures inherited from the past, creating a complex pattern that is spatially and temporally heterogeneous.

It is in frontier areas like Mato Grosso that the political and economic institutions of rural neoliberalism can expand and take on, to some degree, a life of their own. Similar to the expansion to the west in the United States more than a century ago, ethical and legal safeguards tend to be suspended or overlooked due to the alleged need to occupy adverse territory and then sustain the production of the most marketable and profitable goods. Mato Grosso has also seen, curiously, repeated attacks on the apparatus of the Brazilian state by agribusiness farmers, precisely those who have been the major beneficiaries of state investments and regional development policies since the opening of the agricultural frontier four decades ago. This betrays the opportunism and peculiar production of tailored market-friendly rationalities, which are oddly promoted between the demands of transnational corporations and rural elites. The state apparatus remains the main ally and the preferred villain of neoliberalised agribusiness, as it is both constantly despised and perennially prey to manipulation and corruption.

In search of critical thinking

This book is an attempt to question the main features of agribusiness in the world today and to rethink the socio-ecological impacts of the consolidation of agro-neoliberalism in Brazil. A lot has happened in the country in recent decades, particularly in agricultural frontier areas like Mato Grosso, which still defy interpretation and demand adequate intellectual techniques able to connect the local, short-term and particular with global, long-term and general trends. It is also a publication dedicated to the search for alternatives in addition to, and beyond, the common attention to agronomic practices and innovative technologies that often neglect equally important political and ecological challenges. Anyone interested in agri-food studies is probably already tired of reading repeated calls for a 'new production paradigm', and references to 'sustainable farming' or the need to establish 'local' markets or fairs for organically produced food. It seems that the undisputed hegemony of conventional agribusiness is being mirrored by the much weaker voices narrowly calling for technological and commercial transformations that cannot happen without a concomitant removal of wider politico-ecological pressures. If hunger can start with the pitfalls of food production, the fundamental failures of agriculture have their genesis in unequal property relations and in the violence of the mechanisms of socio-ecological exploitation. These serious problems, nonetheless, presuppose the conditions of their solution. As affirmed by Marx (1947: 55) the working class 'ought to understand that, with all the miseries it imposes upon them, the present system simultaneously engenders the *material conditions* and the *social forms* necessary for an economical reconstruction of society'. In practice, the adjustments that most people want for agriculture and food availability require a simultaneous, and directly related, consideration of both everyday politics and large-scale, civilisational politico-ecological sensibilities.

The present work is also an invitation to begin an interdisciplinary dialogue around the fact that agribusiness is one of the most significant battlegrounds of contemporary socio-ecological politics. The contentious features of neoliberalised agribusiness are also relevant in terms of helping to explain the challenges, risks and responsibilities of agriculture in an increasingly urbanised and technified world. This type of agriculture is carried out by highly specialised professionals, but it has had major macroeconomic repercussions, such as the mitigation of the failures of socioeconomic policies promoted by governments subordinate to the prevailing neoliberal paradigm. At the same time, it is based on the long history of territorial politics and technological improvements introduced at the turn of the 20th century. As much as sophisticated technology and precision machinery, agribusiness is increasingly associated with clashes involving non-unionised peasants and labourers, indigenous groups and descendants of slaves, and the outlook is grim, with levels of violence likely to increase. All these discursive, subjective and material aspects of agro-neoliberalism need to be properly understood, and clearer connections need to be made between specific situations in individual localities and regions, and the broader macroeconomic trends. Against the rhetoric of progress and creativity, a more attentive examination should question the actual contribution of agribusiness to local, regional and national economies, as corporate, industrial-scale agribusiness practices make the invisible visible again, resurrecting certain elements of capitalism which were thought to have died out (as discussed by Derrida, 1994). The full historical, geographical and political complexity of this multi-dialectical phenomenon needs to be considered, with appropriate theoretical, methodological and investigative elaboration.

Taking into account the intellectual propositions and conceptual references that fill these pages, it is possible to summarise the book's analytical approach as an intense historical–geographical investigation into the imbricated scales, times and spaces of agro-neoliberalism. The analysis follows the Marxian association of processes unfolding in distinct but interconnected directions, as suggested by Ollman (2003) and also the recommendation of Callinicos (2007), to concentrate on the main dimensions of power, especially economic activity, ideologies and various patterns of political domination. In schematic terms, the analytical approach can be represented by the political nexus that links ideologies, socio-cultures and the politico-ecological context with processes evolving at significantly different times, scales and places. This approach, illustrated by Figure 0.1, is informed by the Lefebvrerian theory of space production – that is, space is constructed through the practices and performances of different groups and social classes, and embodied and material inequalities (Lefebvre, 1991). In that sense, this field of study encapsulates many tensions, which become constructed and reconstructed through empirical research. The analysis of agro-neoliberalism was carried out against the backdrop of the wider politico-ecological context of capitalist agriculture, characterised by increasing commodification, production for the market and subordination of producers and consumers to the money-making priorities of corporations and the development plans of national governments.

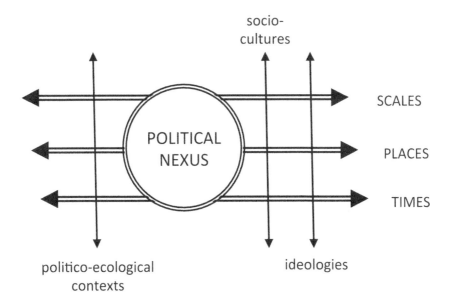

Figure 0.1 Analytical approach for the assessment of agro-neoliberalism and agribusiness frontiers

Source: Author

Agro-neoliberalism emerges and expands under the influence of social and cultural factors, such as issues related to racial discrimination, the role of women and young people, religious practices and ethical conduct, and levels of industrialisation and urbanisation.

The proposed analytical approach centres on the political dimension of agro-neoliberalism and the concurrence of processes happening at different speeds, in different places and at different scales. As proposed by Braudel (1992), to understand recent and current experiences of agro-neoliberalism it is necessary to consider other interconnected times and their respective speeds. There is the history of socio-ecological interactions, the history of society and then the history of events and individuals. In the case of our study, when focusing on the national experience of agro-neoliberalism, it was equally necessary to consider different time frames, from the short-term processes of frontier-making in Mato Grosso to the longer history of agricultural modernisation, the larger canvas of natural resources and labour exploitation since the colonial period, and the problematic incorporation of the Amazon into national integration and development plans (Martins, 2009). Agro-neoliberalism contains within its own history the early organisation of capitalist agriculture in the 19th century, the worldwide transformations caused by the Green Revolution in the 20th century, and the impending agri-food and environmental crisis of the first half of the 21st century. Similarly, there are dynamic synergies and tensions between the multiple places where agro-neoliberalism is planned (e.g. government and corporation offices), implemented (e.g. farms and processing units) and realised (e.g. financial centres and areas of capital circulation and accumulation).

In addition to these interconnected historical contexts, it was necessary to consider local and specific processes in relation, and as integral components, to the more general tendencies of agri-food globalisation. It is not sufficient to talk about agribusiness and agro-neoliberalism in the abstract; the concepts of these regimes must be tempered with attention to localised trends, multiple forms of historical agency and the failures of the food sector at different geographical scales. The range of activities that constitute the agro-neoliberal process connect different scales, because although experienced at the local level, they reflect a politicised construction of scale, given that inequality is constituted through (and constitutive of) scale differences and conflicts (Wolford, 2008). This suggests a need for analysis of the extra-local scales (as well as times) implicated in the creation of localised tensions and problems. The local and regional scales are therefore nested within higher scales of agri-food activity, but all scales interact and affect each other. Rather than being ontologically given, the different scales of agro-neoliberalism are inherently political in nature, inasmuch as resistance unfolds through scales that are constantly produced, contested and reorganised.

The empirical data on which most of the book is based (excluding Chapter 6, which deals with specific, forward-looking research) were obtained during three fieldwork campaigns (lasting around one month each) conducted between 2013 and 2016, which comprised repeated visits to cropping areas and plantation farms, private companies, research centres, and indigenous and subsistence farming communities, as well as attendance at public meetings and semi-structured interviews carried out in the city of São Paulo (where the representatives of the main agribusiness entities, social movements and corporations are based) and in the state of Mato Grosso (in the municipalities of Cuiabá [the state capital], Rondonópolis, Sinop, Cláudia, Campo Novo do Parecis, Porto dos Gaúchos, Juína, Lucas do Rio Verde and Sorriso). Two sets of questions were prepared, one for national players in São Paulo and one for farmers and local authorities in Mato Grosso (all participants in those two broad clusters of social groups were asked similar questions about the process of change, about public policies and the negotiation of conflicts, and about impacts and future trends, although the wording of the questions differed according to the national or regional geographical focus). With the tacit help of local academics, interviewees and informants were identified, initial contacts were set up, and the research then followed a snowball approach. Based on preliminary information, a database was developed to guide further interviews, documentation analysis and the collection of background information.

With the mapping of sectors and organisations, their discourse and stated aims, it was possible to compare intra- and inter-group differences and the range of alliances or disputes (ranging from those strongly against to others fiercely in favour of the prevailing agri-food system among agribusiness farmers, subsistence farmers, urban populations, agro-industrial entrepreneurs, policy-makers and politicians, representative agents and the general population). Semi-structured interviews and participant observation were complemented with analysis of documents, statistics, websites, leaflets, presentations and newspaper articles found in university libraries and in the archives of public agencies and private entities. The research strategy consisted of an 'embedded case study', which started by considering subunits of social action (e.g. municipalities, urban and rural locations, groups of farmers, economic sectors, etc.); these were then scaled up to identify common patterns in larger geographical spheres. Interviews and other qualitative material were transcribed, coded and assessed in Portuguese (only the extracts reproduced in the book were translated into English). Empirical data were analysed, making use of politico-ecological concepts and searching for evidence of the configuration and advance of agro-neoliberalism, rhetorical and material manifestations of power relations, and signs of problems, tensions and contradictions.

The study of a single country (Brazil) and the focus on one specific state (Mato Grosso) obviously entailed intrinsic methodology problems, including generalisation (i.e. how to generate general conclusions on the basis of individual case studies), causation (i.e. how to attribute socioeconomic inequality or ecological degradation to agro-neoliberal policies), and comparison (i.e. how to compare agro-neoliberal processes that occur across different scales, times and places). For the sake of a critical assessment, it was important to take all possible measures to avoid presenting agro-neoliberalism as a monolithic entity and giving it undue prominence and power. In addition, it was necessary to deal with the tension between theorising 'agro-neoliberalism' or 'agro-neoliberalisation' as an abstract concept and researching it by examining its instantiations. The research strategy required an understanding that each localised or sectoral development internalises wider, underlying guiding forces, but it was also necessary to be aware of how agro-neoliberalism relates to specific locations, 'messy' practices, types of socionature (i.e. complex entanglements between human and more-than-human life) and multiple politico-economic repercussions. It is remarkable that, right in the middle of the fieldwork carried out for this book (in June 2014, ahead of a highly disputed presidential campaign when all sides praised the contribution of agribusiness activity to the national economy), one of the most influential Brazilian magazines, *Veja*, was conducting a countrywide tour of locations identified as 'economic successes'. The journalists recorded alleged examples of efficiency and progress ahead of the presidential elections later in the year. This coincidence of the expedition with our analysis confirmed the importance of assessing the distinctive achievements and shortcomings of the Brazilian agribusiness sector.

Structure of the book

The book is organised into chapters that each represent an attempt to explain agro-neoliberalism and its contradictory outcomes. The book begins with a broad discussion of the capitalisation of agriculture and agro-neoliberalism in general, before moving on to focus specifically on Brazilian agribusiness, and on various economic and spatial aspects of the agricultural frontier in Mato Grosso and in new, increasingly influential, soybean production areas. The chapters are all connected and complementary, but they can also be read individually (which implies a little repetition in the contextualisation of problems and description of the study area). After these introductory pages, Chapter 1 will situate the discussion in the context of a growing agri-food crisis ultimately caused by the transformation of agriculture into agribusiness (defined as agriculture-cum-agribusiness). The chapter considers the long academic tradition of studying the relationship between agriculture and capitalism, focusing on issues like agrarian disputes, the Green Revolution, the concept of food regimes and the transition to post-productivist agriculture. It then examines two of the most relevant alternatives to agribusiness – namely, agroecology and food sovereignty. Finally, the chapter presents the conceptual references of this study needed to connect changes at local and farm level with wider national and international forces, and to explain the association between the public and private sectors, and the adoption of multiple, mutually reinforcing, practices and strategies.

Chapter 2 first reviews the intricacies of neoliberalism and its repercussions on agri-food systems. Agro-neoliberalism is defined as a dynamic, socio-ecological process that embraces three main areas of interaction: renewed public–private alliances, novel techno–economic strategies that intensify socio-ecological exploitation, and the hegemonic containment of critical reactions. The rest of the chapter examines the importance of export-led agribusiness for the consolidation of macroeconomic policies and the preservation of political interests in Brazil. Commercial agriculture is increasingly seen by the national population and by the international business community as a great success; however, the impressive growth in agriculture production and productivity conceal growing socio-ecological impacts and uneasiness in old and new production areas. While the neoliberal agribusiness sector has succeeded in crafting a positive image of technological and economic achievement, the federal government and the wider business community have become highly dependent on the export of primary commodities, particularly soybeans to China, and subject to the influence and demands of agribusiness leaders with political influence. The Brazilian state has played a key role in the promotion and legitimation of agro-neoliberalism through the mobilisation of resources and coordination of measures, not in the interest of domestic food security, but primarily for the purpose of capital accumulation via national and transnational networks. The final part of the chapter examines the main trends of the unfolding experience of agro-neoliberalism in the country, particularly in terms of spatial changes, financialisation and mystification.

The next three chapters territorialise the analysis and concentrate on the state of Mato Grosso, where the country's most significant regional developments in agro-neoliberalism are currently taking place. Chapter 3 provides a historical and geographical overview, from the early cycle of colonisation and the first decades of independence up until the Paraguayan War, and then examines the evolution of the legislation and institutional framework established for the partition of state-owned land and the advance of the agricultural frontier since the 1970s. At the frontier, the politico-economic institutions of agribusiness, and later of agro-neoliberalism, were able to expand and take on, to an extent, a life of their own. Furthermore, an examination of the agricultural frontier of Mato Grosso tells us a great deal about the mechanics of contemporary capitalism and why the neoliberal economy still presupposes the continued opening of new spatial and sectoral frontiers. Agribusiness was particularly promoted at the agricultural frontier in Brazil because it is in itself an economic, ecological and ethical frontier. The role and intervention of the state is not a frequently discussed or particularly controversial topic in the region. Given that the state is often blamed for the everyday problems of agribusiness, such as the cost and quality of transport, the lack of affordable loans or subsidies, and the failure to resolve agrarian conflicts, it is also important to remember that the state is ultimately a safety net which, in bad years, should compensate farmers for unfavourable meteorological conditions, plant diseases, low prices, etc. Reflecting on the regional circumstances, it can be concluded that in areas where agribusiness has recently expanded, the possibilities, contradictions and, ultimately, failures of agro-neoliberalism are all the more evident. Unique, place-specific mechanisms for capital circulation and accumulation exist, but at the same time lower moral standards, illegalities and manipulations, and even serious violence are common issues on the agricultural frontier.

Chapter 4 follows up the analysis with a focus on rent. The chapter analyses the political economy of the agricultural frontier to question the basis of the productivist argument commonly presented by the agribusiness sector. The assessment makes use of the category of rent, considered as a proportion of exchange value diverted from production for payment to landowners and their class-based allies. The agricultural frontier in Mato Grosso had three main rent extraction periods: the first when rent was forged by the state apparatus (1970s–1980s), the second during a time of serious turbulence and macro-economic transition (1980s–1990s) and the third with more complex flows of rent due to the neoliberalisation of agribusiness (since the late 1990s). At the frontier of agribusiness, agricultural activity depends on combined strategies of rent creation and rent extraction. Empirical results suggest that rent is more than just the extraction of value from the use of land, but there is a wider capture of value from the network of relations that maintain land in production. Rent derives from land through the formation of a powerful network connecting the state, landowners and the private agro-industrial sector, which provides the conditions for rent extraction.

Chapter 5 further discusses Mato Grosso, but from the perspective of place-making. The chapter investigates the spatial logic and different moments of place-making during the expansion of the agricultural frontier informed by three conceptual concerns – namely, the tensions between representation and experience, between humanist and class-based explanations, and between the intensity of place-making and place-framing. Empirical results demonstrate that socio-spatial changes in the last four decades evolved due to the complementary pressures and controversies of displacement (particularly in the 1970s–1980s) and replacement (in the 1990s–2000s), which have eventually resulted in a widespread sense of misplacement due to accumulated inequalities and entrenched forms of socioeconomic exclusion. The main conclusion is that the places dominated by agribusiness in Mato Grosso have evolved around a totalising spatial strategy that has undermined alternative forms of production and livelihoods that do not fit into the export-oriented agricultural model.

Chapter 6 examines the situation of forest-dependent communities in the lower Tapajós River Basin, where neoliberal agribusiness and soybean production are steadily advancing. The chapter is a reflection on poverty and development in the Amazon, moving beyond the conventional view that places the blame on infrastructure deficiencies, economic isolation or institutional failures. It examines synergistically connected processes that form the persistent poverty-making geography of the Amazon region. The text specifically gives voice to the forest-dependent poor and articulates their concerns over degradation and deforestation. The immediate and long-term causes of socioeconomic problems have been reinterpreted from the politico-ecological perspective required to investigate the apparent paradox of impoverished areas within rich ecosystems and abundant territorial resources. Empirical results demonstrate that, first, development is enacted through the exercise of hegemony over the whole of socionature and, second, because poverty is the lasting materiality of development it cannot be alleviated through conventional mechanisms of economic growth based on socionatural hegemony. The main conclusion is that overcoming the imprint of poverty on Amazonian ecosystems entails a radical socio-ecological reaction. Additionally, the multiple and legitimate demands of low-income groups do not start from a state of hopeless destitution, but from a position of strength provided by their interaction with forest ecosystems and with other comparable groups in the Amazon and elsewhere.

The final pages, in Chapter 7, revisit and summarise the contradictions of neoliberalised agribusiness, in Brazil and elsewhere. Because of systematic attempts to control agricultural trends and manipulate public policies according to the priorities of elites, the impacts of agribusiness are considered, essentially, to be manifestations of corruption. The inherent corruption of agribusiness develops in two main directions, one that is synchronised with other, more immediate forms of corruption, and one that is diachronic and related to the violence and degradation that has occurred at previous points in the history of agriculture and economic activity in general. The chapter then analyses the future prospects for agribusiness, the risks and uncertainties, the perennial asymmetry of gains and the persistence of food insecurity, setting up an agenda for future research.

It should be conceded that all the chapters in this book were influenced by the personal experience of the author, who lived as a child in the Central-West region of Brazil after his family moved there in 1975 to take part in the opening of the new agricultural frontier. He thus experienced at first hand the frantic activity of people and cargo, the spatial transformations in urban and rural areas, the anxiety and excitement of the newcomers as they faced the reality of much larger farms and harvests, and the constant struggles with precarious infrastructure, evolving policies and uncertain markets. As a young boy, the author witnessed the hardship of life in entirely new agricultural areas, without proper roads, communication, electricity or warehouses. He also observed the dramatic removal of the original *cerrado* vegetation and the tensions between different groups of Brazilians who previously knew very little about each other. The many troubles and challenges faced by his parents' generation were evident, as uncles and friends struggled to survive, make money, appropriate new technologies, regularise the land, interact with neighbours and employees, and attract the attention of regional and national politicians. These rich memories certainly belong elsewhere and should fill the pages of a memoir, but suffice to say that the 1970s were a time of both great enthusiasm and major uncertainty, while the early 1980s were characterised by growing (state-funded) profitability and extravagance, which in turn were followed by crisis and reorganisation around the turn of the 1990s. During this process, many of the author's relatives lost their land and had to move further afield or return to their original homes in the southern state of Rio Grande do Sul. This personal situation may add some authority to the text of this book, but it also posed a difficult dilemma for the author: how to objectively analyse the agricultural frontier without disassociating from such vivid reminiscences and experiences. Rather than try to claim total neutrality or deny the influence of his personal trajectory, the best solution was to both admit the positionality of the conclusions and, more importantly, put impressions and subjective knowledge to work in diverse ways to enhance the analysis. The actual result will always be subject to criticism, but the reader is the best judge of its success and coherence.

Note that earlier versions of some chapter sections originally appeared in the following journal articles: Ioris, A.A.R. 2016. The Politico-ecological Economy of Neoliberal Agribusiness: Displacement, Financialisation and Mystification. *Area*, 48(1), 84–91 [incorporated in Chapter 2]; Ioris, A.A.R. 2017. Encroachment and Entrenchment of Agro-neoliberalism in the Centre-West of Brazil. *Journal of Rural Studies*, 51, 15–27 [Chapters 2 and 3]; Ioris, A.A.R. 2016. Rent of Agribusiness in the Amazon: A Case Study from Mato Grosso. *Land Use Policy*, 59, 456–466 [Chapter 4]; Ioris, A.A.R. (2017). Places of Agribusiness: Displacement, Replacement, and Misplacement in Mato Grosso, Brazil. *Geographical Review*, 107(3), 452–475 [Chapter 5]; and Ioris, A.A.R. 2016. The Paradox of Poverty in Rich Ecosystems: Impoverishment and Development in the Amazon of Brazil and Bolivia. *The Geographical Journal*, 182(2), 178–189 [Chapter 6]. These are reproduced here with permission, and the author greatly appreciates the support received from the various journal editors and referees.

Before moving on to the next chapter, the contributions of many colleagues, researchers and students to the preparation of this book must be acknowledged. It is impossible to nominate everybody, but the logistical support and intellectual input of colleagues at the Federal University of Mato Grosso (UFMT) need to be mentioned, in particular Vitale Joanoni Neto, João Carlos Barrozo and Daniel Carneiro Abreu. At the State University of Mato Grosso (UNEMAT), Edison Antônio de Souza was always a source of ideas and assistance. Colleagues in other organisations and universities provided precious help and encouragement, including Embrapa, UNESP and UFRGS in Brazil, and academics at Exeter, City, Essex, Aberdeen, Edinburgh and Cardiff universities in the United Kingdom. The work was carried out through various research projects funded by CAPES and FAPESP (Brazil) and by the ESRC, ESPA and the Newton Fund (UK). Between 2012 and 2015, the author held a Special Visiting Researcher fellowship (PVE) under the Science without Borders programme. Incidental help from various sources also made possible additional travel, meetings and workshops, particularly from UFMT, Edinburgh University, the Scottish Alliance for Geoscience, Environment and Society (SAGES), UNESP, FAPEMIG, FAPEMAT and the International Celso Furtado Centre for Development Policies. Also extremely important was the help received from a number of farmers, peasants, workers, agronomists, civil servants, urban residents, activists, union leaders, Indians and young people who agreed to be visited and interviewed over the years. Their personal stories, family trajectories, material conditions and socio-cultural identities permeate the pages and the conclusions of this book. It is impossible to thank them enough. Last, and, as ever, not least, I thank the lovely family that sustains me. Mato Grosso is definitely quite far away, and the work invested in this research was intense, which means that I had to spend long periods of time away from my family, and terribly missed the company of Adriane and our beautiful little son Antônio. This book is also, and primarily, for the two of you.

References

Braudel, F. 1992. *Écrits Sur l'Histoire*. 2nd edition. Arthaud: Paris.

Callinicos, A. 2007. *Social Theory: A Historical Introduction*. Polity: Cambridge.

Del Casino, V.J. 2015. Social Geography I: Food. *Progress in Human Geography*, 39(6), 800–808.

Derrida, J., 1994. *Specters of Marx*. Routledge: London and New York.

Hopewell, K. 2016. *Breaking the WTO: How Emerging Powers Disrupted the Neoliberal Project*. Stanford University Press: Redwood City, CA.

Ioris, A.A.R. 2012. The Neoliberalization of Water in Lima, Peru. *Political Geography*, 31(5), 266–278.

Ioris, A.A.R. 2014. *The Political Ecology of the State: The Basis and the Evolution of Environmental Statehood*. Routledge Studies in Political Ecology. Routledge: London.

Ioris, A.A.R. 2015. Theorizing state-environment relationships: antinomies of flexibility and legitimacy. *Progress in Human Geography*, 39, 167–184.

Lara, J.B. and López, D.L. 2007. The Harvest of Neoliberalism in Latin America. In: *Imperialism, Neoliberalism and Social Struggles in Latin America*, DelloBuono, R.A. and Lara, J.B. (eds). Brill: Leiden and Boston, MA, pp. 17–35.

Lefebvre, H. 1991. *The Production of Space*. Trans. D. Nicholson-Smith. Blackwell: Oxford.

Martins, J.S., 2009. *Fronteira: A Degradação do Outro nos Confins do Humano*. Contexto, São Paulo.

Marx, K. 1947 [1898]. *Wages, Price and Profit*. Progress Publishers: Moscow.

Ollman, B. 2003. *Dance of the Dialectic: Steps in Marx's Method*. University of Illinois Press: Chicago.

Peck, J. 2008. Remaking Laissez-faire. *Progress in Human Geography*, 32(1), 3–43.

Peck, J. 2013. Explaining (with) Neoliberalism. *Territory, Politics, Governance*, 1(2), 132–157.

Rocha, C., Burlandy, L. and Magalhães, R. (eds). 2013. *Segurança Alimentar e Nutricional*. Fiocruz: Rio de Janeiro.

Saad-Filho, A. 2005. The Political Economy of Neoliberalism in Latin America. In: *Neoliberalism: A Critical Reader*, Saad-Filho, A. and Johnston, D. (eds). Pluto Press: London and Ann Arbor, MI, pp. 222–229.

Schmink, M. and Wood, C.H., 1992. *Contested Frontiers in Amazonia*. Columbia University Press: New York.

Wolford, W. 2008. Environmental Justice and the Construction of Scale in Brazilian Agriculture. *Society & Natural Resources*, 21(7), 641–655.

1 The political ecology of agri-food systems

From agriculture to agribusiness

The production, distribution and consumption of food are subjects for some of the most controversial and, perhaps, poorly understood debates in the world today. In the words of Patel (2007: 23), the 'food system is a battlefield, though few realize quite how many casualties there have been'. The system consists of processes unfolding at different scales, with profound historical and geographical significance, as they involve territorialised transformations that interconnect disputes and collaborations between social groups across different localities, countries and regions. One could say, with no exaggeration, that the problems of agri-food vividly encapsulate the maelstrom of present-day globalised economies and their increasingly alienated societies (considering not only political, marketplace and cultural alienation, but alienation in the strict politico-economic sense of a fundamental separation from the control of production and consumption). If one thinks carefully about supermarket shelves and TV advertisements, the nutritional and cultural dimensions of agriculture and food often seem to be overlooked today, as the sector is increasingly dominated by industrialised goods, standardised diets and intercontinental transactions. Most of our food comes from obscure and often unreliable sources, which are more influenced by market pressures and shareholder expectations than by health requirements, farmer demands or nutritional and environmental concerns. As Friedmann (2005: 124) points out, 'agriculture and food have all along invisibly underpinned relations of property and power in the world system'. Even the most remote corners of the planet are now exposed to the advance of Westernised lifestyles, as is the case in the Upper Negro River, on the border between Brazil and Colombia, visited by the author in June 2016, where local shops are becoming mere distribution points for frozen chicken and ready-to-cook food packed thousands of miles away from the Amazon. More than anything else, this demonstrates that the relations of global capitalism 'are now so deeply internalized within every nation-state that the classic image of imperialism as a relation of external domination is outdated' (Robinson, 2008: 42).

An obvious consequence of such rapidly changing production and consumption patterns is that any investigation into agri-food issues needs to consider the material, subjective and discursive dimensions of market globalisation and the multiple contradictions, as well as achievements, of contemporary capitalist agriculture. A central question of this debate – a true 'elephant in the room' – is the fact that the technological and managerial practices of commercial agriculture are largely determined by the activity of mega-corporations selling agro-chemical inputs (e.g. pesticides, fertilisers, herbicides, etc.), machinery and equipment, and by the complementary activity of agri-food companies controlling the purchase and distribution of goods. As observed by Clapp and Fuchs (2009), large corporations and their commercial allies hold different and interrelated forms of power, including instrumental power (the ability to lobby governments and influence social actors), structural power (influence over the public agenda and rule setting) and discursive power (shaping the public debate and the choices presented to wider society). The power of agri-food corporations, including lobbying and pressure on governments, is never far away. While agro-industries pursue high field productivity, and large supermarkets operate extensive delivery networks, the great majority of the population is dangerously reliant on a small number of supply chains and the narrow menu of fast-food restaurants. The colourful shelves of most shops seem to offer a range of food options and a variety of choices, but are in fact dominated by a small list of plant species and animal breeds. Mass selling of convenient, ready-to-eat options is achieved at the expense of food's nutritional value, traceability and contribution to local economies. The influence of corporate interests is particularly significant among urban populations and on the periphery of large cities, where there is a growing tendency to buy cheap sugary food or consume frozen microwaveable meals. The perverse appeals of convenience and standardisation have seriously affected not only the daily diets and health of both younger and older generations, but also the power of farmers to decide what to produce.

The aggressive modernisation and industrialisation of agri-food can be described as a disturbing movement from food-as-nutrition and agriculture-as-social-integration to a situation in which agri-food operations are carried out primarily to circulate and accumulate capital. In other words, the role of agriculture as a source of nutrition and livelihood is being increasingly supplanted by the imperatives of money and profit, which is happening in the wider context of a globalised market-based society in which everything is prey to commodification. This is the first main contention of this book: notwithstanding many other biophysical, cultural and circumstantial problems, the basic disconnection between food and nutrition, together with the firmly established nexus between food and money-making, are the twin causes of the widespread agri-food crisis faced by governments and society. The ideological and practical reduction of food to the realm of commodities, exploitation and profit also represents a decisive barrier to the resolution of nutritional and environmental problems. In synthetic terms, this is a gradual shift, which began at the end of the 19th century, from *agriculture-cum-food* to *agriculture-cum-agribusiness*. The essential feature of agri-culture-cum-agribusiness is the deliberate incorporation of agri-food processes into mechanisms of profit maximisation, social exclusion (via privatisation of the commons) and socio-ecological exploitation and alienation.

The word 'agribusiness' was only coined in the 1950s, but its structural bases – that is, the brutal transformation of agriculture due to the advance of capitalist relations of production and reproduction, were already evident in the Global North at the turn of the 20th century. The 'business of the agro' gradually became less about sustenance and health and significantly more concerned with short-term financial gains and the legitimisation of hegemonic agri-food systems. Under neoliberalising pressures, from the final three decades of the last century onwards, such totalitarian features were magnified by the systematic adoption of market-based responses to social and ecological problems created by capitalist expansion itself (for instance, in the case of policies and market mechanisms aiming to internalise the costs of environmental degradation and health risks). What happened to most of agriculture (i.e. its conversion into agribusiness) has many elements of what Polanyi (2001) describes as markets – which are essentially power relations – becoming disembedded from social and ecological grids and, echoing Marx's analysis of contingent social relations, the creation of fictitious commodities, as in the case of land, money and labour. Agriculture-cum-agri-business has increasingly become detached (disembedded) from existing socio-cultural and socio-ecological relations, and been reshaped according to the abstract logic of global markets and the elusive measure of money. These transformations have occurred through complex interactions with wider socioeconomic and political phenomena mediated and legitimised, primarily, by the apparatus of the state.

There are specific historical and geographical reasons for this widening gap between agri-food and basic socio-ecological goals. For many centuries, going back to ancient farming and Babylonian irrigation, agriculture was a source of staple food and raw materials, with only a fraction of production commercialised or exchanged in (almost exclusively) local markets. Although some pre-capitalist societies did achieve sizeable food surpluses, this happened over long periods of time and vast territories (as in the case of Aztec, Roman, Chinese, Indian and Islamic agri-food systems). More importantly, pre-capitalist agriculture was not 'premised on a state- and market-enforced productivity model', but 'with the transition to capitalism, the new property relations propelled a process of dispossession and differentiation that enabled rising labor productivity in agriculture and rising food surplus' (Moore, 2015: 242). In this process, the life-sustaining and socio-cultural properties of agriculture were progressively disregarded in favour of commodified versions of food. Capitalist agriculture changed not only in terms of the scale of production, but its fundamental qualities were also transformed as food was transmuted into commodity. It is worth remembering that Marx, in the first page of his main book, affirmed that the 'commodity is, first of all, an external object' (Marx, 1976: 126) and, consequently, commodified food is inescapably impoverished, diminished food. This is a highly politicised phenomenon, with both local and geopolitical repercussions. For instance, the need to secure cheap, commodified food for a growing layer of non-agricultural labourers was a key feature of the early expansion of capitalism and was pivotal to the rise of the Dutch and British world hegemonies, as well as North American world supremacy later in the 20th century (Moore, 2010).

The chief consequence of commodification, which should come as no surprise, is the reinforcement of malnourishment and socio-ecological degradation due to combined distortions in both the production and consumption sides of agri-food systems. Shameful levels of food waste and scandalous distribution losses only aggravate the problem and betray the narrow rationality of mainstream agri-food. Every night, around 800 million people in the world still go to bed hungry and almost a billion suffer from extreme poverty, according to the highly regarded report *The State of Food and Agriculture* (FAO, IFAD and WFP, 2015). Ironically, and sadly, most of these people live in rural areas and depend on agriculture-related jobs for most or all of their income. Nonetheless, the public debate on the causes of hunger and poverty is currently dominated by simplistic claims and technocratic, largely neo-Malthusian and neo-Positivistic, calls for increases in production and productivity. The official discourse of agricultural development and food security adopted by national governments and multilateral agencies emphasises that the aggregate number of people suffering from hunger (vaguely defined as 'chronic undernourishment') has declined in recent decades due to technological and managerial improvements. This claim is apparently supported, at least in part, by the statistical evidence. The year 2015 marked the end of the monitoring period for the two internationally agreed targets for hunger reduction included in the famous Millennium Development Goals (MDGs). The number of people in developing countries suffering from hunger was to be halved compared with the base years of 1990–1992 (from 23.2 to 11.6 per cent). The recorded percentage in 2014–2016 was 12.9 per cent, implying that the goal has almost been met. However, if we analyse the results in terms of undernourished people, the figures are rather different; since 1990–1992, the number of undernourished people in developing regions has fallen from 991 million to 790.7 million, but the goal was 495 million (half of 991 million), meaning that the target has not in fact been met (FAO, IFAD and WFP, 2015: 8–12).

Although any reduction in hunger should be celebrated, there are serious concerns about the reliability and significance of such statistics and, more importantly, the unwillingness to question mainstream agri-food operations. Estimates of hunger are highly problematic due to the difficulty of accurately defining the term, debatable thresholds and inconsistent methodologies, and we all know that national statistics are fraught with imprecision. Governments and multilateral agencies are constantly moving the goalposts with redefinitions of key concepts, data revisions and adjustable targets (Butler, 2015). On the whole, while the MDGs have concentrated on eradicating extreme poverty and eliminating hunger, a major food crisis is affecting both those with and without easily available food. The difficult conditions of those suffering from hunger and malnutrition remain concealed behind aggregate data and the persuasive discourse of agriculture modernisation advanced by agribusiness corporations. Beyond cold statistics, the crux of the matter is really whether agriculture should serve the desires of a small minority of the population and merely support economic growth, or whether the industry should be concerned with social justice and the promotion of socio-ecological sustainability. In practical terms, this is not just about changing global and national trends, but also about fostering alternative solutions and creative strategies at the local and individual levels. In any case, it is becoming clear that business-as-usual (or agribusiness-as-usual, to make an unavoidable pun) is a risky and hopeless option that is not serving the needs and expectations of farmers, consumers and wider society.

This is because mainstream agri-food approaches remain firmly within the established paradigm of market solutions and mitigatory, end-of-the-pipe measures. For example, the aforementioned report by the Food and Agriculture Organisation of the United Nations (FAO) and partners makes clear that investment in agriculture remains the single most effective way to provide opportunities to generate income and improve nutrition, especially for women and young people in rural areas, but very little is said about the underlying causes of rural deprivation (such as violence against subsistence farmers and unequal distribution of land and policy support). Ultimately, documents like these can obscure the prevailing forces of dispossession and displacement promoted by market globalisation and enacted by national governments and their allies. The influence of state policies, including environmental regulation, produces results that can either benefit wider society or, in other cases, concentrate gains in the hands of corporations or powerful landowners (for instance, in the United Kingdom, the payment of farm subsidies to billionaire Saudi princes, dukes and even to Queen Elizabeth II, who received £557,706.52 in 2015, as mentioned in BBC, 2016). Likewise, the prominence of global commodity markets and top-down rural development masks the agroindustrial and financial priorities that pervade the production, distribution and consumption of food. An emblematic example of this controversy can be found in the World Bank's attempts to improve the productivity of small farmers in order to integrate them into commercial chains controlled by powerful, normally foreign, players. It is also the case that, despite any progress, the vast majority of those suffering from hunger live in the Global South, where more than six decades of international development promises have not resolved the matter. It is said in many official reports that Latin America is the region with the best record in terms of increasing food security, but this has been achieved through the controversial expansion of agribusiness and the short-lived success of neoliberalised agri-food policies (as discussed in subsequent chapters).

It is highly relevant that an expanding number of critical studies have demonstrated that conventional agri-food systems and neoliberal agribusiness activities no longer produce food that is safe and healthy, and this cannot can be sustained in the long-term. For McMichael (2010: 64), liberalisation and privatisation are combined 'to accelerate food circulation globally and restructure food production and retailing along corporate lines'. It is also worth remembering the observation of Derrida (1994: 64) that 'never, never in history, has the horizon of the thing whose survival is being celebrated (namely, all the old models of the capitalist and liberal world) been as dark, threatening, and threatened'. The key question therefore posed for society, academics, politicians and farmers is how to reject the configuration and repercussions of agriculture-cum-agribusiness in favour of diversified, largely localised, agricultural practices owned by producers and consumers. Those aims can only be achieved through the simultaneous construction of a new socioeconomic order and novel patterns of production, consumption and ecological conservation. This agenda of radical change vividly and inescapably connects the local with the national and the international. The transition to a more sustainable agriculture and fairer agroindustry will be the result of social mobilisation at different levels, from small-scale agriculture systems to the profound transformation of national and global markets. Moreover, and contrary to the claims of many academics and activists, such changes must necessarily involve more stringent economic, health and environmental regulation and better informed consumers, but these alone will not be sufficient. The transformation of food and agriculture must necessarily contribute to, and follow, wider politico-economic, ethical and technological reconstructions.

Taking into account these challenges and their multiscale ramifications – from household to global scale, and connecting past, present and future – this book is located in the tradition of critical social theory, and aims to contribute to the search for radical alternatives in an attempt to reinstate food as food, farmer as food producer and markets as allocation tools. It is also part of the endeavour to remove the distortions and falsifications of the hegemonic agri-food system that feeds contemporary, market-based society. It is increasingly evident, at least among critical academic and activist circles, that the technologies inherited from the Green Revolution (and its more recent version, the 'Gene Revolution' associated with genetically modified organisms and genetic engineering, and closely related to digital technologies and precision agriculture) were limited in terms of their impact in reducing food supply and distribution problems; the main challenge continues to be a search for politico-ecologically viable and socio-culturally acceptable options. At the moment, there are more hard questions than convincing answers: How do we achieve transformations in the food system to promote a holistic and sustainable approach to food production based on local, place-based food interactions? Why do we have a situation where millions of people are hungry while a billion are overweight? Why is agriculture acknowledged as a major contributor to climate change and ecosystem loss, while millions of farmers are evicted from the countryside? How did we get here? Who are the winners and who are the losers? What are the trajectories of the current model of production, distribution and consumption, and what and where are the alternatives?

If are there no easy answers or predetermined routes to follow – on the contrary, the agenda of change is wide open – it should at least be asserted that these are all questions that animate the discussion and will provoke in-depth reflection throughout the pages of this book. The central element of this debate is necessarily political and should operate at different levels: from the farm and community level to alliances with informed, conscious consumers, other economic sectors and changes in public policies and environmental standards. Responses to the dominance of agribusiness will fail to achieve long-term results unless local and global food systems undergo major, fundamental transformations. It is really fascinating to realise that these multiscale changes will, more than anything else, be felt at the local scale where people work, live and dine (obviously under the influence of wider national and global pressures). Rather than being a pre-structured phenomenon, rural localities are 'reproduced, and the social relations therein recomposed, by virtue of their contemporary magnetism for relocation due to the wider discontinuities of capital activity' (Cloke *et al.*, 1990: 15). Consequently, local and interpersonal interactions are as important as more general, structural dimensions.

Before presenting our interpretative approach, it is necessary to briefly review the evolution of agri-food and agrarian studies and the alternatives offered by two of the most prominent critical approaches.

Walking through agrarian and agri-food studies

The declining role of agriculture-cum-food and its replacement with agriculture-cum-agribusiness has certainly attracted the attention of scholars from different disciplines. Starting from the understanding that industrial and financial capital have become the driving forces of Western societies and economies, many academics began to question the economic and socio-cultural functions of agriculture and traditional forms of landed capital. The role of agriculture in the expansion of industrial, and progressively post-industrial, societies has become a favourite topic for critical researchers interested in the intricacies of late capitalism and its long-term perspectives. The dilemmas of present-day agriculture are accordingly examined in the light of the long evolution of mercantile and industrial capitalism, and the inherent inability of capital to fully control agriculture production. None of this is entirely new, as the classic political economists were already greatly concerned with the role of agriculture in the nascent capitalist economy. The interplay between the rural aristocracy, industrial capitalists and the peasantry were given special consideration by Adam Smith (1998: 272), who warned that investments in commerce and manufacturing by any country were less durable than the capital invested 'in the cultivation and improvement of its lands'. A few generations later,[1] particularly in his non-economic texts and notebooks, Marx extensively examined the idiosyncratic unfolding of capitalism in the rural areas of peripheral societies such as Russia, India, China, the United States and Ireland (Anderson, 2010). Marx (1973: 252) argued that modern landed property 'cannot exist, without capital as its presupposition, and it indeed appears historically as a transformation of the pre-ceding historic shape of landed property by capital so as to correspond to capital'. Consequently, it is 'in the development of landed property that the gradual victory and formation of capital can be studied'.

From the time of the Second Industrial Revolution, at the end of the 19th century, agriculture in the advanced capitalist countries of Western Europe and North America became increasingly dependent on fossil fuels, agrochemicals and, more recently, genetically manipulated seeds, as well as on advanced forms of imperialism, European migration and transcontinental trade. Industrial and financial capital increasingly encroached upon rural property and agroecological systems. This gave rise to many studies on agrarian issues and on the transformative capacity of capitalist expansion. Probably the most influential and controversial work of the time was Kautsky's analysis (initially published in 1899 in Stuttgart) of the turbulent relationship between industrial capitalism, the exploitation of peasants and farm labourers, and the desired transition to socialism. For Kautsky (1988), a Czech–Austrian philosopher who, after the death of Engels in 1895, became one of the most important and influential theoreticians of Marxism during the Second International, the agrarian question was essentially political, in the context of the struggles around the advance of capitalism, rather than merely an economic or technological issue. In the first decades of the last century, other critical authors tried to clarify the role of the peasantry and the reproduction of rural elites in a world increasingly defined by industrial and financial capital. One of the most significant debates took place among Russian revolutionaries and their political allies, intrigued by the unique features of a still largely agrarian capitalism undergoing rapid industrialisation and urbanisation. While those inspired by the Narodnik movement, which in the 1860s and 1870s revolted against Tsardom, considered the peasantry to be the revolutionary class that would overthrow the monarchy, Lenin was rather more doubtful and saw in the peasants the main driver for the development of capitalism in the countryside; by contrast, Chayanov understood that the behaviour of the peasants and the inequalities among them were not primarily due to their class identity, but rather evidence of specific geographical circumstances (Bernstein, 2009; Lenin, 1977).

A more fruitful appraisal of agrarian and socio-cultural transformations was carried out by sociologists, particularly in the United States. Rural sociologists were initially concerned, in the early 20th century, with the social fabric of rural community life; their work then evolved to incorporate socio-psychological perspectives that conceptualised those involved in agriculture as actors responding to new stimuli (such as technologies, education and occupational opportunities), and gradually came to focus on the political economy and the internal structure and dynamics of agriculture (Buttel *et al.*, 1990). This subdiscipline became firmly established in the decades after the Second World War, rejecting any rural romanticism introduced in the 1920s. Most academic research in the 1950s was dominated by the agriculture modernisation project, an authoritative and ever-expanding model that was reshaping global political economy, and there was also a focus on power relations, through the integration of manufacturing and agriculture in both developed and developing nations. However, it was a highly positivistic line of research that basically regarded technological intensification and competent management as a panacea. The result was an over-simplified description of the mechanisms of change and the marginalisation of rural distinctiveness (Marsden, 2006). The limitations of rural sociology in the post-Second World War years became increasingly evident, particularly because of its excessive focus on 'rurality' rather than on the commodification of agriculture;

as pointed out by Friedland (1982: 594), capitalist agriculture is 'no longer a phenomenon based on rural society; it is a process of production, like all other processes of production'. New development strategies, such as the European Union Common Agricultural Policy (CAP), introduced in 1962 to foster production and self-sufficiency through subsidies and market protection, further defied rural sociologists' established views on agricultural communities and rural populations.

In response, from the 1970s onwards, novel approaches to agriculture and food were sought, through what became known as 'new rural sociology', complemented in the 1980s with the 'new sociology of agriculture'. Informed by neo-Marxist and neo-Weberian ideas, this emerging field of work challenged the Western orthodoxy of rural development (whereby it was conceived as a universal, linear and rational process) and was directly influenced by wider social phenomena, such as the social consequences and environmental impacts of agriculture, and conflicting interests around the state. Different conceptual and methodological frameworks attempted to explain the encroachment of capital into agroecological systems, the evolution of landed property, the basis of rural development, the causes of environmental degradation and related political disputes. Many researchers went back to the original texts of Marx, Lenin and Kautsky, among others, to find elements for new theorisations and to develop a strong normative basis for critical analysis. In particular, a number of authors became concerned with the (apparently paradoxical) survival of peasant farming in a context of intense, market-dominated agriculture. According to Mann and Dickinson (1978), some spheres of agriculture, even in advanced capitalist countries (such as local food and organic production), remained largely incompatible with capitalist rationality, and these gave peasants the opportunity to occupy the interstices left vacant by capitalism. Nonetheless, this apparent dichotomy between the rising capitalisation of agriculture and peasant reproduction was challenged by Friedmann (1978), who observed that family farmers are more flexible and are therefore able to outcompete capitalist firms in the production of some crops (sold on the same markets). Mooney (1983) went further, claiming that the dichotomy between family farming and capitalist enterprises was false, given that both were part of the same overall system and subject to a similar logic of exploitation.

Scholars have since adopted different theoretical positions to try to explain the evolution of the agri-food crisis of global capitalist society. For instance, influenced by regulationist theory – essentially, economic and non-economic relations that provide temporary stability to specific capitalist regimes of accumulation – and by world systems theory, Friedmann and McMichael famously adopted the concept of food regimes to historicise global food systems and demonstrate the relevance of food in the geopolitical order of industrial and imperial capitalism (Friedmann, 1987, 2005; Friedmann and McMichael, 1989; McMichael, 2009). Food regimes fix capital accumulation trends both temporally and spatially within the long-term political economy of food. For Araghi (2003), the food regime is essentially a political regime of global value relations that can be used to analyse the contradictions of capitalist processes across time and space. According to proponents of the concept, the first food regime (which lasted from the 1870s until the 1930s, and was known as the Settler–Colonial food regime) was dominated by British strategies for consolidating imperial power and maintaining the supply of agricultural goods from British colonies; this was followed by a second food regime (lasting from the 1950s until the 1970s, the Mercantile–Industrial food regime), under the authority primarily of the United States, which combined intense domestic production and global markets, economic recovery and development strategies (e.g. the Marshall Plan) and protectionist policies such as the European CAP; and a third food regime (from the 1980s onwards, described as the Corporate or Neoliberal food regime) whereby food production is increasingly dominated by mega-supermarkets and transnational corporations, but is also subject to the influence of social and ecological mobilisations and operating in a different geopolitical setting after the collapse of the Berlin Wall and the fast growth of the Chinese economy.

The study of food regimes attempts to embrace political, economic and social features and processes that are relevant to an understanding of the role of food production and consumption relations. According to McMichael (2000), the post-Second World War food regime (the second one in their framework) subverted the argument of classical political economy which defined the division of labour between urban-industrialisation in the core Western economies and primary commodities coming from the largely agrarian countries. Likewise, the third, ongoing, food regime is characterised by a peculiar combination of neoliberal policies, novel technological developments, environmental concerns, and alliances of globalised society and pressure groups. Actors within the corporate food regime, in particular the powerful transnational corporations, are ordinarily united by their class status as ruling elites and their commitment to neoliberal ideology and practice. The food regime theory was later complemented by the commodity systems approach that focuses on commodity chains and networks, and together they form what is often described as agri-food theory, which, according to Murcott and Campbell (2004) is a conceptual and analytical device that encompasses the whole chain from farm production to domestic consumption of food. Agri-food theory examines present day, multiscale complexity by taking into account relationships from rural fields to plate, and the range of social groups in different parts of the world that have a stake in the governance of food (including industry groups, primary producers, consumers, distribution industries and retailers, government regulators, public interest groups, indigenous peoples and rural communities).

However, the applicability of the concept of food regimes has also been questioned – for example, because of what is perceived to be an overly simplistic periodisation of agriculture, mirroring the exogenous evolution of industry or the wider periods of the capitalist economy (among others, by Goodman and Watts, 1997). According to these authors, the concept of 'food regime', as a *longue durée* approach that privileges structures over events, can also obscure the complex interaction of multiple phenomena and the range of disputes that respond to the evolution of agribusiness. In this case, the periodisation that underpins the food regime theory of agricultural evolution has been imported from the parallel patterns of industrialisation, and hence represents an exogenous, artificial explanatory tool. The capitalisation of agriculture, for instance, is substantially different from the vertical integration in the industrial sector, particularly because of the critical relevance of local interactions. Because of agriculture's unique characteristics, the sector faces a much higher level of biological, climatic and logistical obstacles that complicate the constitution of 'food regimes'. For instance, the growth of agricultural biotechnology has never been straightforward, but rather has always met with resistance and scepticism from various groups of farmers and wider civil society (Newell, 2009). For Goodman and Watts (1994: 20), the notion of a food regime poses difficult questions about the degree of coherence of this structure and the means or logic 'by which the rules are established globally', risking hyperstructuralism and reification. On one hand, the idea of overall food regimes may be helpful in the sense that it signals the trends and historical evolution of technology, policies and markets. If disentangled from its regulationist theory biases, the concept of food regimes could be used to inform a labour-oriented perspective on imperialist capitalism as a relation of production embedded in global value relations. On the other hand, this underplays the wider complexity of agriculture and the simultaneous processes of land grabbing and peasant survival, production intensification and post-productivism, the homogenisation and specialisation of agriculture goods, and other issues.

Because of the perceived limitations of all-embracing approaches to food and agriculture, such as food regime theory, there has been a growing emphasis on agri-food governance and the more nuanced and diffused manifestations of power. It has been necessary not only to account for purely economic trends, but also to deal with subjectivities, interconnections and the non-linear evolution of rural development. With the end of the Cold War, the focus shifted from location, context and diversity to a range of approaches informed by behavioural research, actor-network schemes, class-based insights, food regimes and regulation theory (Robinson, 2004). Since the late 1980s, by contrast, research has given increasing space to so-called 'food studies', demonstrated by the growing interest in issues beyond the farm gate, as in the case of commodity system analysis, renovated food regime approaches and research on regulation and market dynamics (Carolan, 2012). The agrarian question was likewise largely converted into a 'question of food' and related to the multiple forms of peasant resistance that combine issues of class, ethnicity, gender and ecology in an attempt to reframe development (McMichael, 1997). The emerging geographies of food, in particular, seek to examine the food chain and systems of food production and consumption, paying attention to culture and trying to reconnect several unhelpful dichotomies: farming and food, food and politics, food and nature, and farmers and agency (Winter, 2003). This line of research considers food practices, which are permeated by symbolism and embody multiple social relations. Authors associated with the geographies of food demonstrate that food is not only biological and economic, but also cultural, social and political. It is also a highly spatialised phenomenon due to its uneven distribution, context-specific technologies and diets, and inter-locked scales of development.

An especially important contribution of food studies during the last three decades has been the examination of the partial and contradictory transition from the productivism of the conventional systems that predominated during most of the past century to an alleged post-productivist and multifunctional agriculture that followed the introduction of post-Keynesian policies (both phases being firmly grounded in the turbulent connection between capital, labour and landed property). According to Ilbery and Bowler (1998), while productivism can be theorised as an agriculture regime characterised by commercialisation (transforma-tion of traditional farming by intense supply–demand relations), commoditisation [or commodification] (farmers becoming dependent on goods and inputs obtained in the market and acquiring income through market exchanges) and industrial-isation (transformation of production into industrial-like activities and increasing utilisation of non-agricultural raw materials), post-productivism is associated with interrelated transitions to extensification, dispersion and diversification of rural activities (obviously within the constraints of capitalist relations and related ideological constructs). Evidence of productivism includes the mechanisms of intensification, concentration and specialisation, whereas post-productivism can be demonstrated by pluriactivity, set-aside farmland (for economic or environmen-tal reasons) and the increasing importance of environmental goods. The debate has continued and advanced in different directions, for instance the controversial notion of embeddedness as the necessity of social relations in all economic transactions (Murdoch *et al.*, 2000). Much more than a simple techno-ecnomic phenomenon, this reconfiguration of agriculture is a socio-political project developing through the struggle between different class fractions of capital (Potter and Tilzey, 2005). These last authors claim that what actually exists today is not a post-productivist agriculture but rather a neoliberal regime of market productivism based in the intense circuits of agri-food capital.

The academic work on agri-food issues has, therefore, moved in various new directions and is based on multiple theoretical and analytical assumptions. It basically reflects the complexity of contemporary agri-food systems, as well as the hegemony of mainstream agribusiness. There is now a convergence between pro-ductivist and post-productivist trends, while non-commercial farming persists and alternative production systems emerge. But this complex reality is subject to the defining influence of powerful market forces, growing commodification and mounting financial speculation. Particularly with the end of the long period characterised by cheap food – precipitated by the commodity boom, which lasted roughly from 2000 until 2014 – productive investment has increased in tandem with the growth of speculative activities. Global investment in food commodities jumped from US$65 billion to US$126 billion between 2008 and 2012, with speculative investment in food commodities amounting to 20 times more than the total spent on agricultural aid by all countries combined (Time, 2012). This investment involves massive flows of capital into stock market ventures that use commodity futures and derivatives to hedge the risk of their portfolios through index funds, exchange traded funds and over-the-counter swap agreements. A number of hedge funds and pension funds now speculate on food prices in financial markets, which is likely to be causing increases in commodity volatility and drastic price swings in staple foods such as wheat, maize and soy (although the association between speculation and prices is not easily demonstrated, according to Zuppiroli, 2015). For instance, food prices were relatively stable for more than a decade, but from 2002 there was a steady increase culminating in the spike of 2008, followed by a sharp fall and then another rapid increase in prices, culminating in a second spike in 2010, after which prices fell again. In addition, there has been an aggressive grabbing of land and other natural resources in the Global South, which several concurring discourses attempt to rationalise by citing such justifications as the pursuit of food security, and is conducted through strategic alliances between transnational companies, international capital and state institutions (Borras *et al.*, 2012).

Overall, the remarkable supremacy of the agri-food corporations, closely associated with the behaviour of investment banks, large-scale landowners and mainstream politicians, matches the definition of 'Empire' put forward by Hardt and Negri (2000), as the fundamental basis of contemporary sovereignty which encompasses a spatial totality, cementing the existing state of affairs and violently exercising biopower. More importantly, the politicised and contested configuration of agri-food systems has become increasingly associated with neoliberalising strategies that try both to enhance the competitiveness of productivist activities and win new markets, and to placate political resistance through a discourse of multi-activity and environmental responsibility that typically permeates post-productivism (Dibden *et al.*, 2009). Consequently, the prevailing agri-food systems today bear the distinctive imprint of neoliberalism, not as a rigidly defined plan, but rather as a multifaceted phenomenon aimed at the renovation of capitalism through the reconfiguration of socio-ecological processes and socioeconomic institutions. As important as examining the shortcomings of agro-neoliberalism and the legacy of earlier phases of the capitalisation of agriculture (this will be covered in Chapter 2), is assessing the other approaches commonly presented as alternatives to agriculture-cum-agribusiness. In the next section, the prospects and limitations of agroecology and food sovereignty will be examined, and this examination will then help to inform the formulation of our own interpretative approach.

Characteristics and shortcomings of two main alternatives

The vast work of agrarian and agri-food scholars, only briefly mentioned above, has served to question the modernisation of agriculture through the advance of capitalist relations of production and reproduction. For the purposes of this book, however, proposing fairer and viable options for mainstreaming agri-food operations is as important as identifying problems and contradictions. The arguments in favour of two experiences in particular – namely, agroecology and food sovereignty, deserve to be scrutinised here. This will help to shed light on the complexity of the challenges ahead and, in particular, the difficulty involved in fulfilling the transformative potential of critical responses. Examining these two alternatives reveals many unresolved conceptual and practical gaps, meaning that further theoretical and experimental efforts will be required. This brief analysis will demonstrate that, although agroecology is receiving more and more attention, and is seen as a sensible way forward, it is not sufficiently focused on the politics of agricultural development, or critical enough of anthropocentric interpretations of ecology. Likewise, food sovereignty certainly places significant emphasis on issues of inequality and power disputes, but it is less concerned with the socio-cultural and subjective elements of agricultural procedures.

Starting with the debate on agroecology, Altieri *et al.* (2001: 123) define the concept as 'a science that provides ecological principles for the design and management of sustainable and resource-conserving agricultural systems'. It emerged in the 1960s as a response to the intensification and specialisation pressures of the Green Revolution, and was initially considered a scientific discipline based on the application of ecological principles to agriculture production (Wezel *et al.*, 2011). Agroecologists were also interested in the ecological features of traditional farming systems and, since the 1980s, have focused on sustainability goals and the study of agroecosystems (a term famously introduced by Eugene P. Odum to describe 'domesticated ecosystems', intermediate between natural and fabricated ecosystems). Agroecology has broadened in recent decades to include a clearer focus on traditional management systems and indigenous knowledge, and there has also been a rearticulation of the concept in terms of 'sustainability'. Social, economic and cultural aspects were also increasingly incorporated throughout the 1990s and 2000s. This means that agroecology is no longer just an academic discipline, but also a social movement, embracing a set of practices, principles and techniques. At the same time, however, in Europe and the United States many agroecologists are still dedicated to the study of agricultural processes per se rather than exploring broader and deeper questions. Numerous groups in these countries remain 'largely grounded in natural science research with a primary focus on analyses at different scales of the agricultural production process, not the agri-food system' (Méndez *et al.*, 2013: 6). Nonetheless, the idea of a purely scientific agroecology is challenged by interpretations that argue that science must incorporate a social and political dimension – the so-called 'human dimension'. This is the case of Dalgaard *et al.* (2013: 44), who maintain that agroecology necessarily combines hard and soft scientific principles, in line with recent epistemological trends that accept the role of human activities as part of the systems under investigation.

For many authors, there is a clear difference between agroecology and organic farming. The latter is broadly defined as a method of crop and livestock production that rejects the use of pesticides, fertilisers, genetically modified organisms, antibiotics and growth hormones; however, the boundaries of organic farming are not fixed. Organic farming does not always rely only on external inputs such as organic fertiliser, may produce single or a few varieties of crops or livestock rather than diversified production, and may not always prioritise holistic principles like water conservation or the use of renewable energy. The main contrast with agroecology, however, is that most organic farmers have also established multiple connections and continuities with mainstream agro-industrial companies, and their position is more of cohabitation than confrontation with agribusiness. Agroecology, on the other hand, tends to be focused on non-commercial farmer knowledge and community forms of production organisation, and is often viewed as a means of challenging top-down food institutions and corporate interests. Many proponents of agroecology have therefore consistently emphasised its transformative potential as a practice-based social movement. There is a commitment to using alternative modes of food production to bring about broader changes for the better in social and ecological outcomes. Agroecology is considered distinct from mainstream agriculture techniques which rely on monocrops, high use of chemical fertilisers and pesticides, and commodified inputs such as patented seeds. It is also regarded as separate from fair trade or small-scale farming, and from organic farming, in that it calls for a whole-system approach with minimal external inputs.

These alleged characteristics suggest that agroecology is a technical and social counter-movement against both conventional and narrow organic farming. Moreover, the political content of most agroecological debate is often too implicit, with an emphasis on concepts like conservation and sustainability rather than an overtly political outlook. Connected with this, Wezel *et al.* (2011: 40) note that agroecology can be a 'vague, confusing and ineffective' term, open to use by a variety of actors with potentially contradictory agendas (in that regard, it is highly revealing that even the World Bank has appropriated the term and produced specific policies on agroecology). There are ongoing debates around the role and nature of knowledge in agroecology, particularly around how to generate creative, democratic and transformative research projects, and concerning the heterogeneous and context-specific nature of claims to transformative participatory knowledge. According to Gonzalez de Molina (2013), agroecology is often still dominated by scientist thinking, but should engage more openly in politics given that agroecosystems are socio-ecological constructions organised through power relations. Political agroecology, the direction favoured by Gonzalez de Molina, considers food production as inherently contested, and calls for conceptualisations of agroecology which foreground power and politics. The remit of political agroecology should be primarily the promotion of small-scale agriculture in which peasants and farmers are empowered through secure land tenure, community seed banks and appropriate credit policies, as well as an emphasis on sustainable technological practices like reuse, recycling and bricolage. Those techniques should emerge from independent experimentation rather than dependence on high-tech equipment from external suppliers and expertise provided by agri-food corporations (Altieri and Toledo, 2011).

Although scholars of agroecology have become more politicised and sensitive to social issues, there is still a long way to go in terms of eliminating the technological excesses of most agroecological approaches (Sanderson Bellamy and Ioris, 2017). There is a need for greater attention to the nature of the relationship between farmer actions and changes demanded at different levels (Sevilla Guzmán-Casado and Woodgate, 2013). The excessive technical and biological concerns and localised focus of many agroecological experiences have been rightly exposed by the work and narratives of those advocating food sovereignty as the necessary response to agriculture crises and socio-ecological degradation. Authors writing about food sovereignty ask whether organic and agroecological methods could replace intensive and input-heavy conventional farming on the same land base, while maintaining, and even increasing, food supply. The fundamental critique of this proposition is that agroecology and organic farming can be easily appropriated by mainstream distribution channels and large supermarkets through under-theorised power relations and restricted engagement with the structural dilemmas of rural, regional and national development. For instance, many agroecologists define resilience and organic practices in individualised terms, as adjustments made at the farm and shop levels, overlooking wider, trans-sectoral responses. While the definition of food sovereignty is still being debated, it generally includes the idea that the means and modes of production of food should be controlled by those who consume it. This concept is related to the right to food principle, recently mainstreamed by organisations such as the United Nations, and food justice, defined generally as 'ensuing that the benefits and risks of where, what and how food is grown and produced, transported and distributed, and accessed and eaten are shared fairly' (Gottlieb and Joshi, 2010: 6).

Social movements have encouraged a broadening of the concept of sovereignty to critically address dynamics of decision making and rule- implementation power within and among all human organisations that shape food systems. On the basis of a more politicised critique of conventional agroindustrial systems, the concept of food sovereignty must therefore constitute an attempt to challenge notions that the state has supreme authority over agri-food. It also reveals the multivalent hierarchies of power and control that exist in mainstream agri-food systems. Beyond the mere emphasis on access to food (as the main goal that permeates superficial calls for food security), the notion of food sovereignty must incorporate 'the right of peoples and sovereign states to democratically determine their own agricultural and food policies' (IAASTD, 2009: 113). Quaye *et al.* (2009) describe food sovereignty as the concurrence of four rights: (a) the right to nutritious, safe, sufficient, and ethnically suitable food; (b) the right to access land, water, seeds and biodiversity; (c) the right to produce food sustainably and in an ecologically acceptable manner; and (d) the right to access trade and local markets. Food sovereignty is explicitly couched in discourses of struggle against dominant food powers and systems of production, and is therefore to be distinguished from technocratic framings that denote 'simple adequacy of supplies and nutritional content, with the food itself produced and delivered under any conditions, including far-off, chemical-intensive industrial agriculture' (Edelman *et al.*, 2014: 914). While claiming that greater productivity is an attraction for agroecologists, Altieri (2002) argues that all-round food supply is more important than single-species productivity. This author deals directly with Latin American agroecological farming and claims that peasant farming makes a substantial contribution to food security in the region despite poor conditions and low input use. Rosset *et al*. (2011: 164) further affirm that 'in the South peasant agroeco-logical systems average a higher level of total productivity than conventional monocultures'.

The most well-known example of a practical food sovereignty movement is *La Vía Campesina*, an international organisation established in 1992 which rejects the power of globalised agribusiness and claims to represent the voice of small farmers in their attempt to develop, and struggle, for a common vision. In 1996, the members of La Vía Campesina defined the food sovereignty framework as the:

> right of peoples to healthy and culturally appropriate food produced through ecologically sound and sustainable methods, and their right to define their own food and agriculture systems. It puts those who produce, distribute and consume food at the heart of food systems and policies rather than the demands of markets and corporations. It defends the interests and inclusion of the next generation.

It is true that La Vía Campesina subscribes to scientific and practical definitions of agroecology, but only while emphasising above all the transformative and political aspects of the model. The movement recognises the importance of agroecological practices, as these can help to increase autonomy from inter-national markets, putting peasants in control of their own production systems, restoring degraded ecosystems and improving the economic viability of peasant agriculture. At the same time, La Vía Campesina prioritises political issues, viewing technical and scientific agroecology as useful insofar as it can help bring about wider transformations. Wittman (2009) particularly emphasises the role of the co-operatives of Brazil's MST (*Movimento Sem Terra* – Landless Workers' Movement) as an example of a non-mainstream collective currently using agroecological principles, particularly ideas of food localism and agrarian land reform, to provide a genuine challenge to dominant agri-food systems.

Having considered the strengths and vulnerabilities of these two approaches, it is clear that the situation is complex. However, debates about both agroecology and food sovereignty are often framed in oversimplified ideas of resistance against capitalism by a vaguely defined peasantry (Bernstein, 2014). Most critical narratives deploy an imagined moral reserve and make assumptions about the social or ecological superiority of peasant or small-scale farming, including generalisations around 'technology vs. traditional techniques', 'capitalist dispossession vs. social cohesion', 'ecological destruction vs. back-to-nature imaginaries', and idealised visions of 'the community'. However, the idea that all small-scale farmers share agroecology's rejection of chemical inputs and technology is not always borne out in the real world. In effect, peasant opposition to capitalism is multiform and strategic, including open confrontation, small-scale reactions and more subtle mechanisms of appropriation of new technologies and restoration of peasant farming. Based on studies in Cuba, Jansen (2015) argues that agroecological players tend to romanticise the idea of an agrarian revolution and that agroecology does not reflect the day-to-day practices of peasants who can adopt flexible attitudes to technology and markets. Likewise, the political agroecological literature, particularly when advocating family and community work, local livelihood diversification strategies, localised food provision and local markets (e.g. Martínez-Torres and Rosset, 2014), appears to have a tendency to undertheorise and fetishise the category of 'community'. The claims made by proponents that small-scale agroecological farming promotes food sovereignty on the basis of an idealised community consequently need greater examination in terms of the farmers' approaches and the relationships between members of this highly heterogeneous group.

Other scholars have argued that proponents of the food sovereignty approach have been too optimistic, and detail several unanswered questions which are of considerable relevance to supporters of agroecology. These include issues regarding the relationship between food sovereignty and food export, and whether food sovereignty is possible in a system where small farmers produce food for export. Such authors criticise a lack of theorising around the institutions and territorial arrangements that could bring about and govern food sovereignty, particularly around land and property relationships. Bernstein (2014) observes that the purported relationship between rejections of genetically modified crops and food sovereignty have not been properly established, and that there are major barriers to critical approaches such as food sovereignty occupying more space and coming to be seen as viable alternatives to mainstream agriculture. Further questions include the relationship between normative and ideological calls for food sovereignty and the realities of farmers' experiences, and the levels of pluralism and diverse approaches that might be acceptable under a normative political vision of food sovereignty. Roman-Alcalá (2016) contends that what is necessary is a relational view of power, whereby reactions to food sovereignty encompass both the quantity and quality of political disputes and their ramifications for different levels of interaction.

An important question which remains is how to connect the issue-specific context of agriculture with the wider peculiarities of national and global capitalist trends. Local changes and circumstantial struggles need to receive proper consideration rather than being met with deterministic biases, and must be dynamically associated with the confrontation against hegemonic politico-economic structures. In order to move beyond the neo-Malthusian biases of the Green Revolution and the technocratic, non-political basis of contemporary policies (i.e. more food should be made available regardless of socio-ecological impacts, the quality of the food and the asymmetry of power and benefits), critical agri-food studies also need to question the simplistic political assumptions of agroecological theory and the dualistic residues (artificial separation of society and the rest of nature) of propositions for food sovereignty. A more sophisticated, nuanced and insightful conceptualisation and analytical approach is required.

Considering the vast agri-food literature, including the work on agroecology, food sovereignty and agrarian reform, there are some significant gaps that essentially reflect the difficulty of dealing with different epistemological positions and connecting activities from different sectors and at embedded scales. A key task is to embrace and make sense of the totality of relations – that is to say, agriculture can only be understood in the context of a national and global system of forces. This is because the fundamental problems of agri-food systems are not specific to the sector, but located in wider politico-economic structures and relations. On one hand, the industrial-scale commodification of food and financialisation of agriculture are integral facets of the reconfiguration and interconnections of scale that underlie present-day capitalism. Contemporary agroindustry is a powerful driver of the homogenisation of goods and the abstraction of food from the ecological and socio-cultural conditions of production. On the other hand, it is necessary to understand issues of agency and subjectivity that evolve over time and contribute towards the production of new spaces. Agency is historically and spatially moulded according to certain political and socio-ecological conditions (Martins, 2009). It does not deny the importance of structural pressures (e.g. commodification, alienation, globalisation), but both depends on and subverts structure. For instance, through active agency and intergroup interaction, peasants and large-scale farmers can help to either commodify or decommodify agriculture practices depending on a number of local and global factors.

To understand the possibilities and limitations of the two alternatives mentioned above, it is important not to idealise the lived reality of peasants and farmer communities, but also to avoid superficial and over-schematic critiques of large-scale farmers, politicians and agri-food corporations. As shown by Schneider and Niederle (2010) in the south of Brazil, peasants can either increase production for selling and processing (thus adding value), can take jobs elsewhere (meaning that they earn more money), or, depending on the circumstances, can expand the area used for subsistence (destined to family consumption). Likewise, it is necessary to connect the multisectoral dilemmas of areas subject to different agricultural situations, as in the case of established regions and new frontiers for the expansion of agribusiness (where the obsolescence and redundancy caused by ultra-modern agribusiness are even more evident). Local, alternative initiatives are highly relevant (as recorded in Cruz *et al.*, 2016) in that they have the power to denounce exploitation, waste and disconnection between producer and consumer, but they must be strategically and systematically articulated with larger scale reactions and other fields of social struggle (i.e. labour, housing, transport, recognition, health, etc.). All these questions share a strong and crucial political dimension that needs to be recognised by producers, consumers and regulators. This political core is not just deeply socioeconomic, but clearly ecological (in the sense that food is both produced and consumed according to concrete ecological realities). Ultimately, and crucially, it is crucial to take into account, and make creative use of, a framework centred on the political ecology of agri-food. The next section will summarise the main conceptual and methodological elements of this political ecology conceptualisation.

For a political ecology of agri-food

The central concern of this chapter has been the expansion of capitalist agriculture –defined above as agriculture-cum-agribusiness – and the creation of global networks of food production and distribution. The powerful commodification of food and its insertion into money-making ventures have been cleverly justified by governments and strong private players through the neo-Malthusian rationalisation of hunger threats and the consequent imperatives of production and productivity. The paradox is that the more agribusiness is naturalised and accepted as given, the more political it becomes, but the less visible is its political substance. Capitalist agriculture depends on the persistent reinforcement of this paradox to maintain reliable streams of profit and private gains, even if this comes at the price of alienated, but still deeply ecological, relations. Because of this central distortion, modern agribusiness has been allowed to destroy the commons (including the material and cultural components of ecosystems) and to dramatically transform locations and regions according to the anti-political pressures of homogenisation, exploitation and commodification. The displacement of rural communities, the use of genetically modified organisms and the related exploitation of labour are all examples of how capitalist agriculture works through the colonisation of social life, biology and production efforts. At the same time, however, critical reactions and the formulation of alternatives have failed to properly relate local challenges and shared responses to wider dilemmas and associated opportunities of late modernity. The main consequence is that the agri-food debate remains entirely open, with clear demands for innovative translations of uneasiness and criticism into concrete measures, while avoiding artificial simplifications of highly complex processes of diversification, resistance and legitimation.

In order to address the complexity of contemporary trends, capitalist agriculture (agribusiness) must be considered as an intrinsically political (contested) and ecological (vital) activity, occurring at the trialectical interface between state, society and the rest of socionature (Ioris, 2012). Both examinations and the denunciations of agribusiness have to grasp its politico-ecological ontology. Agriculture- and food-related activities are intrinsically ecological, first and foremost because they are practised by and for people who are unavoidably part of socionature. Human beings are an integral part of a socionatural world – that is, a universe that is simultaneously social and more-than-social (or, to use more loosely defined terms, a world that is both 'social' and 'natural'). Therefore, capitalist agriculture is a locus of exploitation, property disputes and accumulation resulting from a reconfiguration of socionatural features according to the rationality of capital. The consequence of this fundamental ontological observation is that the separation of nature from society is not only unhelpful, but creates major obstacles to fully understanding multiple agri-food crises. The acceptability and success of modern agriculture-cum-agribusiness depends on the orchestrated denial of the fundamentally political (because anti-ecological) basis of agri-food today. Yet, the majority of critical authors also reproduce a modernist, dichotomic ontology in which nature is theorised in externalised and mechanistic terms and abstracted from the socio-political domain. Goodman (1999) specifically warns that the theoretical and political relevance of most agri-food studies is significantly weakened by the perverse influence of modernist biases, in particular the dualist separation of nature and society. For Goodman and other authors, agri-food processes are metabolised corporally and symbolically as food – that is, food is not something pre-given but the relational result of multiple, politicised socionatural interactions. Rather than being purely organic entities, agri-food systems are hybrid networks where both the natural and the social are perpetually co-produced and co-determined.

Beyond the rigid disciplinary interpretations of economists, sociologists and other similar scholars, the political ecology of agri-food systems is a growing field of investigation, as it integrates different approaches to the study of economic development and environmental change, combining historico-geographical accounts with political and socio-cultural factors (O'Neal Campbell, 2013). While agriculture is essentially ecological – at the intersection between the human and more-than human dimensions of the totality of the world – the incorporation of agriculture into capitalist relations of production and reproduction triggers an increasing, and irreversible, politicisation of food. As observed by Arendt (1998: 138), 'tilling the soil not only procures means of subsistence but in this process prepares the earth for the building of the world'. Commercial agriculture – i.e. agriculture-cum-agribusiness – relies on the private appropriation of agriculture's ecological attributes for the circulation and accumulation of capital. If the crisis of the global food system has led to calls for technological fixes and yield boosting under a 'new Green Revolution' (Sharp and Leshner, 2016), political ecologists have emphasised the growing role of global agribusiness and transnational corporations, as well as the negative impacts of new technologies and market pressures (Watts and Scales, 2015). Place-based interactions and local contexts have been increasingly recognised by political ecologists; it matters where food is produced and consumed, and how it gets from farm to plate. In addition, the success or failure of modernising technologies, such as GMO soybean, are not only dependent on the organisation and functioning of capitalist agricultural systems, but also greatly influenced by the materiality of the crops themselves (Carroll, 2016). However, what is still missing in the academic literature is the application of politico-ecological knowledge to interpret cross-scale connections and the plurality of sectoral and group agendas that underpin agribusiness activity. By approaching capitalist agriculture as a contested socio-ecology, and analysing agricultural frontiers as lived spaces of politico-ecological, institutional and personal experimentation, this research provides a radically new perspective on the achievements, risks and prospects of hegemonic agri-food systems and development strategies.

What is required, as a pioneering research approach, is to unite separate bodies of knowledge and investigation through two associated 'short-circuits'. The first 'short-circuit' involves incorporating subjectivities and interpersonal relations into politico-ecological considerations of conflicts, risks and contradictions (more-than-materialist political ecologies), while simultaneously taking into account how materiality affects subjectivities (more-than-human agencies). Rather than merely ascribing particular behaviours and monodimensional agency to individuals and groups, political ecology should go beyond such intransigent epistemologies to connect these with broader social and economic contexts (Duff, 2016), abandoning the ontological differentiation of subjects and objects, individuals and contexts and instead focusing on how action and agency are generated in unpredictable encounters (DeLanda, 2006). This is the application of 'assemblage thinking' (Marcus and Saka, 2006) to political ecology's class-based thinking, which will be invaluable in terms of understanding how subjects and contexts are ultimately made in experience, as well as for appreciating the material and discursive basis of lived problems and impacts that result from unfair and discriminatory relations of production and reproduction. This same 'short-circuit' will help to connect everyday, localised food with developmental, global-ised trends. Instead of creating a false dichotomy between structure and agency, this methodological approach considers the centrality of social actors, as indi-viduals full of creativity, initiative and contradictions, but also people who are constrained by their social and historico-geographic conditions. As recommended by Long and van der Ploeg (2011), rural development research should take into account the social construction of the world, prioritise individual and collective agency, and consider the social properties that emerge from (politicised) interactions. In addition, this must be a humanist exercise, but equally a class-based approach that is also mindful of issues beyond class, such as gender, culture, intergenerationality, religion and even affection (Sultana, 2015).

The second, incremental, 'short-circuit' is to conflate the materiality and sub-jectivity of contested political ecologies with the profoundly dynamic, and also socio-ecological, ontology of the state apparatus. The state is not simply a detached administrator of environmental pressures; its involvement in socionatural issues has direct effects on its organisation, functioning and legitimisation. The state apparatus is actually an institutional and political permanence which involves unique public–private entanglements. For instance, the expansion of new Brazilian frontiers coincided with the strengthening of environmental regulation and regulatory agencies; this apparent paradox can be explained by the failure of the regulatory apparatus to curb the expansion of production areas and the willingness of the regulators to accommodate farming demands through a selective choice of environmental problems. Nonetheless, scholarly work has often fallen short of establishing the politicised connections between socio-ecological pressures, spatial dynamics and the changing patterns of the state apparatus. This 'second short-circuit' is still necessary in order to examine the failures of emerging governance systems introduced in the course of wider state reforms. The governance of agriculture and environmental change has been particularly influenced by political theories about flexibility and legitimacy, which have facilitated the advance of capitalism over the more-than-human spheres of socio-nature, mediated and promoted by the contemporary state. By conflating those three bodies of theoretical and practical research – represented in Figure 1.1, below

– this book will make sense of the evolution of agro-neoliberalism, particularly in new agricultural frontier areas. As indicated by Harvey (1996), it is through a careful articulation of conceptual and investigative synergies and the pursuit of dialectical reasoning that other 'possible realities' of the world can be explored.

Making use of this overall conceptual framework, political ecology has a lot to contribute to critical agri-food investigation. It is an established field of multidisciplinary research, concerned with power and politics in socio-environmental issues, control and access to resources and territories, questions of identity and justice, and issues of accumulation through the enclosure of resources and dispossession of people. Most work done in this area has so far focused on land grabbing and access to resources, disputes related to commodity circulation, environmental degradation, transnational politics of agri-food chains and the range of responses and global networks (Hall, 2015). Therefore, a strong focus on the political ecology of agri-food systems can further inform an examination into the human aspects of the nature–development–state nexus, particularly the asymmetric distribution of winners and losers, the ways in which unequal access to resources is structured and negotiated in capitalist relations, by major institutions and policies, and by social relations and situated understandings of

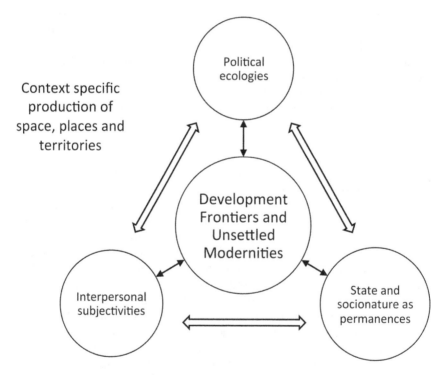

Figure 1.1 Analytical framework for the study of the frontiers and fissures of neoliberalised agribusiness

Source: Author

nature. This is an exciting and evolving line of research that can, and should, be invigorated by different traditions of critical thinking, in particular the mobilisation of political ecology ideas applied to agri-food. The debate can directly benefit from the examination of issues such as technological changes, ecosystem degradation and persistent malnutrition, drawing attention to power relations such as class and gender which produce uneven access to land and promote specific agricultural practices. In very practical terms, the interpretation of agri-food questions, as some of the most crucial and controversial questions of contemporary society, can be inspired by a commitment to a politico-ecological perspective, which can be schematically described as follows:

1   Agri-food systems are predicated upon socio-ecological foundations, class-based antagonisms and the politico-economic goals of the social groups involved (which are embedded and contribute to shape specific spatial configurations from the local to the national and international scales of interaction).

2   Modern, capitalist agriculture (i.e. agriculture-cum-agribusiness) fundamentally relies on the creation of artificial boundaries and cleavages between society and the rest of nature, manifested, for instance, in the encroachment on commons, territories and cultures for the purposes of circulation and private accumulation of capital.

3   The economic and technical success of modern agriculture simultaneously depends on the strict manipulation of its ecological basis and on the maintenance of anti-political narratives (which naturalise and justify agriculture-cum-agribusiness).

4   The more agriculture modernises, globalises and becomes massively commodified, following the imperative of agribusiness, the more abstract and alienated it becomes (i.e. disconnected from concrete geographical settings);

5   These contradictions are encapsulated, negotiated and (partly) accommodated in the apparatus of the state; the state apparatus is itself also a politico-ecological entity fraught with social and ecological disputes and susceptible to power pressures.

6   Reactions to the politico-ecological tensions associated with the expansion of agri-business and with the biased interventions of the state depend on socionatural mobilisation and overcoming alienation; politico-ecological agency is not only a human process, but the rest of socionature also shares with humans the ability to actively respond to degradation and exploitation.

7   Since the 1980s, the advance of agro-neoliberalism and its hegemonic influence around the planet has maintained and exacerbated the contradictions and limitations of agriculture-cum-agribusiness; technological advances encapsulate the achievements and frustrations of the modern world (not the other way around – that is, with modernity leading to technological improvements as undisputed gains).

8   The tensions and contradictions of agro-neoliberalism are more conspicuous at the frontiers of agribusiness expansion, because of the constraints of the

state apparatus, the ease with which norms can be transgressed and the disorganised nature of political resistance.

Informed by these eight points, what follows in the next chapters is a space-sensitive assessment and theorisation of social relations and socioeconomic trends across different scales. The analysis will focus on the intensification of Brazilian agribusiness as a privileged entry point into the politicised geography of globalised agri-food. Because of new production areas and persistent productivity gains, Brazil has consolidated its position as a paradigmatic example of agribusiness activity. The importance of agribusiness expansion within the wider politico-economic context of Brazilian neoliberalism will be demonstrated. Agribusiness was a central part of the conservative response to the crisis of capitalist accumulation in the 1980s, and the exhaustion of a model of development largely based on direct state support from the 1930s until the 1970s. As an alternative to agrarian reform and local food, as demanded by large proportions of the Brazilian population, the mainstream solution was to intensify and update production according to neoliberal goals. The quest for modernisation and efficiency in Brazil pervaded the enthusiastic rhetoric of agribusiness leaders, influential landowners and associated politicians (Ioris, 2016). Neoliberalised agribusiness in Brazil has entailed the realisation (actualisation, in the Hegelian sense) of technological advances and economic relations of production initiated almost a century earlier. However, as Friedland (1982: 602) rightly claimed, efficiency is 'a slippery phenomenon' and cannot be defined only in terms of inputs and outputs, but must take into account other factors. Moreover, the complex and controversial bases of agribusiness are reinforced daily through various mechanisms of self-justification and criticism of other rural activities considered archaic and inefficient, despite the fact that most of the food consumed is produced by small, family-based agriculture. As in other parts of the globe, Brazilian agribusiness has sparked disputes about actual beneficiaries, uncertain prospects and negative impacts. Ultimately, it reveals an ambivalent combination of tradition and (conservative) modernity – that is, a new social order amid old political structures.

Note

1   Some of David Ricardo's contribution will be discussed in Chapter 4.

References

Altieri, M.A. 2002. Agroecology: The Science of Natural Resource Management for Poor Farmers in Marginal Environments. *Agriculture, Ecosystems and Environment*, 93(1), 1–24.
Altieri, M.A. and Toledo, V.M. 2011. The Agroecological Revolution in Latin America: Rescuing Nature, Ensuring Food Sovereignty and Empowering Peasants. *Journal of Peasant Studies*, 38(3), 587–612.
Altieri, M.A., Rosset, P. and Thrupp, L.A. 2001. The Potential of Agroecology to Combat Hunger in the Developing World. In: *The Unfinished Agenda*, Pinstrup-Andersen, P. and Pandya-Lorch, R. (eds). IFPRI: Washington, DC, pp. 123–127.

Anderson, K.B. 2010. *Marx at the Margins: On Nationalism, Ethnicity, and Non-Western Societies*. Chicago University Press: Chicago and London.

Araghi, F. 2003. Food Regimes and the Production of Value: Some Methodological Issues. *Journal of Peasant Studies*, 30(2), 41–70.

Arendt, H. 1998 [1958]. *The Human Condition*. 2nd edition. University of Chicago Press: Chicago and London.

BBC. 2016. Farm Subsidies: Payment to Billionaire Prince Sparks Anger. Available at: www.bbc.co.uk/news/uk-politics-37493956 (29 September 2016).

Bernstein, H. 2009. V.I. Lenin and A.V. Chayanov: Looking Back, Looking Forward. *Journal of Peasant Studies*, 36(1), 55–81.

Bernstein, H. 2014. Food Sovereignty via the 'Peasant Way': A Sceptical View. *Journal of Peasant Studies*, 41(6), 1031–1063.

Borras Jr, S.M., Franco, J.C., Gómez, S., Kay, C. and Spoor, M. 2012. Land Grabbing in Latin America and the Caribbean. *Journal of Peasant Studies*, 39(3–4), 845–872.

Butler, C.D. 2015. Revised Hunger Estimates Accelerate Apparent Progress towards the MDG Hunger Target. *Global Food Security*, 5, 19–24.

Buttel, F., Larson, O.F. and Gillespie, G. Jr. 1990. *The Sociology of Agriculture*. Greenwood Press: Westport, CT.

Carolan, M. 2012. *The Sociology of Food and Agriculture*. Routledge: London and New York.

Carroll, M. 2016. The Sticky materiality of Neo-liberal Neonatures: GMOs and the Agrarian Question. *New Political Economy*, DOI: 10.1080/13563467.2016.1214696

Clapp, J. and Fuchs, D. (eds). 2009. *Corporate Power in Global Agrifood Governance*. MIT Press: Cambridge, MA.

Cloke, P., Le Heron, R. and Roche, M. 1990. Towards a Geography of Political Economy Perspective on Rural Change: The Example of New Zealand. *Geografiska Annaler. Series B, Human Geography*, 72(1), 13–25.

Cruz, F.T., Matte, A. and Schneider, S. (eds). 2016. *Produção, Consumo e Abastecimento de Alimentos: Desafios e Novas Estratégias*. UFRGS: Porto Alegre.

Dalgaard, T., Hutchings, N.J. and Porter, J.R. 2003. Agroecology, Scaling and Interdisciplinarity. *Agriculture, Ecosystems and Environment*, 100(1), 39–51.

DeLanda, M. 2006. *A New Philosophy of Society: Assemblage Theory and Social Complexity*. Continuum: London.

Derrida, J. 1994. *Specters of Marx*. Trans. P. Kamuf. Routledge: London and New York.

Dibden, J., Potter, C. and Cocklin, C. 2009. Contesting the Neoliberal Project for Agriculture: Productivist and Multifunctional Trajectories in the European Union and Australia. *Journal of Rural Studies*, 25(3), 299–308.

Duff, C. 2016. Assemblages, Territories, Contexts. *International Journal of Drug Policy*, 33, 15–20.

Edelman, M., Weis, T., Baviskar, A., Borras Jr, S.M., Holt-Giménez, E., Kandiyoti, D. and Wolford, W. 2014. Introduction: Critical Perspectives on Food Sovereignty. *Journal of Peasant Studies*, 41(6), 911–931.

FAO, IFAD and WFP. 2015. *The State of Food Insecurity in the World 2015. Meeting the 2015 International Hunger Targets: Taking Stock of Uneven Progress*. UN-Food and Agriculture Organisation: Rome.

Friedland, W.H. 1982. The End of Rural Society and the Future of Rural Sociology. *Rural Sociology*, 47(4), 589–608.

Friedmann, H. 1978. World Market, State, and Family Farm: Social Bases of Household Production in the Era of Wage Labor. *Comparative Studies in Society and History*, 20(4), 545–586.

Friedmann, H. 1987. International Regimes of Food and Agriculture since 1870. In: *Peasants and Peasant Societies*, Shanin, T. (ed.). Basil Blackwell: Oxford, pp. 258–276.

Friedmann, H. 2005. Feeding the Empire: The Pathologies of Globalized Agriculture. *Socialist Register*, 41, 124–143.

Friedmann, H. and McMichael, P. 1989. Agriculture and the State System: The Rise and Decline of National Agricultures, 1870 to the Present. *Sociologia Ruralis*, 29(2), 93–117.

Gonzalez de Molina, M. 2013. Agroecology and Politics. How to Get Sustainability? About the Necessity for a Political Agroecology. *Agroecology and Sustainable Food Systems*, 37(1), 45–59.

Goodman, D. 1999. Agro-food Studies in the 'Age of Ecology': Nature, Corporeality, Bio-politics. *Sociologia Ruralis*, 39(1), 17–38.

Goodman, D. and Watts, M.J. 1994. Reconfiguring the Rural of Fording the Divide? Capitalist Restructuring and the Global Agri-food System. *Journal of Peasant Studies*, 22(1), 1–49.

Goodman, D. and Watts, M.J. (eds). 1997. *Globalising Food: Agrarian Questions and Global Restructuring*. Routledge: London and New York.

Gottlieb, R. and Joshi, A. 2010. *Food Justice*. MIT Press: Cambridge, MA.

Hall, D. 2015. The Political Ecology of International Agri-Food Systems. In: *The Routledge Handbook of Political Ecology*, Perreault, T., Bridge, G. and McCarthy, J. (eds). Routledge: Abingdon and New York, pp. 406–417.

Hardt, M. and Negri, A. 2000. *Empire*. Harvard Press: Cambridge, MA.

Harvey, D. 1996. *Justice, Nature and the Geography of Difference*. Blackwell: Oxford.

IAASTD (International Assessment of Agricultural Knowledge, Science and Technology for Development). 2009. *Agriculture at a Crossroads*. Island Press: Washington, DC.

Ilbey, B. and Bowler, I. 1998. From Agricultural Productivism to Post-productivism. In: *The Geography of Rural Change*, Ilbery, B. (ed.). Pearson: Harlow, pp. 57–84.

Ioris, A.A.R. 2012. Applying the Strategic-Relational Approach to Urban Political Ecology: The Water Management Problems of the Baixada Fluminense, Rio de Janeiro, Brazil. *Antipode*, 44(1), 122–150.

Ioris, A.A.R. 2016. Rent of Agribusiness in the Amazon: A Case Study from Mato Grosso. *Land Use Policy*, 59, 456–466.

Jansen, K. 2015. The Debate on Food Sovereignty Theory: Agrarian Capitalism, Dispossession and Agroecology. *Journal of Peasant Studies*, 42(1), 213–232.

Kautsky, K. 1988 [1899]. *The Agrarian Question*. Trans. P. Burgess. Zwan: London.

Lenin, V.I. 1977. [1899]. *The Development of Capitalism in Russia*. Collected Works, Vol. 3. Progress Publishers: Moscow.

Long, N. and van der Ploeg, J.D. 2011. Heterogeneidade, Ator e Estrutura: Para a Reconstituição do Conceito de Estrutura. In: *Os Atores do Desenvolvimento Rural: Perspectivas Teóricas e Práticas Sociais*, Schneider, S. and Gazolla, M. (eds). UFRGS: Porto Alegre, pp. 21–48.

Mann, S.A. and Dickinson, J.M. 1978. Obstacles to the Development of a Capitalist Agriculture. *Journal of Peasant Studies*, 5(4), 466–481.

Marcus, G. and Saka, E. 2006. Assemblage. *Theory, Culture & Society*, 23(2–3), 101–106.

Marsden, T. 2006. Pathways in the Sociology of Rural Knowledge. In: *The Handbook of Rural Studies*, Cloke, P., Marsden, T. and Mooney, P. (eds). SAGE: London, pp. 3–18.

Martínez-Torres, M.E. and Rosset, P.M. 2014. Diálogo de Saberes in La Vía Campesina: Food Sovereignty and Agroecology. *Journal of Peasant Studies*, 41(6), 979–997.

Martins, J.S. (ed.). 2009. *Travessias: A Vivência da Reforma Agrária nos Assentamentos*. 2nd edition. UFRGS: Porto Alegre.

Marx, K. 1973 [1857–1858]. *Grundrisse: Foundations of the Critique of Political Economy*. Trans. M. Nicolaus. Penguin: London.

Marx, K. 1976 [1867]. *Capital*. Vol. 1. Trans. B. Fowkes. Penguin: London.

McMichael, P. 1997. Rethinking Globalization: The Agrarian Question Revisited. *Review of International Political Economy*, 4(4), 630–662.

McMichael, P. 2000. Global Food Politics. In: *Hungry for Profit: The Agribusiness Threat to Farmers, Food, and the Environment*, Magdoff, F., Foster, J.B. and Buttel, F.H. (eds). Monthly Review Press: New York, pp. 125–143.

McMichael, P. 2009. A Food Regime Genealogy. *Journal of Peasant Studies*, 36(1), 139–169.

McMichael, P. 2010. The World Food Crisis in Historical Perspective. In: *Agriculture and Food in Crisis: Conflict, Resistance, and Renewal*, Magdoff, F. and Tokar, B. (eds). Monthly Review Press: New York, pp. 51–67.

Méndez, V.E., Bacon, C.M. and Cohen, R. 2013. Agroecology as a Transdisciplinary, Participatory, and Action-oriented Approach. *Agroecology and Sustainable Food Systems*, 37(1), 3–18.

Mooney, P. 1983. Toward a Class Analysis of Midwestern Agriculture. *Rural Sociology*, 48(4): 563–584.

Moore, J.W. 2010. Cheap Food and Bad Money: Food, Frontiers, and Financialization in the Rise and Demise of Neoliberalism. *Review*, 33(2–3), 225–261.

Moore, J.W. 2015. *Capitalism in the Web of Life*. Verso: London and New York.

Murcott, A. and Campbell, H. 2004. Teoria Agro-alimentare e Sociologia dell' Alimentazione. *Rassegna Italiana di Sociologia*, 4, 571–602.

Murdoch, J., Marsden, T. and Banks, J. 2000. Quality, Nature, and Embeddedness: Some Theoretical Considerations in the Context of the Food Sector. *Economic Geography*, 76(2), 107–125.

Newell, P. 2009. Technology, Food, Power: Governing GMOs in Argentina. In: *Corporate Power in Global Agrifood Governance*, Clapp, J. and Fuchs, D. (eds). MIT Press: Cambridge, MA, pp. 253–283.

O'Neal Campbell, M. 2013. *The Political Ecology of Agricultural History in Ghana*. Nova Science Publishers: Hauppauge, NY.

Patel, R. 2007. *Stuffed and Starved: From Farm to Fork the Hidden Battle for the World Food System*. Portobello Books: London.

Polanyi, K. 2001 [1944]. *The Great Transformation: The Political and Economic Origins of Our Time*. Beacon Press: Boston, MA.

Potter, C. and Tilzey, M. 2005. Agricultural Policy Discourses in the European post-Fordist Transition: Neoliberalism, Neomercantilism and Multifunctionality. *Progress in Human Geography*, 29(5), 581–600.

Quaye, W. Frempong, G.K. and Jongerden Juivenkamp, G. 2009. Exploring Possibilities to Enhance Food Sovereignty within the Cowpea Production-Consumption Network in Northern Ghana. *Journal of Human Ecology*, 28(2), 83–92.

Robinson, G. 2004. *Geographies of Agriculture: Globalisation, Restructuring and Sustainability*. Pearson: Harlow.

Robinson, W.I. 2008. *Latin America and Global Capitalism: A Critical Globalization Perspective*. The Johns Hopkins University Press: Baltimore, MD.

Roman-Alcalá, A. 2016. Conceptualising Components, Conditions and Trajectories of Food Sovereignty's 'Sovereignty'. *Third World Quarterly*, 37(8), 1388–1407.

Rosset, P.M., Machin Sosa, B., Roque Jaime, A.M. and Ávila Lozano, D.R. 2011. The Campesino-to-Campesino Agroecology Movement of ANAP in Cuba: Social Process Methodology in the Construction of Sustainable Peasant Agriculture and Food Sovereignty. *Journal of Peasant Studies*, 38(1), 161–191.

Sanderson Bellamy, A. and Ioris, A.A.R. 2017. Addressing the Knowledge Gaps in Agroecology and Identifying Guiding Principles for Transforming Conventional Agri-food Systems. *Sustainability*, 9(3), 330; DOI: 10.3390/su9030330

Schneider, S. and Niederle, P. A. 2010. Resistance Strategies and Diversification of Rural Livelihoods: The Construction of Autonomy among Brazilian Family Farmers. *The Journal of Peasant Studies*, 37(2), 379–405.

Sevilla Guzmán-Casado, E. and Woodgate, G. 2013. Agroecology: Foundations in Agrarian Social Thought and Sociological Theory. *Agroecology and Sustainable Food Systems*, 37(1), 32–44.

Sharp, P.A. and Leshner, A. 2016 (4 January). We Need a New Green Revolution. *The New York Times*.

Smith, A. 1998 [1776]. *Wealth of Nations*. Selected edition. Oxford University Press: Oxford.

Sultana, F. 2015. Emotional Political Ecology. In: *The International Handbook of Political Ecology*, Bryant, R.L. (ed.). Edward Elgar: Cheltenham, pp. 633–645.

Time. 2012. Betting on Hunger: Is Financial Speculation to Blame for High Food Prices? Available at: http://science.time.com/2012/12/17/betting-on-hunger-is-financial-speculation-to-blame-for-high-food-prices (12 December 2012).

Watts, N. and Scales, I.R. 2015. Seeds, Agricultural Systems and Socio-natures: Towards an Actor–Network Theory Informed Political Ecology of Agriculture. *Geography Compass*, 9(5), 225–236.

Wezel, A., Bellon, S., Doré, T., Francis, C., Vallod, D. and David, C. 2011. Agroecology as a Science, a Movement and a Practice. In: *Sustainable Agriculture Volume 2*. Springer: Netherlands, pp. 27–43.

Winter, M. 2003. Geographies of Food: Agro-food Geographies – Making Reconnections. *Progress in Human Geography*, 27(4), 505–513.

Wittman, H. 2009. Reworking the Metabolic Rift: La Vía Campesina, Agrarian Citizenship, and Food Sovereignty. *Journal of Peasant Studies*, 36(4), 805–826.

Zuppiroli, M. 2015. Recent Developments in Agri-food Commodity Prices and the Impact of Financial Speculation. *Progress in Nutrition*, 17(1), 23–35.

2 Realising agro-neoliberalism in Brazil

Agriculture, capitalism and agro-neoliberalism

The aims of this chapter are, first, to outline the main characteristics of agro-neoliberalism, and then to analyse its politico-economic repercussions in Brazil, making use of a conceptual framework that embraces three main areas of inter-action – namely, renewed public–private alliances, novel techno-economic strategies that intensify socio-ecological exploitation and the containment of critical reactions. The critical importance of export-led agribusiness in Brazil will provide a paradigmatic opportunity to test this conceptual framework and investigate the specificities of agro-neoliberalism. The chapter will offer a critical assessment of the implementation of neoliberal policies and the evolution of political and ideological mechanisms alongside forces of geographical change. It will specifically discuss recent politico-economic adjustments that have followed neoliberalising pressures and also early signs of weakness in Brazilian agro-neoliberalism, despite its undisputed hegemony. However, it is important to emphasise that agro-neoliberalism is a slippery concept with unclear boundaries and multiple continuities with previous phases of capitalist agriculture; in addition, not all economic processes and institutional changes to agriculture that have occurred in recent years can be associated with neoliberal reforms. Neo-liberalism is certainly widespread and very influential, but it is not everywhere all the time; other economic paradigms continue to function in the world today, even in impure forms (such as colonialism, statism and Stalinist-industrialisation). But by ignoring these nuances, many authors have exaggerated the scale and distinctiveness of neoliberalism, overstating the importance of some individual features while disregarding the wider economic history and geography of capitalism.

In basic terms, neoliberalism is a variegated, geographically uneven and path-dependent process that represents a 'historically specific, unevenly developed, hybrid, patterned tendency of market-disciplinary regulatory restructuring' (Brenner et al., 2010: 330). Neoliberalism is not only an economic and social phenomenon, but also constitutes an assertive development strategy aimed at displacing some of the prevailing politico-economic mechanisms adopted before the 1970s (Connell and Dados, 2014). It is about a new global rationality in which people are no longer only governed, but increasingly self-governed – that is, through new forms of collective and personal discipline according to a business-centred doctrine (Dardot and Laval, 2010). Neoliberalism has also entailed the extension of market-based competition and commodification into previously insulated realms of politico-economic life (created or protected by Keynesian economic policies). The fluidity of neoliberalisation includes a specific set of ideological tenets and policies aimed at renovating capitalism through increased market liberties, which, sooner or later, intensify mechanisms of exploitation and alienation. For instance, neoliberalism has always been anchored in its control of some of the last frontiers of modernity, such as new oil reserves, the deruralisation of China, cheap food and debt-driven trade liberalisation. Considering the dynamic and uneven basis of neoliberalism, it could be argued that most of the existing academic and grey literature exacerbates the division between state and market strategies, which is a false dichotomy often employed to rationalise neoliberalising reforms (i.e. the market as the realm of efficiency and rationality, and the state as the realm of inefficiency and paternalism). Practical experience around the world shows that even governments with distinct neoliberal façades continue to make use of direct interventions in market forces, such as fiscal or non-tariff restrictions. This is why Busch (2014) affirms that neoliberalism is mythical, as the concept is ultimately based on myths and ideological constructs about state and market, even though its power and disruptive impacts are real.

As discussed in the previous pages, the complex role of agriculture in industrial, and increasingly post-industrial, economies has been a favourite research topic for many of those studying the patterns and perspectives of contemporary capitalist societies and Western-based modernity. The high levels of financialisation of agri-food systems, the deep causes of agrarian disputes, the class identity of different groups of farmers and the various types of rural property, among other related issues, continue to be matters of great academic and policy interest. More importantly, the modernisation and intensification of agriculture are key factors in present-day capitalism (Busch and Bain, 2004) and, in particular, the transition to post-Fordist modes of production under the sphere of influence of neoliberalism (McMichael, 2009). The agri-food sector today increasingly bears the imprint of neoliberalism, not as a rigidly defined plan, but rather as a multifaceted phenomenon aimed at the reconfiguration of socio-ecological processes and socioeconomic institutions. The various techno-economic innovations introduced in commercial agriculture – including land and gene grabs, biotechnology, dispossession of common land, etc. – are all approaches that combine old and new features of the wider capitalist economy. One of the arresting features of this debate is that, although agricultural activities have increased considerably in the last few years (at least in absolute terms), various problems still affect food supply reliability and undermine the basic demands of rural and urban populations. The substantial questions associated with the neoliberalisation of agriculture include a lack of access to affordable, nutritious food, the impacts of agrochemicals on communities and ecosystems, and the enormous concentration of power held by a small number of mega-supermarkets and agri-food corporations that control food production, distribution and consumption.

If neoliberalism – seen as both the contemporary phase of capitalism (Moore, 2015) and as a complex, inherently variegated ideology of critical importance across scales and regions (MacArtney, 2009) – comprises beliefs and practices centred on the idea that market efficiency is the best mechanism for regulating socioeconomic relations and renovating politico-economic strategies (Schmalz and Ebenau, 2012), its influence on agriculture is a highly idiosyncratic process that combines free-market pressures and flexibilisation approaches with renewed forms of protectionism, trade barriers and labour movement restrictions (Potter and Tilzey, 2005). Since the end of the 1980s at least, the agenda of international development, led by multilateral agencies such as the World Bank, has been to reconcile agricultural economic growth and the reduction of rural poverty with incentives and institutional adjustments aimed at increasing land productivity and promoting free trade and land markets (Pereira, 2015). The creation of the World Trade Organization (WTO) in 1995 was the most eloquent attempt to liberalise global markets and reduce the importance of price controls and stock formation. In 1996, the final declaration of the World Food Summit in Rome affirmed that the pursuit of food trade policies would 'encourage our producers and consumers to utilise available resources in an economically sound and sustainable manner'. This triggered measures ranging from adjustments in small-scale farming and local economies to the escalation of agroindustrial production, the monopolisation of trade (upstream and downstream to the farm gate and the household), the widespread financialisation of agriculture (including future markets and agriculture derivatives) and the subjugation of public policies to private pressures (Clapp and Fuchs, 2009). As a result, contemporary agri-food systems are increasingly focused on short-term economic gains and the legitimisation of political hegemonies at the expense of issues of nourishment and health.

Neoliberalised agriculture is also an important element and a central component of a class-based project to restore the basis of exploitation and profitability that is guided by the imperatives of flexible capital accumulation, globalised markets and renewed forms of public–private interaction (Duménil and Lévy, 2004). Agri-food has certainly become one of the most globalised sectors in the neoliberalised economy, as the production and consumption of its products are now truly global affairs (Bonanno and Constance, 2008), and in this process the interests of farmers and customers have increasingly been subordinated to those of large corporations and their commercial allies, who have developed multiple strategies to benefit from the globalisation of markets and to lessen regulatory restrictions. As observed by McMichael (2010: 64), liberalisation and privatisation have combined 'to accelerate food circulation globally and restructure food production and retailing along corporate lines'. Nonetheless, most of the critical literature has so far focused on neoliberal agriculture's more readily identifiable features, such as the intensification of trade and financial flows or the evident influence of transnational corporations, but left rather too implicit the foundations and geographical specificities of what can be called 'agro-neoliberalism'. For instance, Wolf and Bonanno (2014) offer a very interesting set of examples of

results, contradictions and reactions to neoliberalism, but largely fail to con-
ceptualise the term itself beyond market solutions and private sector protagonism. Although agroneoliberalism is a sectoral expression of state and market
reforms under the influence of flexibilisation and financialisation pressures
(Harvey, 2005), it is necessary to further theorise and examine its ramifications
and unique praxis. For instance, in an otherwise fascinating article, Hollander
(2004) focuses on 'agriculture trade liberalisation', while in effect agro-
neoliberalism goes far beyond commerce and includes politico-ideological
dynamics, influencing economic production and social reproduction 'all the way
down'. Goodman and Watts (1994) appropriately recommend that rural questions should be situated within the wider canvas of social theory, emphasising,
for example, the territoriality of the agro-food complex and the simultaneous
territorialisation and deterritorialisation under globalising and neoliberalising
influences.

Overall, agro-neoliberalism is a complex, context-specific phenomenon that
aims to remove the constraints of Keynesian and Fordist approaches, create
new political and economic prospects and reinforce class-based hegemony.
However, neoliberalised agri-food is more than just a simple sectoral manifestation
of broader neoliberal calls for market-based solutions to the problems created
or neglected by the state apparatus; it is also qualitatively distinct from other
areas under the influence of neoliberal pressures, particularly because of a
tailored combination of simultaneous pleas for free-market and sustained
protectionism (Otero, 2012). In particular, the neoliberalisation of agri-food
largely follows the fetishism of free-market relations while at the same time
perpetuating or even amplifying calls for state interventions aimed, for instance,
at mitigating price oscillations and preventing over-production. Agro-neoliberalism is essentially the result of a contingent convergence of various production
and commercialisation practices organised according to an ideological construct
that privileges market-based policies and the intensification of capital circulation
and accumulation without ever removing the intervention and mediation of
the state apparatus. In addition, agro-neoliberalism incorporates complex historico-
geographical processes that are undoubtedly connected with other sectors and
public policies, such as environmental governance (as in the case of the management of resources and biodiversity), public services (e.g. provision and supervision
of transport and health) and commercial legislation (e.g. labelling, corporate
liability, customer rights).

Departing from the existing academic literature, and in order to facilitate the
analysis of the complex relationships between agriculture and neoliberalism, it is
possible to identify three main dimensions, or key features, of agro-neoliberalism,
as follows:

1 **Renewed public–private alliances (Dimension 1):** The central promoter of
agro-neoliberalism, despite all the rhetoric of free market rationality,
continues to be the national state, but often operating through new
partnerships with the private sector and through multilateral organisations,

such as the World Trade Organization, Bretton Woods institutions and regional blocks (e.g. Mercosul, European Union, NAFTA, etc.). The neoliberalised state strives both to address the insufficiencies of previous developmentalist policies and also to forge a more market-friendly institutional context – what is commonly described as a movement from 'government' to 'governance' (Ioris, 2013). This means that the interventionist policies of the post-Second World War years were partially replaced by a multi-level structure of food and agriculture governance that, crucially, included emerging associations between public and private agents (Marsden *et al.*, 2010). The state has remained central in the deployment and transcendence of agro-neoliberalism, and needs to be understood not as an isolated entity above society and socionature, but as an inherent locus of power that emerges from social and socio-ecological interactions and class-based compromises (Ioris, 2014). Because of this, public policies and regulatory approaches are subject to the powerful influence of the transnational corporate sector, which systematically attempts to both capture new markets and organise agriculture production and commercialisation. On one hand, the apparatus of the state remains in control of market re-regulation, knowledge production, organisation of health and labour, trade agreements and monetary policies, protection against market and agro-climatic risks, the promotion of food-security, etc. On the other hand, agro-neoliberalism grants the private sector, particularly corporations, influence that extends beyond their market share, through complex networks and carefully crafted discourses.

2   **Novel techno-economic strategies that intensify socio-ecological exploitation (Dimension 2)**: Agro-neoliberalism has benefited from capital-intense technologies and science-based solutions (which help to reinforce the position of the best-equipped and best-trained farmers), such as genetic engineering, computer systems and sophisticated transport, information and communication technologies (Busch, 2010). Moreover, agro-neoliberalism is not only an economic or technological process, but also a politico-ecological project that has deepened and intensified the multiple mechanisms of labour and nature exploitation required to maximise exchange values. It was not by chance that biotechnology was adopted commercially in the 1980s in tandem with the expansion of neoliberal reforms. The expansion of agro-neoliberalism, after the transition period in the late 1980s and early 1990s, was based on calls for market competition and promises that higher productivity and economic efficiency would reduce the costs of agri-food goods. Agriculture commodities (sugar, coffee, soybean, etc.) are increasingly treated like any other investment, such as gold or petroleum. The neoliberalisation of agri-food has become the embodiment of aggressive processes of commodity export, land concentration or reconcentration, marginalisation and proletarianisation (Murray, 2006). Due to growing proletarianisation, new technologies and rising productivity, neoliberalism coincided with the cheapest food in world history, considered in terms of calories produced per

labour hour in the commodity system (Moore, 2015). Ultimately, neoliberal agricultural policies have produced uneven, but generally negative, results for the agricultural sectors of poor countries, exacerbating social differences and marginalising many social groups (Oya, 2005).

3 **Containment of critical reactions (Dimension 3):** Agro-neoliberalising strategies have been employed to appease socio-political resistance through a discourse of supposed gains in terms of environmental responsibility and food security (Dibden *et al.*, 2009). Various types of power work together, from instrumental and discursive rationality to structural manifestations of political control determining what is produced and what sort of food is consumed (Newell, 2009). The widespread repercussions of agro-neoliberalism have also contributed to reinforcing the 'sanctity' of private property and the creation of entirely new markets, including the commodification of ecosystems, water and biodiversity. In this process, traditional farming is systematically displaced and the ability of producers to counter the effects of capitalist agriculture is significantly undermined (Guthman, 2008). None-theless, even with impressive levels of production and trade, advocates of agro-neoliberalism have not been able to eliminate uncomfortable questions about the displacement of family farming, the grabbing of land and other natural resources, growing risks and legitimacy gaps. There are increasing questions about the legitimacy, material coherence and instabilities of neoliberal agri-food systems (Wolf and Bonanno, 2014). Social movements and critical groups have established international protest networks that attempt to draw attention to renewed mechanisms of exclusion and exploitation (e.g. *La Vía Campesina*). At the same time, the hegemony and appeal of agro-neoliberalism have complicated grassroots reactions, and consequently opposition to agro-neoliberalism often replicates the very things it purports to resist, as in the case of commodification and private property rights (Guthman, 2007). As a result, the powerful influence of agro-neoliberalism has influenced the pursuit of technological and socioeconomic alternatives, as in the case of agro-ecological farming and organic production, which are increasingly captured and contained within the realm of corporate-friendly institutions.

The above three dimensions of agro-neoliberalism represent the specific conceptual framework used in this chapter to analyse the Brazilian agribusiness experience. Because of new production areas and growing productivity, Brazil has consolidated its position as a global leader, and even as a 'model' of commercial, integrated crop production (Collier, 2008). Unlike other economic sectors (such as industrial production and the retail market), neoliberalised agribusiness is considered an island of prosperity and economic dynamism, and is currently claimed to be the 'main business of Brazil' (Furtado, 2002: 203). Due to promotional campaigns and assertive public policies, the term 'agribusiness' has a particularly positive, and strategic, meaning in Brazil, where it is commonly used with reference to large plantation farms and, to a lesser extent, in reference to food processing and trading companies (the latter is the characterisation typically used in the United States). In general terms, Brazilian agribusiness is composed of four sectors: raw materials, agriculture, industry and distribution (Buainain and Garcia, 2015). At this point, a quick note on terminology is in order: the expression 'agribusiness', although quite vague, has helpful explanatory value here as it encapsulates the multiple activities of present-day commercial agriculture. It elusively reveals the 'agro' being transformed and reshaped according to the capitalist rationality of commodification, privatisation and intense exploitation needed to secure profitability. This is related to the observation of Debord (2009: 37) that the 'commodity's *independence* has spread to the entire economy it now dominates'. The imprecision of the term 'agribusiness' is nothing new, given that (capitalist) agriculture also has no rigid boundaries. It is not by chance that

> lobbyists and politicians generally get around the complexity of the farm industry by neglecting to define agriculture. Often, the goals of agricultural policy are simply stated in terms of unstable and low farm incomes. [. . .] agricultural policy design is ill-conceived because the farm problem itself is not well defined.
>
> (Schmitz *et al.*, 2002: 30–32)

While agriculture and agribusiness have no firm definitions, the concept of agribusiness makes evident the local specificities of intensive farming and also its insertion into the cross-scale features of capitalist agriculture. The origin of the term is attributed to Davis and Goldberg (1957), who define agribusiness (based on previous references made to agroindustry and entrepreneurial agriculture) as all the operations involved in the manufacture and distribution of farm supplies and the storage, processing and distribution of farm commodities. Agribusiness became associated with a large agroindustrial complex under concentrated forms of corporate ownership and management. Seen from a critical perspective, agri-business appears to be more than just a commercial agriculture regime practiced in high-tech farms, but rather constitutes a particular approach to the management of rural properties, the mobilisation of resources and the financing and commercialisation of production. The consolidation of agribusiness in the name of agriculture – that is, agriculture-cum-agribusiness – not only exposes the supremacy of industrial and financial capitalism, but also reveals a striving for territorial expansion and new market penetration. The adjustments that followed the introduction of neoliberalising ideas in recent decades need to be understood in the context of the increasing capitalisation of agriculture associated with the consolidation of agribusiness. Agro-neoliberalism, basically realised through the expansion and renovation of agribusiness, changed agriculture from its role as supplier of food, material and cheap labour into a strategic area for rapid capital circulation, diversification of investments and contingent (circumstantial) stabilisation of the socio-ecological contradictions of capitalism.

The transition from conventional to neoliberalised agribusiness has been only partially accomplished given that, although the neoliberalisation of food and agriculture has been a calculated attempt to fix the systemic crisis of Fordist agri-food, it failed to prevent the reappearance of instability, protest, socio-ecological degradation and, ultimately, legitimacy deficits (Wolf and Bonanno, 2014). The contradictions of neoliberalised agribusiness are repeatedly played down by those who praise its material and socio-political achievements, although there is mounting criticism from those who oppose agribusiness-led forms of development. The impacts cited by the latter group include the disruption of traditional food, utilisation of mechanised deforestation, and concentration of landed property. In particular, the removal of subsidies and the dismantling of state enterprises resulted in higher levels of vulnerability affecting low-income populations, which ultimately encourages migration as a negotiated response to new public policies and practices (Torres and Carte, 2014). The complexity and shortcomings of agro-neoliberalism are even more evident when positioned in relation to the uneven geographical development and world-ecology of the global capitalist economy (Moore, 2010). In the case of Brazil, the neoliberalisation of agribusiness has proved central to the country's insertion into globalised markets, but it has also revealed a peculiar amalgamation of tradition and modernity evolving through both new socio-spatial orders and the maintenance of old political structures. Repeated assertions of the success of agribusiness in Brazil have paved the way for consolidation of the political hegemony of agro-neoliberalism as a highly idiosyncratic phenomenon progressing through distinctive associations between the state apparatus and the national and international private sector. It is to this contentious national experience in South America that we now turn.

The realisation of agro-neoliberalism in Brazil

Brazilian agriculture has evolved, since colonial times, through the strategic association of export crops cultivated in vast latifundia and staple food produced by subsistence farming at the margins of the large properties. Unlike the mineral-rich parts of South America under Spanish rule (e.g. the vice-royalty of Peru), Brazil was initially established as an agricultural colony of Portugal for the cultivation and export of cane sugar. Over the following centuries the country became an important source of coffee and other agricultural and extractive products. The production of goods for northern markets relied on a politico-economic alliance between powerful rural elites and the apparatus of the colonial and, later, national state (Oliveira, 2007). As in comparable regions of the world during the 'first food regime' (see Chapter 1), initial attempts to modernise agriculture were already in place at the turn of the 20th century (largely involving migrants from Italy, Germany and Japan; the main agricultural colleges and research centres in Brazil were also established during this period), without altering the overall balance of agrarian power between large-scale and subsistence farmers. Agribusiness-like agriculture was initiated in the extreme south of the territory, with the irrigation of rice and, a few decades later, the cultivation of wheat, maize and, increasingly, soybean. It remained a typically dualistic agri-culture with an 'efficient' segment dominated by large-scale farmers producing for foreign markets alongside what was considered an 'inefficient', family-based sector of basic food production (Muir, 2014).[1]

The agribusiness translation (i.e. reconfiguration) of agriculture intensified after the Second World War, in the context of the Green Revolution and with the state apparatus promoting organisational and technological changes, especially via subsidies, credit, technology and minimum prices. Despite technological advances and increasing agricultural production, hunger and malnutrition persisted and continued to plague the country. Castro (1954) famously demonstrated the existence of a true 'geography and geopolitics of hunger' in which perverse socioeconomic inequalities, inherited from the past, play a more important role than production and distribution issues. The modernisation of agriculture and rural development received a much larger stimulus during the twenty-one years of military dictatorship (1964–1985), with the incorporation of different forms of capital, new methods of production and the formation of agroindustrial chains (Gonçalves Neto, 1997). Priority was given by the authoritarian governments of the time to national-developmentalist policies inspired by Keynesian principles and national security concerns (Graziano da Silva, 1988). Policy instruments included further and targeted fiscal incentives, subsidised credit, efficiency measures and the integration of farming and industry (Delgado, 2012). It was essentially a plan to intensify and expand agriculture via an increase in its technical composition and subordination to the interests of industrial and financial capital. Brazil became an important exporter of key commodities, especially soybean, red and white meat, sugar and paper pulp due to the incorporation of old and new areas, technological improvements and mobilisation of a large workforce. The expansion of Brazilian agribusiness was also helped by developments elsewhere. Between 1971 and 1973, the USSR purchased a significant proportion of the crops produced in the United States, which caused a general rise in grain prices. In addition, because of the El Niño, there was a reduction in the harvest of anchovy in Peru and diminished peanut production in Africa, for which the main substitute was soybean meal. The United States declared an embargo on its soybeans, which opened an important market space for the Brazilian agribusiness (Warnken, 1999).

Regarding the social consequences of the expansion of agriculture-cum-agribusiness, instead of facilitating access to land and opportunities for the majority of subsistence farmers, the federal government focused on promoting crop production throughout the country (Oliveira and Stédile, 2005) as an 'anti-agrarian' reform that further concentrated land ownership and reinforced old agrarian trends. Traditional communities and ecosystem processes were removed to make space for commercial agriculture in what is described by Araghi (2009) as a mechanism of accumulation by displacement. The problems of the agribusiness model promoted by the military, however, went far beyond social inequalities and environmental degradation. After remarkable rates of growth, the state-centralised mode of agricultural intensification started to show its serious limitations, particularly as Brazil was suffering from a public debt crisis, escalating rates of inflation and macroeconomic instability. International loans also became significantly more expensive and more difficult to obtain because of the increasingly stringent requirements of multilateral banks after the oil price shocks of the 1970s. The inadequacy of developmentalist policies is what O'Connor (1973) defines as the 'fiscal crisis of the state' – that is, a public sector increasingly unable to cope with economic demands because of the discrepancy between the available tax base and high social expectations. The Brazilian agribusiness sector went through a period of turbulence and uncertainty in the mid-1980s, which coincided with the collapse of the military dictatorship and a protracted restoration of political and electoral rights (with limited effects on social inclusion and equality). Interest rates rose significantly and government support schemes (e.g. subsidies, guaranteed prices, investments in infrastructure, regional development plans, etc.) were scaled down.

The concurrence of strong political, economic and ideological pressures led to a gradual transition to new bases of production and commercialisation, which essentially occurred because of the contradictions intrinsic to the conservative modernisation of agriculture championed by the Brazilian state and the increasingly favourable opportunities in globalised markets. Agribusiness in Brazil has gradually shifted towards a 'new rural model', as described by Campanhola and Graziano da Silva (2000), characterised by higher levels of agroindustrial integration, more direct intervention from large corporations, adoption of biotechnology and digital technologies, specialisation and economic concentration. This new configuration of agribusiness was directly associated with the wider neoliberal reforms introduced in the early 1990s. Inflation reduction and macroeconomic stabilisation policies – known as the Real Plan, launched in 1994 and maintained by President Cardoso (1995–2002) – dramatically reorganised the economy and paved the way for the advancement of agro-neoliberalism as the preferred strategy for the revitalisation of national agribusiness. Initially, however, agriculture suffered from higher interest rates and the strengthening of the national currency, the real (R$), which facilitated agroindustrial imports while at the same time creating circumstantial barriers to the export of Brazilian goods (Ioris and Ioris, 2013). After this temporary volatility, the situation soon improved and the production of crops for export was again encouraged by more favourable exchange rates following the 1999 mega-devaluation of the Brazilian currency (Siqueira, 2004) and by extraordinarily advantageous commodity prices during most of the 2000s (Richards *et al.*, 2012). It was not by chance that Brazil sustained a long fight against protectionism in the WTO as part of its attempt to further liberalise global markets and preserve the interests of its export-driven agribusiness sector (Hopewell, 2013).

Production has since increased year on year and the Brazilian agribusiness sector now accounts for approximately 25 per cent of GDP, 35 per cent of exports and 40 per cent of national jobs in the country (MAPA, 2012). At the time of writing, there are expectations that the largest total agricultural production in the country's history will be achieved in 2017, based on data from Brazil's National Supply Company (Conab) published in November 2016 (projections indicate an increase of up to 15.6 per cent compared with 2016, with total harvests between

210.9 million and 215.1 million tons). The speedy recovery of Brazilian agriculture and the fulfilment of neoliberalising reforms were certainly enabled by a combination of public and private measures (Petras and Veltmeyer, 2003). The state apparatus remained firmly in charge of rural development, but at the same time forged close partnerships with an ever-stronger private agribusiness sector (Schneider, 2010). It is curious that under the populist, neo-developmentalist administrations of Presidents Lula (2003–2010) and Dilma (2011–2016), agro-neoliberalism has become, perhaps paradoxically, more deeply entrenched, with a return to some of the state-led policies of the military regime, although within the neoliberal frame introduced in the 1990s. In this process, both established transnationals (Monsanto, ADM, Bunge, Cargill, Dreyfus, etc.) and newly transnational Brazilian companies (Amaggi, BR Foods, JBS, Marfrig, etc.) have played an increasingly decisive role. Transnational corporations directly contributed to the advance of agro-neoliberalism in Brazil by working in collaboration (and sometimes in competition) with national companies, agribusiness farmers and even small-scale farmers (the latter can benefit circumstantially, for example, from periods of high commodity prices that induce them to cultivate cash crops).

An interesting peculiarity of populist, neo-developmentalist policies was the allocation of massive public funds from state-owned banks for the consolidation and internationalisation of the new Brazilian TNCs. Direct support was given within the framework of the Productive Development Policy (PDP), with the National Bank for Economic and Social Development [*Banco Nacional de Desenvolvimento Econômico e Social* – BNDES] as sponsor, direct investor and agent for mergers, and the acquisitions of a series of foreign companies based in various countries. Another integral element of Brazilian agro-neoliberalism was the persistence of rural credit offered by state-owned banks – with annual interest rates of around 5 per cent, significantly lower than the standard rates offered by commercial banks – which expanded from R$15 billion per year in the 1990s to R$133 billion in 2013 and R$156 billion in 2014 (O Estado de São Paulo, 2014). Despite a demagogic discourse aiming to please both agribusiness and small-scale farming, such public funding was overwhelmingly directed towards the agribusiness sector, (e.g. for the 2013–2014 harvest, R$115 billion were invested in corporate agriculture and only R$18 billion in family farming). Needless to say, much of the investment in family farming also supports the purchase of machinery to modernise production, and acts as a stimulus for the agroindustrial sector.

Together with generous state support, various new financial instruments have played a crucial role in the advance of neoliberalised agribusiness, such as self-financing, financial cooperatives, input supplier companies and trading companies, filling the gap created by the inadequacies of previous federal government-administered schemes (Serigati, 2013). Some of these instruments are not new in Brazil and have been available for several years, but have been expanded and reformulated to satisfy the financial needs of neoliberalised agribusiness. A significant proportion of rural credit is now provided by transnational corporations and through a massive increase in bank-like transactions (normally called 'green soybean' [*soja verde*]) made available at the beginning of the growing season.

Another notable illustration of the widespread use of financial instruments was the 2004 legislation that created the Agribusiness Receivables Certificate (CRA), among other titles traded on the São Paulo Stock Exchange. The CRA is a registered credit instrument which links a promise of future payment in cash to the debt claim issued by the securitisation company (MAPA, 2010). By 2013, the amount of traded CRAs had reached R$1.2 billion (around US$550 million), but this is expected to grow 30 times more over the next few years (ISTOÉ Dinheiro, 2013). An early confirmation of this projection was the trifold increase in investments between January and December 2015; a total of R$6.4 billion was invested over the year, according to the management and registration company Cetip. The situation in Brazil is consistent with the international experience – worldwide, the neoliberalisation of agribusiness has entailed, among other adjustments, increases in the use of financial instruments by the agri-food sector (Fuchs *et al.*, 2013).

In the case of Brazil, the increased financialisation of crop production and distribution (further discussed below) has not only affected the relations of production, but directly transformed the nature and destination of what is produced. Government investments in agriculture-related infrastructure and technological development have become more selective, targeting primarily biofuel and export commodities, as in the case of soybean (Bernardes, 1996). In addition, there has been a partial replacement of previously dominant north–south trade priorities (especially trade with the European Union) with increasing south–south interconnections, particularly between Brazil and Asia (FIESP, 2008). Commercial exchanges between Brazil and China reached US$77 billion in 2011 (Brazil exported goods worth US$44.3 billion and imported goods worth US$32.8 billion), with agriculture-based exchanges increasing from US$1.7 billion in 2003 to US$14.6 billion in 2011, according to MAPA (2012). The Economist (2010) has even named Brazil the first tropical food giant, mainly because of the influence of Chinese demand. Soybean is by far the most important agricultural commodity in Brazil and the 'soybean complex' accounts for 80 per cent of agricultural exports to China. Soybean is not just an emblematic symbol of Brazilian agro-neoliberal modernity and the success of production reorganisation; soybean production also involves significant geopolitical repercussions in terms of Brazil's influence, especially in Africa and South America. Jepson *et al.* (2010) highlight the high demand for soybean among transnational corporations due to its market value and industrial uses.[2] And the national sectoral organisation ABAG asserts that 'soybean production was born modern' and that it is an example of the best the country has to offer (Furtado, 2002: 135).

Considering the changes and adjustments carried out during the last two decades, the three dimensions of agro-neoliberalism, as described above, are clearly manifested: novel public–private alliances (replacing previous forms of collaboration primarily established around the apparatus of the state), techno-economic modernisation (for example, genetically modified seeds, new agrochemicals and sophisticated machinery) and the use of developmentalist discourses by left-wing, populist administrations to justify neoliberalising policies and prevent opposition.

It is true that both right-wing (Cardoso and, since 2016, Temer) and left-wing governments (Lula and Dilma) have accepted the necessity of agro-neoliberalism and its crucial contribution to the functioning of Brazil's macroeconomic system. The overall impacts and key repercussions of the agro-neoliberal experience can be summarised in four basic points.

First, despite positive results in terms of increased production, financing and commercialisation, the success of neoliberalised agribusiness has left Brazil dangerously over-reliant on primary commodities and the appetites of distant markets. On one hand, the country has become the main global exporter of soybean (contributing 44 million of the 105.1 million tons traded in 2013) and the soybean complex continues to expand unabated (8.2 per cent in 2011–2012 and 18.5 per cent in 2012–2013, when it accounted for almost US$31 billion of export revenues, according to CEPEA, 2014). According to a FAO communiqué published in 2016, the country will be the world's largest soybean producer by 2025, overtaking the United States. Projections by the Brazilian ministry of agriculture (MAPA) indicate that by 2019 the country will be responsible for 40 per cent of the global trade in soybean grains [*soja em grão*] and 73 per cent of soybean meal [*farelo*]. On the other hand, the Brazilian economy has faced progressive deindustrialisation, increased dependence on foreign investments and rising imports of intermediate inputs and capital goods.

From 2004 to 2013, manufacturing dropped from 55.0 per cent to 38.4 per cent-of GDP, while primary production increased from 29.5 per cent to 46.7 per cent (MDIC, 2013). Between 2000 and 2010, export earnings from primary goods increased from 25 per cent to 45 per cent, while those from manufactured goods declined from 56 per cent to 43 per cent (Delgado, 2012). After the 2008 global financial crisis, the dependence of the Brazilian economy on the success of agribusiness extended even further as the export of agricultural commodities became the 'green anchor' of the economy (Acselrad, 2012). Between 2012 and 2013, total national exports fell by 0.2 per cent, but agribusiness exports increased by 4.3 per cent; in the same period, total national imports increased by 7.4 per cent, while agribusiness imports increased by only 4.0 per cent (CONAB, 2014). In 2014 the trade balance showed the worst performance since 1998 (a deficit of US$4.036 billion in 2014, according to the MDIC database) with agribusiness appearing as one of the few sectors with positive foreign exchange results. As shown in Table 2.1, while agribusiness grew proportionally less than the national economy, and its percentage contribution to the national economy actually decreased between 2007 and 2015, its contribution to the national surplus (in dollar terms) was critical. Agricultural exports in 2013 reached a value of US$99.97 billion (4.3 per cent more than the previous year) with a net surplus (i.e. minus imports) of US$82.91 billion (including US$30.96 billion from soybean exports alone). The contribution of agribusiness was even more impressive considering that the average price of commodities on international markets fell by 7.5 per cent between 2012 and 2013 (Barros *et al.*, 2014). In subsequent years, the contribution of agribusiness to the national trade balance has remained highly significant, although it has

Table 2.1 Agribusiness and the Brazilian economy (selected years)

	2007	2013	2014	2015
GDP Brazil (R$)	3.58 trillion	4.49 trillion	6.14 trillion	5.90 trillion
GDP agribusiness sector (R$)	833.6 billion	1.02 trillion	1.26 trillion	1.27 trillion
Participation of agribusiness in the Brazilian GDP	23.30 %	22.80 %	20.56 %	21.46 %
National trade balance (US$)	40.0 billion	2.2 billion	(4.0 billion)	19.7 billion
Agribusiness trade balance (US$)	49.7 billion	82.9 billion	80.1 billion	75.1 billion

Data consolidated from various bulletins of CEPEA (at the University of São Paulo) / SECEX (Brazilian Foreign Trade Secretariat)

gradually declined because of less favourable agriculture commodity prices on international markets.

Second, as observed in Figure 2.1, while the difference between export and import values ('price x quantity bought', in US$ figures) is dwindling in Brazil and even tending towards a negative result, the surplus (gross income – i.e. total exports minus total imports) produced by the agribusiness sector is positive and growing. One of the most perverse consequences of the steady expansion of agribusiness surpluses is that the contemporary Brazilian state, which combines neoliberalising priorities with elements of populism and neo-Keynesian developmentalism, greatly depends on agriculture to help manage its monumental public debt (the public deficit in the year 2015 was more than US$1.2 trillion) and to sustain politically relevant welfare-related programmes (such as the important conditional cash transfer scheme known as the Family Grant [*Bolsa Família*]).

Third (and directly related to 'Dimension 3' above), the positive economic results produced by agribusiness have served to unify the interests of rural conservative groups and renew processes of political hegemony and class domination (Bruno, 2009). The ambiguous structure of the federal government directly reflects class inequalities and disputes, as agribusiness exerts great influence over the Ministry of Agriculture (i.e. MAPA), while the interests of family and subsistence farming are overseen by the much weaker Ministry of Agrarian Development (the MDA, which was eventually incorporated into a larger department by President Temer's administration). It was highly indicative of the political influence of agribusiness that President Lula started his first term in office with the 'Zero Hunger' programme and ended his second mandate openly defending the agribusiness sector and making significant concessions on regulation and environmental legislation (Canal Rural, 2009). Because of its political significance, the agribusiness sector has actively managed to protect its interests, especially with an organised and prominent presence in the National Congress, where around one third of the senators and deputies belong to, or support, the Parliamentary Farming and Cattle Raising Front [*Frente Parlamentar da*

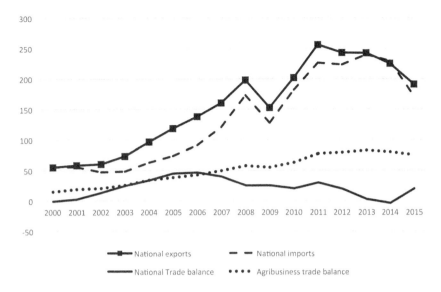

Figure 2.1 Brazil's trade balance and the contribution of agribusiness (in billions of dollars)

Source: Author

Agropecuária – FPA], with the number of FPA parliamentarians increasing after the 2014 general election. An important initiative of the FPA is its determined effort to remove any environmental and social regulation that could prevent the expansion of production. One of its key members is the hard-line Senator Kátia Abreu, president of the National Confederation of Agriculture and Livestock (Ms Abreu was re-elected in 2014 and was Minister of Agriculture in the second Dilma government from January 2015 until the removal of the president by the National Congress in May 2016). Senator Abreu repeatedly stated that environmental conservation aggravates the food crisis and that, consequently, climate change deserves much less attention from government and society alike (The Guardian, 2014).[3]

Fourth (and directly related to 'Dimension 2' above), there have been growing tensions between global commodity chains led by Brazilian agribusinesses and social, grassroots movements calling for corporate responsibility, environmental protection, quality food and labour rights (Wilkinson, 2011). However, due to the vital role played by agribusiness in maintaining macroeconomic stability, and thanks to the political legitimisation of populist governments, the sector has managed to secure increasing regulatory concessions (such as more flexible labour and forestry legislation) and its political capital has served to mitigate bad publicity generated by environmental impacts and the regressive social agenda advanced by representatives of agribusiness. Systematic campaigns orchestrated by influential representative entities (for instance, the Brazilian Agribusiness

Association, the National Confederation of Agriculture and Livestock, and the Federation of Industries of the State of São Paulo) have tried to refute and dismiss the prevalent image of large-scale farmers as perpetrators of injustice against small-scale farmers and indigenous groups and as major contributors to environmental damage in old and new production areas.

All things considered, it is possible to conclude that Brazilian agro-neoliberalism has evolved through an intricate process of economic gain and aggressive modernisation intertwined with systematic attempts to justify, and sometimes conceal, strategic alliances between populist authorities and market-friendly ideologies. The sector has maintained steady rates of expansion not only due to constant technological improvements (e.g. new agrochemicals, genetically modified seeds and more sophisticated machinery and digital equipment), but also because of further land grabbing and incursion into new production areas (Borras *et al.*, 2012). To a large extent, the apparent success of agribusiness is the result of policy mistakes (e.g. the financing of new Brazilian TNCs through BNDES) and the need to maintain agribusiness exports as a macroeconomic stabiliser (playing an anti-cyclical role). Regardless of the causes, the bitter consequence is that national economic policies now largely depend on the results of the primary sector, which is considered an island of prosperity and technological success in a context of growing deindustrialisation, low productivity gains and escalating public deficits (Buainain and Garcia, 2015). Circumstantial profitability and positive results are combined with mounting socio-ecological risks and the concentration of power in the hands of corporations and agribusiness leaders, including several elected politicians. Let us now consider the trends and main patterns of the neoliberalisation of agribusiness in Brazil.

The overall trends of Brazilian agro-neoliberalism

The multiple dimensions of the advance of agro-neoliberalism in Brazil (briefly reviewed above) suggest that the intensification of market operations and market-based solutions are at once products and co-producers of the wider modernisation of the national economy. Particularly with the slowdown of the economy since 2014, neoliberalised agribusiness has come to be seen as one of the few islands of prosperity and dynamism in a context of corporate losses and lack of investment, particularly in the industrial sector. The operation of neoliberalised agribusiness has comprised a range of production and distribution processes (rather than an isolated phenomenon with clear-cut boundaries), required for the maximisation of surplus according to a market-friendly discourse and a strong ideology of market liberty. This is relevant because, as observed by Foucault (1998, quoted in Oels 2005: 190), 'it is in discourse that power and knowledge are joined together'. It is also the case that the main agribusiness players have been less concerned with development goals (regardless of the discourse of efficiency and social responsibility) than with short-term capital accumulation strategies and insertion into globalised agri-food markets. Consequently, as in other parts of the globe, agro-neoliberalism in Brazil has sparked huge criticism in terms of its actual beneficiaries and its uncertain prospects. Especially in agricultural frontier areas, such as Mato Grosso in the southern section of the Amazon region, agribusiness seems to thrive on a peculiar combination of tradition and modernity (which will be examined in later pages). Neoliberalised agribusiness has not only reinforced previous developmentalist policies, but has also, through a combination of physical, social and political shifts, displaced, but in some cases also reaffirmed, old capitalist tendencies.

This complexity has been only partially recognised in the existing literature – for instance, in the landmark publication by a range of experts from different parts of Brazil (Buainain *et al.*, 2014), who summarise the 'new agricultural model' in terms of the aggressive influence of financial capital, increased social differentiation (segmentation of winners and losers), continued influence of the state apparatus and restricted access to new technologies. This list certainly captures some important elements of the transition to agro-neoliberalism, but fails to deal with the more politicised and contested pillars of contemporary agribusiness. It further demonstrates that the internal neoliberalising tendencies of Brazilian capitalist agriculture are not easily recognisable beyond the discourse of the supposed achievements of agribusiness. An incisive scrutiny of the entire spectrum of adjustments and adaptation to changes is required. Taking everything presented so far into account, it is possible to identify at least three main tendencies in the advance of agro-neoliberalism in Brazil.

The first leading trend has been the aggressive, although partial, substitution of the previous emphasis on rural development, job creation and infrastructure with a focus on market integration, cost reduction, efficiency gains and technological intensification. The political strength of neoliberal agribusiness actually comes from the consolidation of new economic strategies that have supplanted the developmentalist policies that were hegemonic before the 1980s. This process of substitution has had both sectoral and spatial manifestations. It occurs, for instance, due to technological improvements (e.g. the constant introduction of agrochemicals, genetically modified seeds and sophisticated equipment), inter-country trade (often at the expense of fulfilling national and local needs) and the facilitated interchangeability of different forms of capital in commodity and land markets. The neoliberalisation of agribusiness has benefited from, and contributed to, a wider process of sectoral dislocation due to an emphasis on the import of intermediate inputs and capital goods (to contain inflation and appease consumer demand) and ill-conceived deindustrialisation policies. Although local food production remains important (particularly where food is produced by family farmers and peasant communities), southern countries have been encouraged to expand the export of high-value foods (e.g. expensive soft-fruits, out-of-season vegetables, luxury crops, etc.) to northern markets, and to cultivate biofuel crops under the influence, for example, of mainstream environmental agendas. Sizeable commercial partnerships have been established between Brazil and other countries of the Global South (China in particular) which have, to a degree, replaced the established north–south flow of agriculture goods (the export of soybean from Brazil to the European Union was previously particularly relevant, for example).

The affirmation of agro-neoliberalism was also associated with the migration of farmers and companies to new areas and the incorporation of regions that were not previously agricultural areas or were beyond the reach of global markets. Large parts of Brazil have been transformed by the advance of neoliberal agribusiness due to the intensification, and joint operation, of public and private capital investments. The most emblematic experience was the conversion of millions of hectares of native vegetation in the central region of the country (considered as 'spare farmland') into soybean plantations and cattle ranches in close coordination with ever bigger agro-industries (Barreto *et al.*, 2013). Such neoliberal 'land reform' (in effect, another anti-agrarian reform similar to the one adopted by the military government in the 1970s) was based on the premise that private ownership of land was sacrosanct in the name of democratising capitalism and, more importantly, avoiding the excesses of the state apparatus. The transformation associated with agribusiness is, thus, dialectically related to the transnationalisation of the rural economy, in the sense that activities and processes are (partially) altered at the local or horizontal level only to be then (partial and problematically) integrated into globalised phenomena. This trend is particularly demonstrated by the fact that agriculture continues to be enacted in the localised context of farms and regions, but management, technologies and trade relations increasingly happen in accordance with transnational interactions and priorities. This means that the neoliberalisation of agribusiness is an attempt to maximise production and profitability at the local level through a web of relations that reconstruct agriculture as a 'world farm' (McMichael, 2010). The search for efficiency and the emphasis on competitive advantages have resulted in the dispossession of less successful smallholders by commercial smallholders and large estates that are vertically integrated into agribusiness marketing chains (Amanor, 2009).

The second main tendency has been the growing financialisation of agriculture production as a decisive force behind politico-ecological changes. Since the crisis of Keynesian policies, agribusiness has operated through a gradual shift from the production side to the retail side, and towards novel mechanisms of capital circulation and accumulation. Production obviously continues, but increasingly under the decisive authority of corporations and financial institutions (Burch and Lawrence, 2013). Financialisation is a process whereby transnational corporations, commercial elites and banks acquire even greater influence over rural policy-making and agriculture outcomes (at the expense of the more traditional players of the previous developmentalist phase). Production has also been transformed and it is now common for large-scale farm-management corporations to become the primary vehicle for financial capital (including new entrants into agribusiness production, such as hedge funds, pension funds, etc.) in order to engage in farmland investments and agroindustrial production. This means that most financing for seeds, agro-chemicals, and machinery no longer comes from public banks but from transnational companies themselves (Fairbairn, 2014).

For instance, in several parts of South America, such as Argentina, Brazil and Paraguay, there are now 'pools de *siembra*' (sowing pools), which are transitory enterprises whereby investors work together to finance grain production; each pool forms rent contracts with a large number of landowners – generally located in different regions in order to diversify risks – and then assumes management of the crop production enterprise.

As a result, the entrenched financialisation of food and farming ends up penetrating everyday life and pervading the local, regional and global scales of interaction; as Busch (2014: 516) affirms, 'the grammar of markets has become hegemonic in both social life and individual selves'. Financialisation is not restricted to adjustments in the productive and commercial sectors (including the role of asset management companies, private equity consortia and other financial institutions in acquiring and managing farmland), but is present along the whole agri-food supply chain, at macro- and micro-scales. This all corroborates the claim that neoliberalised agribusiness is now less focused on farm production than during the previous phases of the capitalist economy, as it is centred on off-farm financial activities that increasingly dominate supply chains, logistics and distribution systems coordinated and supported by the state (Whatmore, 1995). The 'food crisis', associated with high commodity prices during the last decade, further discouraged productive investment in industries and infrastructure in favour of speculative activities that produced a massive flow of capital into agriculture. In Brazil, the amounts involved grew from 2.4 billion reais (R$) in June 2006 to 144.7 billion in June 2016. The rise was much sharper after 2011. Between 2012 and 2015, the financial volume grew sevenfold, from R$19.7 billion in 2012 to R$145.4 billion in 2015. The average value of future contracts in the São Paulo Stock Exchange (BM&F Bovespa) increased from U$74 in 2005 to U$312,000 in 2013. The agribusiness sector has the largest share of open capital companies among the economic sectors operating in the BM&F Bovespa, with 21.2 per cent of the total number (Balestro and Lourenço, 2014).

At the same time, the escalating financialisation of agribusiness and the influence of foreign capital help to explain disturbing events such as the bankruptcy of Sadia, the Brazilian food-processing giant, in 2008, with losses of more than $4 billion, due to high levels of exchange derivative speculation. In effect, in 2008 and 2009, soon after the onset of the global financial crisis, some of the largest Brazilian agribusiness corporations made huge losses from financial speculation with exchange derivatives. Likewise, Votorantim Holding's financial losses from exchange derivatives due to the rise of the dollar against the Brazilian real reached R$2.2 billion (as reported in the newspaper O Estado de São Paulo on 11 October 2008). In historico-geographical terms, the financialisation of the agri-food sector has represented an accommodating solution to the ever-problematic combination of the production and plunder spheres of capitalism, which can affect both workers and the general public, as well as those with personal stakes in capitalist activities (Moore, 2010). Related to this, the phenomenon of land grabbing, which has increased as growing numbers of institutional investors have entered Brazilian agribusiness, has also had an impact on land prices over the last decade. Foreign direct investment flow into agriculture jumped from $2.4 billion in 2002 to $13.1 billion in 2012 (Sauer and Leite, 2012), and since then a bill has been under consideration in the Brazilian congress (no. 4059/12) which aims to legalise and facilitate access to land for foreign investors. This controversial proposal received a significant boost in 2016 after the removal of President Rousseff's populist government.

The third main trend is associated with the systematic and well-orchestrated mystification of results and problems. Together with its important technological and economic components, neoliberalised agribusiness has evolved through constant political efforts to disguise and simultaneously justify changes in the contemporary agri-food sector. The representatives of neoliberal agribusiness have cleverly crafted an image of prosperity and accomplishment that is presented in terms of Brazil's geographical advantages and the competence of the farming sector. The Brazilian agribusiness sector is portrayed by most of the mass media and most economic and political leaders as beyond criticism – that is, treated as normal and necessary. Every day, TV, radio and newspapers endorse agribusiness as the ultimate example of economic success.[4] All this has led to a decline in the relative importance given to the material properties of agri-food in favour of more explicit business goals. Despite the rhetoric of food security and the publicity of the major agribusiness corporations claiming to 'feed the world', agribusiness is increasingly about business in and for itself and less concerned with social opportunities, nourishment or food production. The mystification of the neo-liberalisation of agribusiness in Brazil has followed a dynamic of continuity and change, in which practices, interpersonal relations and political strategies have been only partially transformed. The main proof of the domestic performance of neoliberalised agribusiness is often the expansion of domestic agri-food markets, without much discussion about the beneficiaries and distortions associated with powerful market transactions. Money-making objectives are shrouded in discourses of low prices and consumer satisfaction, which mystify the real impacts of the neoliberalisation of agribusiness.

Although the sector makes use of the appealing symbolism of triumph and modernisation, the evolution of agribusiness has served to unify the interests of rural conservative groups and partly renovate processes of political hegemony and class domination. Agribusiness farmers repeatedly emphasise their contribution to regional development and economic growth, but only from the perspective of an intense financialisation of agriculture, while calling for the removal of environmental, social and regulatory constraints. The sector has demonstrated a competent ability to lobby and promote its interests, particularly via the Brazilian Agribusiness Association (ABAG) created in 1993. Similarly, regular technical visits to production areas coordinated by the Round Table on Responsible Soy association, established in 2006, have tried to improve the image of the Brazilian agri-food sector with colourful rhetoric of sustainability, certification and environmental commitment. Other mystification strategies have included the appropriation of the environmental agenda by the agribusiness sector and its conversion into new business opportunities, as in the case of the

Low Carbon Agriculture Programme [*Programa ABC*], launched by the federal government in 2010 to fund the recovery of degraded pastures, cattle-crop integration, forest plantations, etc. which ultimately provided indirect support to commercial agriculture. However, the rhetoric of entrepreneurialism, competence and environmental responsibility obscures the fact that the results of agribusiness have more to do with the flexibilisation of domestic markets, the deeper insertion of Brazil into global trade and, crucially, mounting mistakes and ill-conceived policies that have diminished the prospects of other economic sectors.

Neoliberalised agribusiness is fundamentally intended to further subordinate agriculture production to the extraction of surplus value; it is an aggressive phenomenon that reconfigures old agriculture practices and relaunches them in the circles of transnational capitalism. It has resulted in an increased concentration of power and transactions into the hands of just a few (e.g. in 2005, seven national and international corporations controlled 70 per cent of the soybean harvested in Brazil, according to Bernardes and Silva, 2016). Furthermore, the mystification of the success achieved by the agribusiness sector helps to conceal internal disputes, particularly between the agribusiness farmers themselves and other major players (large-scale farmers and transnational companies). A discourse has been constructed around wealth creation and the macroeconomic value of agribusiness, although behind closed doors there are also signs of disunity and often uneasiness with the way farmers are treated by corporations, banks and other urban sectors. A final element of mystification is the confusion about the role of the federal Brazilian state, which remains the main promoter and defender of agro-neoliberal measures, despite the colourful discourse in favour of market-based solutions and associated strategies.

Conclusions

The previous pages of this chapter discussed the synergies between neoliberalising reforms and their impacts on the evolution of agribusiness, from the conventional model adopted in the middle of the last century to the current insertion of the agri-food sector into globalised markets and flexible mechanisms of capital accumulation. This partial and turbulent transition reveals a great deal about the political, economic and politico-ecological basis of the neoliberalised economy and about the class-based tensions of socio-ecological changes that have followed the modernisation of agriculture in recent decades. Agro-neoliberalism was defined as the convergence of three main forces – that is, renewed public–private alliances, novel techno-economic strategies that intensify socio-ecological exploitation and the containment of critical reactions. It should be noted that this synthetic framework is not without conceptual and methodological limitations, but it should be considered as a starting point for further academic investigations and a tool to foster critical thinking. The proposed analytical framework has significant implications for social sciences research, especially within politico-economy and neoliberalism studies, insofar as it encapsulates interdependent processes that are together responsible for the revitalisation of agribusiness and the legitimisation of global agri-food markets. Thinking specifically about the Brazilian experience, these main drivers have produced fundamental changes in terms of substitution (sectoral and spatial transformations), financialisation (prioritising money-making over agriculture outcomes) and mystification (dissimulation of neoliberalising trends and associated risks and disputes).

The neoliberalisation of agribusiness in Brazil followed the displacement of traditional areas and industrial sectors in favour of the export of agriculture commodities (soybean in particular), the growing financialisation of production, distribution and consumption (especially as articulated by transnational companies and fuelled by the need to generate dollars to stabilise national accounts) and numerous mystification strategies to disguise manifold socio-ecological problems. Because of its short-term results, particularly during the commodity boom in the 2000s, neoliberal agribusiness has hijacked the Brazilian economy and left little space for alternative agricultural production systems (Ioris, 2016). It has favoured a group of powerful political elites in charge of agro-neoliberal reforms, who have established important alliances with speculative landowners, the agroindustrial and financial sectors, and most political parties. Agro-neoliberalism has become so hegemonic in Brazil that it seems naturalised and beyond the sphere of criticism, having secured support from the great majority of politicians. Moreover, the apparent success of the neoliberalisation of agri-business betrays a clear attempt to temporarily assuage the structural contradictions of capitalist agriculture while new tensions and reactions become increasingly evident (such as mounting rates of environmental degradation and social conflicts, and the way the national economy is completely dependent on agri-food exports). At the end of the day, agribusiness production in Brazil has been a privileged arena for the consolidation of flexible capital accumulation approaches, while at the same time being significantly shaped by direct state interventions, widespread violence and the subordination of agriculture to wider, globalised politico-ecological demands.

Also demonstrated above was the importance of contextualising issues of rural and agri-food development within the wider framework of regional and global political economy. The apparent success of the agribusiness sector in Brazil offers an intriguing case study of a temporary, and only partial, suspension of the contradictions of capitalist agriculture. Agribusiness was a conservative response to the crisis of capitalist accumulation in the 1980s and the exhaustion of a model of development based on direct state support. Instead of focusing on agrarian reform and local food production, the conservative solution was to intensify and update production according to neoliberal terms. Yet, despite its distinctive technological and economic accomplishments, the expansion of agribusiness has some disturbing parallels with the formation of agricultural frontiers in previous generations. On one hand, the aggressive expansion of agribusiness since the 1990s has reproduced ideological claims about the crucial role of agronomic science and agriculture modernisation which were invoked to justify production changes at the turn of the 20th century and during the Green Revolution in the 1960s and 1970s.

Neoliberalised agribusiness is a product of the trend towards technological advances and economic relations of production which began over a century ago. On the other hand, agribusiness is a unique phenomenon insofar as it results from the articulation between local scales and transnational flows of capital. The crucial connections between horizontal displacement and vertical transnationalisation are persistently mystified as a necessary element of regional development and macroeconomic stability promoted through agribusiness. Such complex and controversial bases of agro-neoliberalism are reinforced daily through various mechanisms of self-justification and criticism against other rural activities considered archaic and misplaced.

As typically happens with neoliberalising experiences around the world, the political geography of agro-neoliberalism in Brazil was decisively shaped by the flexibilisation of controls and novel incentives advanced by the national state. Given that the state was and remains the main player in neoliberalism (Ioris, 2014), its apparatus moved from a position of supporter and main financer to become the promoter and manager of neoliberalised agribusiness. If the developmentalist state of the post-war decades brought capital to the centre of Brazil, adjusted agricultural technology to tropical conditions with acidic soils and abundant solar radiation, and implemented extensive transport and storage infrastructure, the neoliberal state promotes agribusiness in partnership with transnational corporations and through multiple financing strategies. As analysed by Eakin *et al.* (2014) in relation to other national experiences, neoliberalised agribusiness has even appropriated the language of food sovereignty to justify preferential treatment and novel supporting mechanisms from governments. But there is a fundamental and decisive difference between these two historical periods: in the post-war years, the Brazilian state and the reputation of national politicians were primarily associated with national industrialisation and urbanisation, but they are now increasingly and inescapably dependent on the economic surplus generated by growing agriculture exports and are hostage to the aura of undisputed success associated with agribusiness.

It is central to the present analysis that the advance of agro-neoliberalism in Brazil should be understood as the embodiment of the most progressive and regressive elements of present-day capitalism. This paradoxical situation is clear evidence of capitalist society's perennial and always partial process of 'becoming modern', as the spectre of the new (paraphrasing Marx) which needs elements of the obsolete to function. The obsolete is an integral part of rural capitalist modernity, which is constantly recreating the world and permeating it with chaos and destruction. For instance, the growth of agricultural biotechnology has never been straightforward; rather, it has always been met with resistance and scepticism (Newell, 2009). When confronting political resistance from other social sectors, the industry normally reacts with a pre-established rhetoric of heroism and entrepreneurialism that serves transnational corporations and national politicians more than the farmers themselves. The alleged multifunctionality of today's agriculture (i.e. a range of economic and non-economic outputs beyond traditional farming production) often serves to conceal the neoliberal features of agribusiness

(Potter and Tilzey, 2007) and mask the fact that agribusiness has increasingly failed to produce any significant improvement in productivity or technology (Moore, 2010).

The Brazilian area where the controversies related to agro-neoliberalism are most evident is the state of Mato Grosso, in the Centre-West region, where more than half the economy is now based on highly neoliberalised agribusiness (IMEA, 2014) and where the value of exports jumped from US$254 million to US$8.5 billion between 1990 and 2009 (Pereira, 2012). The intensification of agribusiness in the state since the 1990s has been an attempt to consolidate the agricultural frontier, initially opened in the 1970s, through 'export oriented farming' (Brannstrom, 2009). During our research it was indeed possible to verify that agro-neoliberalism is being practised in the localised context of farms and regions, but management, technologies and trade relations increasingly happen in accordance with globalised, transnational interactions and priorities. Mier y Terán (2016) also rightly points out that agribusiness in Mato Grosso was never a uniform phenomenon, but has been shaped by local particularities because of the heterogeneity of migrants, farming practices, market oscillation and ecological specificities. However, what is still missing in most available publications is a critical examination of the achievements, justification and failures of agro-neoliberalism at the geographical frontier of agribusiness (Ioris, 2015); the goal of the next chapter is to provide such an examination.

Notes

1   In this broad context, most latifundia were used for extensive cattle grazing or purely for land speculation, which contrasted with the small proportion of mechanised and technified large-scale properties involved in crop exports. Such unproductive latifundia were seen by urban groups as a significant obstacle to national development and industrialisation; nonetheless, the power of traditional rural elites never allowed the implementation of any serious programme of agrarian reform and significantly delayed countryside modernisation.

2   The soybean plant (*Glycine max* (L.) Merrill) is a nitrogen-fixing legume and the grain is a hybrid commodity, as it also demonstrates some properties of high-value foods (e.g. its use as meat substitute). In Brazil, commercial production of soybean began in the 1940s in the southern state of Rio Grande do Sul, later coming to occupy larger areas in other states, especially in the savannah [*cerrado*] biome. Interestingly, the relentless increase of soybean production in the Centre-West of Brazil, particularly in Mato Grosso, as discussed in the next chapters, was initially underestimated in most public and private projections, which did not anticipate the measures taken to overcome technical, economic and socio-political difficulties (Warnken, 2000).

3   After being nicknamed 'Miss Deforestation' and 'chainsaw queen' by Brazilian environmentalists for her promotion of deforestation, Kátia Abreu resumed her senatorial duties after the removal of President Dilma Rousseff and gave a surprising, perhaps cynical, interview claiming to have developed environmental concerns and that she was willing to engage in conservation, which bolstered her further political ambitions (Veja, 2016).

4   For example, the presenter of the programme 'The Hour of Agribusiness' [*A Hora do Agronegócio*] on Radio Jovem Pan, declared on 21 December 2015, at 6.30, while I was having some coffee and enjoying a little break from writing the first drafts of these pages, that 'Christmas is agribusiness, milk, meat, the basis of life'.

References

Acselrad, V. 2012. A Economia Politica do Agronegócio no Brasil: O Legado Desenvolvimentista no Contexto da Democratização com Liberalização. Unpublished PhD thesis. UFRGS: Porto Alegre.

Amanor, K.S. 2012. Global Resource Grabs, Agribusiness Concentration and the Smallholder: Two West African Case Studies. *Journal of Peasant Studies*, 39, 731–749.

Araghi, F. 2009. Accumulation by Displacement: Global Enclosures, Food Crisis, and the Ecological Contradictions of Capitalism. *Review*, 32(1), 113–146.

Balestro, M.V. and Lourenço, L.C.B. 2014. Notas para uma Análise da Financeirização do Agronegócio: Além da Volatilidade dos Preços das Commodities. In: *O Mundo Rural no Brasil do Século 21: A Formação de um Novo Padrão Agrário e Agrícola*, Buainain, A.M., Alves, E., Silveira, J.M. and Navarro, Z. (eds). Embrapa: Brasília, pp. 241–265.

Barretto, A.G.O.P., Berndes, G., Sparovek, G. and Wirsenius, S. 2013 Agricultural Intensification in Brazil and its Effects on Land-use Patterns: An Analysis of the 1975–2006 Period. *Global Change Biology*, 19, 1804–1815.

Barros, G.S.C., Adami, A.C.O. and Zandoná, N.F. 2014. *Faturamento e Volume Exportado do Agronegócio Brasileiro São Recordes em 2013*. CEPEA: Piracicaba.

Bernardes, J.A. 1996. As Estratégias do Capital no Complexo da Soja. In: *Questões Atuais da Reorganização do Território*, Gomes, P.C.C., Correa, R.L. and Castro, I.E. (eds). Bertrand Brasil: Rio de Janeiro, pp. 325–366.

Bernardes, J.A. and Silva, E.J.M. 2016. Estratégias das Empresas Comerciais Exportadoras da Cadeia de Grãos na Fronteira da BR-163 Mato Grossense. In: *As Novas Fronteiras do Agronegócio: Transformações Territoriais em Mato Grosso*, Bernardes, J.A., Buhler, E.A. and Costa, M.V.V. (eds). Lamparina: Rio de Janeiro, pp. 83–100.

Bonanno, A. and Constance, D.H. 2008. *Stories of Globalization*. Pennsylvania State University Press: University Park, PA.

Borras, S.M., Kay, C., Gómez, S. and Wilkinson, J. 2012. Land Grabbing and Global Capitalist Accumulation: Key Features in Latin America. *Canadian Journal of Development Studies*, 33(4), 402–416.

Brannstrom, C. 2009. South America's Neoliberal Agricultural Frontiers: Places of Environmental Sacrifice or Conservation Opportunity? *Ambio*, 38(3), 141–149.

Brenner, N., Peck, J. and Theodore, N., 2010. After Neoliberalization? *Globalizations*, 7(3), 327–345.

Bruno, R. 2009. *Um Brasil Ambivalente: Agronegócio, Ruralismo e Relações de Poder*. Edur/Mauad: Rio de Janeiro.

Buainain, A.M. and Garcia, R. 2015. Recent Development Patterns and Challenges of Brazilian Agriculture. In: *Emerging Economies: Food and Energy Security, and Technology and Innovation*, Shome, P. and Sharma, P. (eds). Springer, pp. 41–66.

Buainain, A.M., Alves, E., Silveira, J.M. and Navarro, Z. (eds). 2014. *O Mundo Rural no Brasil do Século 21: A Formação de um Novo Padrão Agrário e Agrícola*. Embrapa: Brasília.

Busch, L. 2010. Can Fairy Tales Come True? The Surprising Story of Neoliberalism and World Agriculture. *Sociologia Ruralis*, 50(4), 331–351.

Busch, L. 2014. Governance in the Age of Global Markets: Challenges, Limits, and Consequences. *Agriculture and Human Values*, 31(3), 513–523.

Busch, L. and Bain, C. 2004. New! Improved? The Transformation of the Global Agrifood System *Rural Sociology*, 69(3), 321–346.

Burch, D. and Lawrence, G. 2013. Financialization in Agri-food Supply Chains: Private Equity and the Transformation of the Retail Sector. *Agriculture and Human Values*, 30, 247–258.

Campanhola, C. and Graziano da Silva, J.F. (eds). 2000. *O Novo Rural Brasileiro: Uma Análise Nacional e Regional*. Embrapa: Jaguariúna.

Canal Rural. 2009. Lula Declara Disposição para Comprar Briga pelo Agronegócio. Available at: www.clicrbs.com.br/especial/rs/expointer-2010/19,0,2558094, Lula-declara-disposicao-para-comprar-briga-pelo-agronegocio.html (25 June 2009).

Castro, J. 1954. *Geopolítica da Fome: Ensaio sobre os Problemas de Alimentação e de População do Mundo*. 3rd edition. Casa do Estudante do Brasil: Rio de Janeiro.

CEPEA. 2014. *Agromensal – CEPEA/ESALQ: Informações de Mercado*. January issue. CEPEA: Piracicaba.

Clapp, J. and Fuchs, D. (eds). 2009. *Corporate Power in Global Agrifood Governance*. MIT Press: Cambridge, MA.

Collier, P. 2008. The Politics of Hunger: How Illusion and Greed Fan the Food Crisis. *Foreign Affairs*, 87(6), 67–79.

CONAB. 2014. Balança Comercial do Agronegócio. *Indicadores da Agropecuária*, 23(1), 62.

Connell, R. and Dados, N. 2014. Where in the World does Neoliberalism come from? The Market Agenda in Southern Perspective. *Theory and Society*, 43, 117–138.

Dardot, P. and Laval, C. 2010. *La Nouvelle Raison du Monde: Essai sur la Société Néolibérale*. La Découverte: Paris.

Davis, J. and Goldberg, R. 1957. *A Concept of Agribusiness*. Alpine Press: Boston, MA.

Debord, G. 2009. *Society of the Spectacle*. Trans. K. Knabb. Soul Bay Press: Eastbourne, Sussex.

Delgado, G.D. 2012. *Do Capital Financeiro na Agricultura à Economia do Agronegócio: Mudanças Cíclicas em meio Século (1965–2012)*. UFRGS: Porto Alegre.

Dibden, J., Potter, C. and Cocklin, C. 2009. Contesting the Neoliberal Project for Agriculture: Productivist and Multifunctional Trajectories in the European Union and Australia. *Journal of Rural Studies*, 25, 299–308.

Duménil, G. and Lévy, D. 2004. *Capital Resurgent: Roots of the Neoliberal Revolution*. Harvard University Press: Cambridge, MA.

Eakin, H., Bausch, J.C. and Sweeney, S. 2014. Agrarian Winners of Neoliberal Reform: The 'Maize Boom' of Sinaloa, Mexico. *Journal of Agrarian Change*, 14, 26–51.

The Economist. 2010. The Miracle of the Cerrado: Brazil has Revolutionised its own Farms: Can it do the Same for others? Available at: www.economist.com/node/16886442 (26 August 2010).

Fairbairn, M. 2014. 'Like Gold with Yield': Evolving Intersections between Farmland and Finance. *Journal of Peasant Studies*, 41(5), 777–795.

FIESP. 2008. *Brazilian Agribusiness: Characteristics, Performance, Products and Markets*. FIESP: São Paulo.

Fuchs, D., Meyer-Eppler, R. and Hamenstädt, U. 2013. Food for Thought: The Politics of Financialization in the Agrifood System. *Competition and Change*, 17(3), 219–233.

Furtado, R. 2002. *Agribusiness Brasileiro: A História*. ABAG/Evoluir: São Paulo.

Gonçalves Neto, W. 1997. *Estado e Agricultura no Brasil: Política Agrícola e Modernização Econômica Brasileira 1960–1980*. Hucitec: São Paulo.

Goodman, D. and Watts, M.J. 1994. Reconfiguring the Rural or Fording the Divide?: Capitalist Restructuring and the Global Agro-food System. *Journal of Peasant Studies*, 22(1), 1–49.

Graziano da Silva, J.F. 1988. *Estrutura Agrária e Produção de Subsistência na Agricultura Brasileira*. Hucitec: São Paulo.

The Guardian. 2014. Brazil's 'Chainsaw Queen' Takes on Environmentalists. Available at: www.theguardian.com/environment/2014/may/05/brazil-chainsaw-queen-katia-abreu-amazon-deforestation/print (pub 5 May 2014).

Guthman, J. 2007. The Polanyian Way? Voluntary Food Labels as Neoliberal Governance. *Antipode*, 39(3), 456–478.

Guthman, J., 2008. Neoliberalism and the Making of Food Politics in California. *Geoforum*, 39, 1171–1183.

Harvey, D. 2005. *A Brief History of Neoliberalism*. Oxford University Press: Oxford.

Hollander, G. M. 2004. Agricultural Trade Liberalization, Multifunctionality, and Sugar in the South Florida landscape. *Geoforum*, 35(3), 299–312.

Hopewell, K. 2013. New Protagonists in Global Economic Governance: Brazilian Agribusiness at the WTO. *New Political Economy*, 18(4), 602–623.

IMEA. 2014. *Conjuntura Econômica*, bulletin no. 4, 29 September 2014.

Ioris, A.A.R. 2103. The Adaptive Nature of the Neoliberal State and the State-led Neoliberalization of Nature: Unpacking the Political Economy of Water in Lima, Peru. *New Political Economy*, 18(6), 912–938.

Ioris, A.A.R. 2014. *The Political Ecology of the State: The Basis and the Evolution of Environmental Statehood*. Routledge: Abingdon, Oxford.

Ioris, A.A.R. 2015. Cracking the Nut of Agribusiness and Global Food Insecurity: In Search of a Critical Agenda of Research. *Geoforum*, 63, 1–4.

Ioris, A.A.R. (ed.). 2016. *Agriculture, Environment and Development: International Perspectives on Water, Land and Politics*. Palgrave Macmillan: Basingstoke.

Ioris, R.R. and Ioris, A.A.R. 2013. The Brazilian Developmentalist State in Historical Perspective: Revisiting the 1950s in Light of Today's Challenges. *Journal of Iberian and Latin American Research*, 19(1), 133–148.

ISTOÉ Dinheiro. 2013. *Milhão com Açúcar*, published on16 October 2013, pp. 83–85.

Jepson, W., Brannstrom, C. and Filippi, A. 2010. Access Regimes and Regional Land Change in the Brazilian Cerrado, 1972–2002. *Annals of the Association of American Geographers*, 100(1), 87–111.

MacArtney, H. 2009. Variegated Neo-liberalism: Transnationally Oriented Fractions of Capital in EU Financial Market Integration. *Review of International Studies*, 35(2), 451–480.

MAPA. 2010. *How to Invest in Agribusiness*. MAPA: Brasília.

MAPA. 2012. *Intercâmbio Comercial do Agronegócio: Principais Mercados de Destino*. MAPA: Brasília.

Marsden, T., Lee, R., Flynn, A. and Thankappan, S. 2010. *The New Regulation and Governance of Food*. Routledge: New York and London.

McMichael, P. 2009. A Food Regime Genealogy. *Journal of Peasant Studies*, 36(1), 139–169.

McMichael, P. 2010. The World Food Crisis in Historical Perspective. In: *Agriculture and Food in Crisis: Conflict, Resistance, and Renewal*, Magdoff, F. and Tokar, B. (eds). Monthly Review Press: New York, pp. 51–67

MDIC. 2013. *Brazilian Trade Balance: Consolidated Data*. MDIC: Brasília.

Mier y Terán G.C., M. 2016. Soybean Agri-food Systems Dynamics and the Diversity of Farming Styles on the Agricultural Frontier in Mato Grosso, Brazil. *Journal of Peasant Studies*, 43(2), 419–441.

Moore, J.W. 2010. Cheap Food and Bad Money: Food, Frontiers, and Financialization in the Rise and Demise of Neoliberalism. *Review*, 33(2–3), 225–261.

Moore, J.W. 2015. *Capitalism in the Web of Life: Ecology and the Accumulation of Capital*. Verso: London and New York.

Muir, C. 2014. *The Broken Promise of Agricultural Progress: An Environmental History*. Earthscan: London and New York.

Murray, W.E. 2006. Neo-feudalism in Latin America? Globalisation, Agribusiness, and Land Re-concentration in Chile. *Journal of Peasant Studies*, 33(4), 646–677.

Newell, P. 2009. Technology, Food, Power: Governing GMOs in Argentina. In: *Corporate Power in Global Agrifood Governance*, Clapp, J. and Fuchs, D. (eds). MIT Press: Cambridge, MA. pp. 253–283.

O Estado de São Paulo. 2014. Governo Aumenta em 14,8% Valor Destinado ao Crédito Rural. Available at: http://economia.estadao.com.br/noticias/economia-geral,governo-aumenta-em-14–8-valor-destinado-ao-credito-rural,185256,0.htm (May 2014).

O'Connor, J. 1973. *The Fiscal Crisis of the State*. St. Martin's Press: New York.

Oels, A. 2005. Rendering Climate Change Governable: From Biopower to Advanced Liberal Government? *Journal of Environmental Policy and Planning*, 7(3), 185–207.

Oliveira, A.U. 2007. *Modo Capitalista de Produção, Agricultura e Reforma Agrária*. FFLCH/Labur Edições: São Paulo.

Oliveira, A.U. and Stédile, J.P. 2005. *A Natureza do Agronegócio no Brasil*. Vía Campesina: Brasília.

Otero, G. 2012. The Neoliberal Food Regime in Latin America: State, Agribusiness. Transnational Corporations and Biotechnology. *Canadian Journal of Development Studies*, 33(3), 282–294.

Oya, C. 2005. Sticks and Carrots for Farmers in Developing Countries: Agrarian Neoliberalism in Theory and Practice. In: *Neoliberalism: A Critical Reader*, Saad-Filho, A. and Johnston, D. (eds). Pluto Press: London, pp. 127–134.

Pereira, B.D. 2012. *Agropecuária de Mato Grosso: Velhas Questões de uma Nova Economia*. EdUFMT: Cuiabá.

Pereira, J.M.M. 2015. Modernization, the Fight against Poverty, and Land Markets. *Varia Historia*, 32, 225–258.

Petras, J. and Veltmeyer, H. 2003. Whither Lula's Brazil? Neoliberalism and 'Third Way' Ideology. *The Journal of Peasant Studies*, 31(1), 1–44.

Potter, C. and Tilzey, M. 2005. Agricultural Policy Discourses in the European post-Fordist Transition: Neoliberalism, Neomercantilism and Multifunctionality. *Progress in Human Geography*, 29(5), 581–600.

Potter, C. and Tilzey, M. 2007. Agricultural Multifunctionality, Environmental Sustainability and the WTO: Resistance or Accommodation to the Neoliberal Project for Agriculture? *Geoforum*, 38, 1290–1303.

Richards, P.D., Myers, R.J., Swinton, S.M. and Walker, R.J. 2012. Exchange Rates, Soybean Supply Response, and Deforestation in South America. *Global Environmental Change*, 22(2), 454–462.

Sauer, S. and Leite, S. 2012. Expansão Agrícola, Preços e Apropriação de Terra por Estrangeiros no Brasil. *Revista de Economia e Sociologia Rural*, 50(3), 503–524.

Schmalz, S. and Ebenau, M. 2012. After Neoliberalism? Brazil, India, and China in the Global Economic Crisis. *Globalizations*, 9(4), 487–501.

Schmitz, A., Furtan, H. and Baylis, K. 2002. *Agricultural Policy, Agribusiness, and Rent-Seeking Behavior*. University of Toronto Press: Toronto.

Schneider, S. 2010. Situando o Desenvolvimento Rural no Brasil: O Contexto e as Questões em Debate. *Revista de Economia Política*, 30(3), 511–531.

Serigati, F. 2013. A Agricultura Puxa o PIB? *Agroanalysis*, 33(2), 13–14.

Siqueira, T.V. 2004. O Ciclo da Soja: Desempenho da Cultura da Soja entre 1961 e 2003. *BNDES Setorial*, 20, 127–222.

Torres, R.M. and Carte, L. 2014. Community Participatory Appraisal in Migration Research: Connecting Neoliberalism, Rural Restructuring and Mobility. *Transactions of the Institute of British Geographers*, 39, 140–154.

Veja. 2016. "Eu Não Mudei de Lado" – Interview with Kátia Abreu, by Thaís Oyama. pp. 13–17 (7 September 2016).

Warnken, P.F. 1999. *The Development and Growth of the Soybean Industry in Brazil*. Iowa State University Press: Ames.

Warnken, P. 2000. O Futuro da Soja no Brasil. *Revista de Política Agrícola*, year IX, no. 2, 54–65.

Whatmore, S. 1995. From Farming to Agribusiness: The Global Agro-food System. In: *Geographies of Global Change: Remapping the World in the late Twentieth Century*, Johnston, R.J., Taylor, P.J. and Watts, M.J. (eds). Blackwell: Oxford, pp. 36–49.

Wilkinson, J. 2011. From Fair Trade to Responsible Soy: Social Movements and the Qualification of Agrofood Markets. *Environment and Planning A*, 43, 2012–2026.

Wolf, S.A. and Bonanno, A. (eds). 2014. The Neoliberal Regime in the Agri-Food Sector: Crisis, Resilience, and Restructuring. Routledge: London and New York.

3   Push and hold the agribusiness frontier
Antecedents of agribusiness in Mato Grosso

The intense activity of tractors, lorries and pickups in the large areas of crop production in the state of Mato Grosso, in the southern section of the Amazon, has been praised as irrefutable evidence of progress and modernisation. The image of success and growth contrasts with most of the rest of the Brazilian economy, which is often considered inefficient and ill-prepared to cope with the pressures of globalisation. Mato Grosso is portrayed as an island of productivity, innovation and, essentially, major achievements. It is undeniable that Mato Grosso is now one of the world's agribusiness hotspots and is currently the national leader in soybean, beef, sunflower, cotton and maize production (IMEA, 2016a). The export of soybean and other goods from Mato Grosso is crucial for macroeconomic stability because of the industry's substantial contribution to trade surplus and growing international reserves. While I wrote the early versions of this chapter in September 2016 – working in a hotel in the old district of the state capital, Cuiabá (located near the geodesic centre of South America – that is, further away from the coast than anywhere else in the continent), trying to systematise multiple datasets and waiting for the next interview or visit to happen – it was easy to perceive a sense of triumph in the speech of the candidates running for public office in the forthcoming municipal elections (I was able to follow it from my hotel room, given that most of the political campaign in Brazil was carried out via dedicated TV and radio broadcasts). The mayoral candidates enthusiastically associated their many plans for the city with the recurrent assertion that Cuiabá is the administrative heart of a prosperous and fast-expanding agribusiness industry, which is metaphorically considered the lifeblood of Mato Grosso.

This chapter and the next two will focus on one of the main soybean production areas in the country, which is located in the north of Mato Grosso, at the transition between savannah [cerrado] and forest ecosystems. It broadly corresponds to the upstream sections of the Teles Pires River Basin,[1] with the main river named after the army Captain Antônio Lourenço Teles Pires, who died in 1890 on a ship that sank in the middle of one of several epic explorations. The time of heroic expeditions to conquer territory and control the natives is certainly over, as now most of the region consists of a monotonous combination of plantation farms along lengthy roads and the sparse remnants of the original vegetation, together with a growing number of towns and cities where the great majority of the local population (including farmers and rural workers) live. In the rainy season (October to March) the landscape is dominated by the green and later the yellow of huge plantation fields of genetically modified soybeans. In the Teles Pires, those who control soybean control major flows of money, and also dominate the political game, to the extent that the currency commonly used for business transactions in the region is not the Brazilian Real (R$), but 'soybean-money' (a reference to the market value of 60 kg bags of soybean, normally used when buying land and other assets or when privately lending money). The expansion of soybean in recent decades has in fact been astonishing: in the municipality of Sinop, the regional administrative and commercial centre, between 1996 and 2006, the soybean production area increased from 11,485 to 344,245 hectares, and production increased from 19,142 to 960,887 tons in that period. Near Sinop is the municipality of Sorriso, which is Brazil's largest producer of soybean, with almost 600,000 hectares and more than 1.4 million tons produced per year (according to data from the Brazilian geographic institute IBGE).

The aim of this chapter is to unpack overall trends and tensions, in particular why the politico-economic and geographical circumstances led to the consolidation of agro-neoliberalism in Mato Grosso. The doors of agriculture-cum-agribusiness in the state opened grandly in the 1970s with the concerted promotion of a new agricultural frontier, greatly improved road access and generous financial support from the federal government (although most of the money flown into the region ended up in the hands of a small proportion of farmers and directly contributed to increased inequality and reduced food security, as demonstrated by Graham *et al.*, 1987). A few years later, in a context of liberalising reforms and technological intensification, agribusiness activity evolved rapidly and, since the end of the 1990s, has become increasingly dependent on global markets and the protagonism of mega-corporations. Due to sophisticated technologies, entrepreneurial competence and convenient alliances between old and new agrarian elites, the belated arrival of agribusiness hypermodernity, mixed with some persistent and disturbing features of the colonial past, has been accomplished in the form of agro-neoliberalism. This is strongly corroborated by growing financialisation strategies and the influence of transnational corporations (TNCs) in the selling off of farm inputs, the provision of credit and the acquisition of crops. The economic and political relevance of agribusiness activity, both in the main production areas of the Teles Pires and the rest of Mato Grosso, is directly related to what Heredia *et al.* (2010) describe as the 'society of agribusiness'. Moreover, to understand the present it is necessary to briefly revisit the past experience of frontier making.

In the early days of its colonisation, in the 17th century, the economy of Mato Grosso was intimately associated with territorial expansion and the advance of an idiosyncratic form of exploratory and mercantile capitalism, always in a subordinate position in relation to stronger political and economic centres in Brazil and Portugal (Ioris, 2012). The Iberian influence in Mato Grosso began in the 16th century – it is worth mentioning the extraordinary journey of Álvar Núñez

Cabeza de Vaca through South America between 1528 and 1537 (Cabeza de Vaca, 1922) – when the first Europeans, including missionary Jesuits, introduced cattle to the region in order to benefit from the extensive pastures of the Pantanal wetland that occupies the centre of Mato Grosso and parts of Bolivia and Paraguay (Wilcox, 1992). Cattle adapted relatively well to the local conditions, characterised by seasonal floods that help to fertilise the fields. Moreover, while the Spaniards arrived first they did not colonise the region and the early settlements established in the Pantanal were soon abandoned. Mato Grosso, like other parts of present-day Brazil, were explored by expeditions of Luso-Brazilians coming mainly from São Paulo, known as *bandeiras* (literally, flags), in search of indigenous slaves and precious metals and stones. The leaders of these expeditions, known as *bandeirantes*, had a reputation for being both brave and violent, and they gradually grew to become highly celebrated figures in the popular imagination. Gold extraction in Mato Grosso commenced in the second decade of the 18th century in the area around Cuiabá, a town that was founded by the Portuguese crown in 1726 (Lucidio, 2013). The Overseas Council [*Conselho Ultramarino*] drew a line of defence of Portuguese America from the Amazon to Mato Grosso and then to the south of Brazil; as part of this effort, the Captaincy of Mato Grosso was formed in 1748. The formal occupation of the region, beyond the initial mines and settlements, only occurred in the second half of the 18th century, after the imperial powers established military fortifications to oversee the uncertain borders.

The 1750 Madrid Treaty, agreed between Portugal and Spain, resolved the two countries' long territorial dispute with the recognition of the rights of Lisbon over most of the Amazon and the west of Brazilian colonial territory. The strategic importance of Mato Grosso for Portugal's colonial plans can be verified in the instructions issued by the powerful Marquis of Pombal, the visionary and proactive prime minister of the Portuguese king between 1756 and 1777, who devoted special efforts to establishing navigable river connections between the Amazon, the mines of Mato Grosso and the southern regions (Silva, 2012). While better integration of the different parts of Brazil was a recurrent goal, although difficult to attain, it was not true, as claimed by the official historiography, that Mato Grosso was almost completely isolated from the rest of the country. On the contrary, the territory of Mato Grosso was strategically important to the colonial, and later national, economy because of its mines and localised commercial centres. The myth of isolation has in effect served to boost the heroic image of conquest and to reinforce the claim that the remote corners in the Centre-South of Brazil owe much to the bravery of São Paulo's trail-blazers [*bandeirantes*] (Lenharo, 1982). Nonetheless, it is also the case that at the time of Brazilian independence in 1822, Mato Grosso was only reachable from the main cities of the new Brazilian Empire (1822–1889) after an arduous journey by land and river. At that time, the province had only a small non-indigenous population, governed by a political elite in constant internal conflict and continuously trying to cultivate alliances with the national political masters (Siqueira, 2002). Similar to what happened in other parts of Brazil during the Regency period (1831–1840), a revolt erupted in Mato Grosso in 1834 against the local government, the conservative political leaders and the remaining Portuguese nationals (accused, rightly or wrongly, of plotting to turn Brazil back into a colony). The revolt was called *Rusga* [disorder] and involved mainly mestizos and non-white liberal dissidents. After some acts of gallantry, it was not difficult for the national government to reinstate order and prosecute the protesters in Rio de Janeiro, then the national capital.

With peace restored in the province, the main problem was again the incipient economy and the lack of a more reliable transportation route. This was why an agreement was signed with the Paraguayan Republic in 1856 regarding permission to navigate along the Paraguay river system. International river navigation in the centre of South America was also a British geopolitical demand and part of the country's imperialist and trade expansion plans. This directly affected the interests of Paraguay, which was at that time the most industrialised and aggressive country in the region. The long, bloody and large-scale Paraguayan War, between 1864 and 1870, began with the occupation of the southern half of Mato Grosso and was largely associated with the control of fluvial navigation (Ioris, 2013). During the conflict, which was the most ferocious in the history of the South American continent, local farmers were forced to supply the troops with meat and leather. The regional economy was decimated and the small number of cattle that survived ended up dispersed and unmanaged. It took some years for settlers to gradually return, and for farms and fluvial navigation to slowly recover. Because of distances and the problems of national integration, farmers and residents had to develop a high level of self-sufficiency in terms of resources, technology and equipment. Strong patrimonialism and widespread corruption facilitated the formation of an unproductive elite in charge of provincial administration and overseeing the extraction of natural resources, such as timber, rubber and minerals, which continued after the proclamation of the republic and end of the monarchy in 1889. (When Brazil became a republic, the imperial provinces were converted into a federation of semi-autonomous states.)

The first decades of the new Brazilian Republic paved the way for the consolidation of a landed oligarchy in control of the public sector and allied with the national, also oligarchic, politicians. Mato Grosso was then managed by a regional elite that included powerful family names, such as Paes de Barros, Ponce and Corrêa, whose descendants are still active in the political process. The first State Land Act of Mato Grosso was introduced in 1892, instituting the first legal provisions for agrarian regularisation and creating an agency specifically in charge of partitioning state-owned land. The new regulatory framework essentially benefited large proprietors or those who illegally occupied vast tracts of common or public land (Moreno, 2007). Society leaders in Mato Grosso not only controlled most of the regional economy (with the tacit acquiescence of the absent and distant national government), but systematically tried to redefine its identity with a peculiar combination of the stereotypes of territorial conquest and the supposed valour of both white and non-white groups that formed the basis of regional society. In the early 1900s, references to the *bandeirantes* as heroes of national expansion were still common, reinforced by the work of the History Institute of Mato Grosso, created in 1919. Local writers, such as the famous archbishop and state governor Aquino Correia, persistently tried to subvert the common feeling of backwardness with claims about the racial purity of the (idealised) American Indians and the pioneer spirit of the regional population.

History and geography took a new turn after the 1930 political coup [*Revolução de 1930*], which deposed the elected president and installed Getúlio Vargas as the new national leader. The 1930 Revolution is considered a milestone in the evolution of Brazilian capitalism as it led to the acceleration of industrial production and urban growth. It was a nationalistic phase characterised by political centralisation and the concentration of power in the hands of federal authorities at the expense of regional oligarchies. The president-dictator Getúlio Vargas – who ruled the country between 1930 and 1945, and was then elected for a second term between 1951 and 1954 (which tragically ended with his suicide) – famously launched the 'March towards the West' [*Marcha para o Oeste*] as a coordinated set of policies for economic development of the hinterland. Regional development strategies and programmes were permeated by the ideology of national integration and the alleged need to 'occupy' empty spaces (considered vast wastelands). The process likewise resembled the description of new economic frontiers by Webb (1952: 29), as territories where nature had to be conquered given that 'man was the only active agent present, and was free to do what he would'. Interestingly, the promotion of new economic and agricultural 'frontiers', as launched by the Vargas administration, had been a recurring phenomenon in the political history of Brazil, especially since the transition of the main centres of coffee production from Rio de Janeiro to São Paulo in the 1880s, a process that corresponds to the first Food Regime mentioned in Chapter 1 and that coincided with the formal end of slavery, the introduction of a paid workforce (including large numbers of migrants from Italy and elsewhere), the conquest of new areas by large-scale landowners and the first phase of national industrialisation.

The experience with coffee production in the southeast of the country had already demonstrated that agricultural frontiers in Brazil are typically promoted by the national state, creating border zones with plenty of money-making opportunities, although in practice only a small number of farmers, traders and politicians really benefited from the new agrarian economy. The advance of the agricultural frontier in the west of São Paulo and north of Paraná in the first decades of the 20th century, for example, evolved as a wave of simultaneous construction and destruction, which consumed ecosystems and existing forms of subsistence agriculture in its drive to make money at all costs; ultimately, the main beneficiaries were the intermediaries and those who had financed the enterprise (Monbeig, 1984). A similar process occurred under the influence of the 'March towards the West', and involved a series of initiatives that were defended as an important contribution and necessary enterprise for the modernisation of the economy and the affirmation of national sovereignty. The narrative was simple, but nonetheless very appealing: after a century of independent history, Brazil finally deserved to be modern and, in that context, the 'useless' lands of Mato Grosso, occupied by vaguely known indigenous tribes still living in the Stone Age, were an awkward, embarrassing situation. The western hinterland was simultaneously perceived as a challenge and a paradise, a vast terrain rich in resources and a concrete opportunity to realise the bright future that the country absolutely deserved (Ricardo, 1970).

The combination of great hardship and imminent transformation was uniquely captured by the French anthropologist Claude Lévi-Strauss in his famous book *Tristes Tropiques*, where the author recorded that, as late as in the 1930s, neighbouring groups in Mato Grosso were practically living in different historical centuries, although they were all increasingly affected by the fierce advance of the process of development. Only a few years after Lévi-Strauss's travels in the region, the state administration aggressively attempted to attract entrepreneurs from other parts of Brazil by regularly selling off vast plots of land that were often converted into agrarian projects and then resold to groups of farmers or investors. Moreno (2007) shows that in the 1950s and 1960s colonisation companies could acquire land from the state at Cr$7–10 per hectare and then resell it for Cr$100–300.[2] At the same time, National Agriculture Colonies were also established by the federal government throughout the Centre-West, in places such as Dourados in the south of Mato Grosso, as part of the agricultural development effort, although many new farmers in those areas soon abandoned their land due to various difficulties with production and commercialisation. The failure of collective projects, among other causes, led to a growing preference for individual-ised and private colonisation approaches in Mato Grosso, as demonstrated in the legal amendments introduced by Governor Fernando Corrêa da Costa during his two terms of office (1951–1956 and 1961–1966) and by subsequent administrators. The state government continued to sell large plots of relatively cheap land (typically measuring around 200,000 hectares) in order to secure revenues to run the public sector and compensate for the limited financial support received from federal authorities.

In the 1950s, the state administration transferred more than four million hectares to private colonisation companies, split into 20 plots of 200,000 hectares each, although some were not cultivated until the 1970s, as the owners decided to speculate on the rising value of land (Barrozo, 2010). The first of many such initiatives was the occupation of *Gleba* (i.e. plot of land) Arinos, from 1955 onwards, by farmers from the south of the country; this later became the municipality of Porto dos Gaúchos (Meyer, 2015). Collective land, which up to that point had been held and used mainly by poor peasant families, extractive communities or Indian tribes, underwent a rapid process of commodification in the name of colonisation and development. 'Land politics had always been part of the game of political party and economic interests, but during the 1950s it was scandalous' (Moreno, 2007: 122). According to the mindset prevailing at that juncture, this was 'no man's land' waiting to be explored or, whenever possible, grabbed with the help of false documents and the assistance of corrupt civil servants and politicians (Souza, 2013). Land titles were typically issued by public agencies with no inspection or visit to the area, informed by a mere desk study based on uncertain geographical references and unclear property limits. Strangely, it was those wishing to acquire the land rather than the public authorities who were obliged to measure the new properties, that led to massive confusion and even to situations where several official documents were issued for the same location (a situation commonly described as 'bunk bed landholding' [*beliches fundiários*]). The corruption and incompetence of the responsible agencies was magnified by the widespread use of violence to remove Indians and peasants from the land they traditionally occupied.

Land grabbing [*grilagem*] was facilitated by the flimsy mechanisms of property transfer: with land prices increasing and the market expanding, speculation and fraud increased from the 1960s onwards, especially with the extensive use of bogus envoys and fictitious proxies who claimed to represent landowners and signed the same document for several buyers (working in coordination with fraudsters, corrupt notaries and public authorities).[3] Another common practice was the granting of 'flying titles' [*títulos voadores*] which could be used by the fraudsters to document any available land (land was frequently made available through violence, normally involving suborned judges and policemen). Corruption was so endemic that it forced brief suspensions of the activities of the state Land Department (DTC, created in 1946) in the years 1951, 1956 and 1961. The situation continued out of control and, because of the absurd level of irregularities, Governor Pedro Pedrossian (1966–1971) even temporarily closed DTC's land titling service. Nonetheless, in the meantime a sister agency (CPP, created in 1948 and with a largely overlapping role, later incorporated by CODEMAT, which was created in 1966) continued to operate and issue land titles. Another agency, Intermat, was opened in 1978, and was also deeply involved in widespread illegality and corruption. The perverse appropriation of the commons that characterised the 'March towards the West' and associated forgery mechanisms accepted by the Mato Grosso government were not only maintained but amplified in the context of the developmentalist initiatives of the post-1964 military dictatorship, analysed below. Despite the rhetoric of the new 'agricultural frontier', there was limited interest in production or economic growth; rather, the main goal of politicians, opportunists and colonisation companies alike was to make quick money from the easy seizure, speculation and reselling of land.

The crude reality was that around 75 per cent of the surface of Mato Grosso had already been titled by 1980, although the rhetoric of 'land abundance' continued to be persistently invoked by all interested players. Everybody knew that the agrarian policies underpinning the agricultural frontier were completely fraudulent and unreliable, but there was no appetite to change a profitable scheme that benefited those in and around the apparatus of the state. At the same time, a bitter price for 'progress' and 'modernity' was being paid by squatters, aborigines and ecosystems that, in the context of a brutal military dictatorship, had no defenders and few spokespeople. It is also important to observe that the initial phase of colonisation, from the 'March towards the West' in the 1930s to the concession of land in the 1960s, added little in terms of agri-food development and agricultural production, but paved the way for the introduction of agribusiness in the following decades, particularly in terms of setting the basis for the prevalence of large rural properties and the adoption of capital-intensive production techniques. Regardless of its many problems and high levels of irregularities, land titling played an important role in terms of establishing a private property rights regime in Mato Grosso (most other parts of the Amazon had no such regime), which later facilitated the introduction of cooperatives and private colonisation projects (Mueller, 2012). Nonetheless, the advance of this specific type of modernity and development preserved elements of the violence, racism and discrimination that had characterised the initial conquest of Mato Grosso in colonial and early independence times. Interestingly, but also tragically, these unpleasant features would reappear in the 1990s, during the promotion of agro-neoliberalism's hypermodernity.

The national-developmentalist period (1960s–1980s)

The economy of Mato Grosso was invigorated under the military dictatorship (1964–1985), which accelerated and expanded the process of territorial occupation initiated in the preceding decades. The intention was to advance agribusiness by following the agroindustrial model adopted in the south of Brazil with the mobilisation of the necessary technological and logistical investments to make production possible in Mato Grosso. The frontier was not simply a line, as famously described by the economist Johann Heinrich von Thünen, but a potential space for imminent agricultural exploitation after minimal factors and infrastructure were established (Mueller, 2012). Motivated by concerns for national security, the federal government, ruled by the generals, adopted comprehensive, though highly technocratic, strategies to radically transform the Centre-West, and the southern and eastern tracts of the Amazon region. This is demonstrated by the creation of new development agencies with joint jurisdiction over the state of Mato Grosso (SUDAM, created in 1966, for the Amazon, and SUDECO, created in 1967, for the Centre-West) and the launch of several development programmes (Table 3.1).[4] Overcoming technological barriers was critical for the success of these initiatives. The Centre-West region was mainly made up of savannah ecosystems, which had hitherto been considered inappropriate for agriculture due to high levels of acidity, low fertility and a low percentage of organic matter.[5] It had been a technological taboo among the original Mato Grosso landowners ('pre-agribusiness') to practise intensive agriculture on savannah farms, so the new cultivation of these areas triggered specific research and technological improvements. New experimental facilities were formed, including considerable cooperation with top North American universities and beyond; the first, and highly influential, generation of Brazilian Ph.Ds in agronomy emerged during this period.

Agricultural development of Mato Grosso, as in the rest of the Amazon, was characterised by a form of 'agro-geopolitics' in which the military government sought to appease social discontent in the rest of the country – notably in areas with agrarian disputes in the South and Northeast regions, where poor families

Table 3.1 Main development programmes launched by the military technocracy

Programme	Period	Main goals
PIN (Programa de Integração Nacional/ National Integration Programme)	1970	Construction of infrastructure (including roads and colonisation), integrate economic frontiers with the rest of the country.
1st PND (Programa Nacional de Desenvolvimento/National Development Programme)	1972–1974	Enhance basic infra-structure (transport and telecommunications), invest in science and technology, and in naval, petrochemical and steel industry.
2nd PND (Programa Nacional de Desenvolvimento/National Development Programme)	1975–1979	Stimulate production of basic materials, capital goods, food and energy.
Prodoeste (Programa de Desenvolvimento do Centro Oeste)	1971–1974	Better integrate the Centre-West region with more developed states; promote infra-structure, secondary roads and sanitation (according to the goals of PND I).
Proterra (Programa de Redistribuição de Terras e Estímulo à Agroindústria do Norte e Nordeste)	1971–1979	Facilitate access to land and stimulate jobs; finance private agro-industrial projects; induce new farming practices and agro-industries; technical assistance; encourage private colonisation schemes.
First, Second and Third PDA (Amazon Development Plans)	1972–74, 1975–79, 1980–85	Assessment of natural resources, investments in economic infrastructure, human resources, Carajás mining project, Tucuruí hydropower.
Polamazônia (Programa de Pólos Agropecuários e Agrominerais da Amazônia)	1974	Occupy the 'empty lands' of the Amazon; promote farming, agro-industry and mining in 15 selected poles (launched in the 2nd PDA).
Polocentro (Programa de Desenvolvimento dos Cerrados)	1975	Stimulate the conversion of 3.7 million hectares of savannah into commercial farming; 12 'poles' in the *cerrado* with superior potential for agricultural growth were selected; investment in infrastructure, land clearing, production, commercialisation, storage, capital goods and harvest operations
Promat (Special Plan for the Development of Mato Grosso)	1977	Related to the split of the state as a series of compensatory measures, in the form of investments and payment of administrative costs of the Mato Grosso administration by the federal government in the period 1979–1989.

Note: other related programmes that focused on specific sectors or geographical areas in the 1970s to the 1990s were Polonoroeste, Prodecer, Probor, Prodiat, Prodien, Prodei, Prodeagro.

struggled to survive because of the power of large-scale landowners and land speculators – and at the same time attempted to favour business interests and foster agroindustry (most public investments at the time were fuelled by petrodollars in the form of foreign loans). Amazonian agro-geopolitics certainly played a crucial role in the spatial expansion and deepening of capitalism in Brazil. The new agricultural frontier also helped to keep salaries low in others parts of the country, reduce expenditure on social services (basically unavailable in most of the Amazon at the time) and ultimately concentrate wealth at all levels (Padis, 1981). As interpreted by Sorj (1980), the movement of people to the eastern and southern sections of the Amazon and the promotion of agroindustry were simultaneous processes of horizontal and vertical 'modernisation' – that is, the spread of a supposed modern world order, essentially through the advance of land speculation, the extraction of surplus value and the transfer of rent. At face value, this seemed a viable and promising plan, even more so under the firm control of an authoritarian administration and with the prospects of an easy appropriation of large, apparently unoccupied, areas, but the reality on the ground was much more challenging and fraught with contradictions (Ianni, 1981).

The first phase of the agribusiness frontier – in broad terms, between the late 1960s and late 1980s – entailed a strong and strategic articulation of public and private agendas that complemented each other in a context of abundant foreign capital, political authoritarianism and availability of land and labour. The main intellectual luminary of the military regime – General Golbery do Couto e Silva – made very clear the government's intention to promote a 'shock of civilisation' to replace a system that was considered highly obsolete. In his words, the aim was to 'humanise, integrate and value the immense territory, which is still largely unused and desert'; this was to be achieved through a 'deluge of civilisation over the Amazon', operated from logistical bases located in the centre of the country (Couto e Silva, 1981: 47). Golbery's development strategy reveals a peculiar combination of right-wing nationalism with an ideology of socioeconomic 'modernisation from the top'. The prevailing perception was that 'Brazil has too much land, but this is not where the men are' and that, with great sacrifices, it was imperative to 'offer them land' (Lambert, 1970: 131). Before long, however, it became obvious that the generals had opened the doors to hell and 'unleashed forces beyond their control, and now the Amazon face[d] its apocalypse' (Hecht and Cockburn, 1989: 141). Economic plans were being formulated in the distant offices of Brasília, with little attention given to socio-ecological impacts and the presence of other groups of Brazilians.

Development was imposed as if the Amazon were 'one of the few empty areas left in the world; we might occupy it and make it Brazilian before the Chinese decide they want it' (*The New York Times*, 1970). Nonetheless, there were at least a quarter of a million peasant families already living in the region, not to mention the Indian population of at least 100,000 people (Branford and Glock, 1985). In actual fact, the displacement and extermination of numerous indigenous tribes in the eastern and southern sections of the Amazon opened the most tragic chapter of this epopeia and remain highly contentious issues to the present day (as large hydropower dams, waterways and roads are increasingly constructed near or through vulnerable Indian reserves, while the agribusiness sector sustains an ongoing attack against these reserves). The tribes were forced either to move to more precarious reserves or be decimated by disease and abject exploitation. As unflinchingly described by Oliveira (2005: 84) the

> occupation of the north of Mato Grosso by agriculture projects financed and stimulated by SUDAM [the state agency responsible for regional development in the Amazon] occurred through the widespread grabbing [*grilagem*] of indigenous land, which amounted to an authentic ethnocide and genocide [of various first nation tribes]

The complexity of the socio-cultural landscape was aggravated by poor–poor disputes for land and opportunities, such as between Indians and small-scale farmers. Particularly during the administration of General Emílio Médici (1969–1974), impoverished farmers and peasants were brought to the Amazon (mainly to the state of Pará) from the southern states, each receiving a plot of land through public colonisation schemes [*assentamentos de reforma agrária*]. The movement of people to the Amazon echoed the strategy adopted by their ancestors, who had left Germany, Italy and other poverty-stricken parts of Europe to move to Brazil in search of the land denied them in their birthplaces (Schwantes, 1989). Figure 3.1 shows one of the sites where immigrants coming to Mato Grosso could find accommodation before moving to their new destination. Attracting poor famers to the region helped to conceal major inequalities and distortions in land allocation and official support. The National System of Rural Credit (SNCR) was established in 1965, and the volume of funds for agriculture increased by several times between the 1960s and the end of the 1970s, but most subsidised credit favoured large-scale producers and the export of non-traditional crops rather than the settlers. This happened because industries, banks and other private companies based in the rest of the country were stimulated to acquire inexpensive land in the Amazon by the promise of generous public incentives and subsidies offered by the development agencies and publicly owned banks. According to Law 5,173/1966, companies were allowed to deduct up to 50 per cent of the income tax payable on all their operations throughout Brazil provided that the money was invested in an approved industrial or farming project or in infrastructure in the Amazon. However, this money was often siphoned off to finance activities in the main economic centres of Brazil rather than production in the Amazon region, as analysed by Cardoso and Müller (1977).

If Pará was the epicentre of this conservative process of counter-agrarian reform, Mato Grosso was considered the 'paradise of private colonisation' projects (Oliveira, 1989: 106). The prominence of public farming schemes during the very first years of economic modernisation was largely superseded, from 1974, by an emphasis on private colonisation coordinated by cooperatives and entrepreneurial companies (Santos, 1993), notably in Mato Grosso, where they could benefit from

Figure 3.1 Accommodation at Posto Gil, a staging post for the migrants on their way to
    the farms and colonisation projects
Source: Author

an existing private property regime in the easily mechanisable areas in the centre
and north of the state (Furtado, 2010). Instead of the small plots of land in agrarian
reform schemes, medium-sized or large properties were the norm in the private
colonisation projects. More than 50 private colonisation companies, as well as
the federal and state public colonisation agencies, were in operation in Mato
Grosso during this period. Around 90 per cent of the new towns and cities at the
agribusiness frontier in Mato Gross are actually result of the colonisation effort
(Arruda, 2009). This was the experience in the current municipalities of Sinop
(founded in 1974 by the colonisation company Sinop), Sorriso (in 1975, by
Colonizadora Feliz), Canarana (in 1975, by Cooperative Copercol), Nova Mutum
(in 1976, by Colonizadora Mutum), Alta Floresta (in 1976, by Indeco) and
Primavera do Leste (in 1979, by Colonizadora Consentino), among others. In
addition, agrarian reform projects, coordinated by the federal agency INCRA, were
implemented in Terranova, Guarantã and Lucas do Rio Verde, which also led to
the creation of new municipalities. Over the years, large-scale farms were
naturalised and accepted as the only viable alternative to the low fertility and
high acidity of *cerrado* (savannah) soils and the related need of capital to invest
in machinery, seeds and agro-chemicals (Wolford, 2008).[6]

For many years, the colonisation companies, with their monumental profits, controlled the local land market and could plan the new towns and rural properties as they wanted. Nevertheless, the advance of agribusiness was not uniform, but influenced by the uneven distribution of vegetation and natural resources. For instance, areas of *cerrado* along BR-163, such as Sorriso, tended to attract colonists with more capital, who were able to adopt mechanised plantation technologies; a subset of these later became powerful agribusiness farmers.[7] In the north of Mato Grosso, on the border with Pará, it was more common to find forested areas that were allocated to peasants and small-scale farmers (it is difficult to know how many came to Mato Grosso, but it is likely that more than 25,000 settlement plots were sold).[8] Throughout the region and in the more distant forested locations, cattle ranchers also played a very important role in terms of land clearing and farm formation. Regional transformation engulfed both rural and urban areas – for instance, in the municipalities situated in areas of forest, like Sinop, timber mills fed with the trees from the new farms defined the first phase of urbanisation. The expansion of the agricultural frontier in Mato Grosso was facilitated by the conversion of the soldiers of the Brazilian Army into a developmental force, which is what happened when two military engineer battalions became responsible for the construction of the motorway (BR-163) that crosses the main production areas in the Teles Pires River Basin. Regional development required the construction of other similar federal motorways (BR-070, BR-158 and BR-364), as well as additional infrastructure (warehouses, research centres, extension and financial services, technical schools, etc.), by the public sector.

Because of its relatively remote location and underdeveloped economy, Mato Grosso was a latecomer to the Green Revolution. However, the belated adoption of the agribusiness model was transformed into an opportunity for the sector to capture economic policies (previously dominated by the old cattle oligarchy). Subsidies (i.e. concessionary-priced credit) became the main instrument of agricultural development and the key catalyst for the building of the new frontier. It was, nonetheless, a highly perverse and quite regressive policy instrument, as it was mostly appropriated by large-scale farmers, aggravating social inequality and stimulating environmental degradation. Graham *et al.* (1987) show that by the mid-1970s, subsidised credit almost equalled the total gross value of agricultural output, creating allocation distortions and diverting funds. Because of high inflation and fixed lending rates, there was in practice a negative real rate of interest, but

> the majority of formal credit to agriculture went to no more than 3%–4% of the producers in the sector. [. . .] Given the extreme concentration of credit to a small proportion of producers within the agricultural credit portfolio and the high ratio of agricultural credit to total agricultural output (for the sector as a whole), those producers fortunate enough to have access to formal credit could not possibly be using it all for the purposes of agricultural production.
>
> (Graham *et al.*, 1987: 24–25)

It was clear that subsidies were being diverted to other, more profitable, forms of investment and particularly towards the acquisition of more land. Marked economic inequalities were rapidly intensifying in the agricultural frontier: total income increased by 149 per cent between 1970 and 1980 (the highest rate in the country, as the last authors point out), but the Gini index deteriorated from 0.339 to 0.503 in the same period. These tendencies can only be properly understood in relation to the power of oligarchic groups and the class-based commitments of the Brazilian state.

In 1977, as part of the technocratic quest to control the new economic frontier, the territory of Mato Grosso was split into two separate federal units (i.e. states). The partition of the vast, practically unmanageable, geographical features of Mato Grosso had long been demanded by political and economic groups in the southern portion of the original state, who despised what was perceived as the backward, indigenous and forested north and repeatedly defied the power of Cuiabá. Interestingly, while the fragmentation may initially have favoured the new southern state (which is now called 'Mato Grosso of the South' [*Mato Grosso do Sul*]), in the long term it was the northern state (which maintained the original name) that gained most from the division. With two separate administrations, Mato Grosso and Mato Grosso do Sul followed even more closely the agricultural tendencies of the more advanced parts of Brazil, characterised by incentives to export processed and semi-processed goods (including tax exemptions and concessionary-priced credit), rapid modernisation and increasing mechanisation (leading to severe land concentration). However, despite the enthusiasm of politicians and their close allies, the first years of the new agricultural frontier in Mato Grosso could hardly be considered a success. Production was diversified and included several crops (coffee, cassava, guarana, pepper, rice, etc.), but most technologies were not suitable for the local agro-ecological conditions, while commercialisation was expensive and very difficult, aggravated by erratic and inadequate support from the government.[9] In addition, Mato Grosso, and the rest of the Centre-West region, had historically been an important producer of domestic food crops (especially rice) and cattle, but that situation was dramatically transformed with the reduction in food-crop area (due to the displacement of subsistence farming).

The lack of appropriate technologies, high production and transaction costs, and dwindling public subsidies forced a change of course and, eventually, the transition to agro-neoliberalism (discussed below). Technical and socio-ecological barriers faced by the new farmers coincided with the national macroeconomic crisis of the 1980s, when the government ran out of cash and defaulted on the payment of international obligations. Nonetheless, from the perspective of the main political and economic players, production and productivity problems were less of an issue. For those in control of the new development frontier, the main source of profit was actually the capture of public land under no specific use, with the help of corrupt authorities, and its subsequent sale to farmers or other land speculators. Land speculation, which was had already been rife for decades, continued at a high speed through the acquisition of cheap land from the state or existing private owners, which was then sold on to new farmers from the south and southeast of the country. In many cases, land was acquired merely to be offered as a guarantee for bank loans, which further accelerated the fast-growing semi-illegal land market. Confusion and criminality reached remarkable levels in the first decade of the agricultural frontier, aided by the lack of political freedom characteristic of the context of military dictatorship.

It is disappointing to observe that speculation and land grabbing actually increased with the return to electoral democracy; Governor Júlio Campos had many political pressures to respond to, and between 1983 and 1986 more than 4 million hectares were conceded to political and business allies (Moreno, 2007: 248). This suggests continuity between formally democratic and authoritarian periods of Mato Grosso's history. The newly elected state administration aggressively promoted new rounds of colonisation and land selling. However, the main strategy was to maintain a high level of confusion and bureaucracy in order to facilitate the concession of land to political allies and the extraction of rent through speculation (aided by the selective construction of new roads and public infrastructure in areas acquired by or under the influence of speculators). Júlio Campos, together with his brother Jayme, also a Governor (1991–1994), were emblematic examples of the regional oligarchy who incorporated populist and developmentalist goals into their political platform. Astonishingly, more land was ultimately sold and grabbed than the total surface area of the state of Mato Grosso, which still has major consequences today in terms of fierce disputes and court cases. Agribusiness flourished in Mato Grosso not in parallel with, but precisely because of this powerful creation of fictitious commodities (in this case, land as the key economic asset) following national-developmentalist policies initially advanced by the military technocracy. The ideology of the agricultural frontier, together with the persistent use of heroic images of the old *bandeirantes*, provided the necessary political justification and the appropriate policies for the violent appropriation of the commons and the reorganisation of the socio-spatial order.

Notwithstanding operation and logistical problems, Mato Grosso was increasingly seen as a promising territory for agribusiness activity, regardless of the social and ecological impacts. From the perspective of landowners and agribusiness mandarins, it was largely unimportant that a significant proportion of farmers could not cope with the bureaucracy and violence involved in the advance of the agricultural frontier. Travelling around the state in the last few years, it was easy to collect narratives from farmers who had lost their properties, become employees on other farms or in towns, migrated elsewhere in the Amazon or returned to the south of the country. This means that, despite the promise of opportunities and land for all, the agricultural frontier was selective from the start, and this selectivity only increased with the insertion of the regional economy into globalised markets from the end of the 1990s onwards. What is central to the present analysis is that the failures of the initial phase of the agricultural frontier, which was certainly painful for the large majority of decapitalised farmers, provided the material and ideological means for the flourishing of agro-

Figure 3.2 Aerial image of the landscape in the Teles Pires
Source: Author

neoliberalism. All in all, it has been a deeply political game, although those in charge try their utmost to deny the significance of opposing voices and the associated risks and inequalities. Let us now consider in more detail the balance of gains and losses of the advance of agro-neoliberalism in Mato Grosso (the resulting landscape is illustrated by Figure 3.2). The specific aim of the next section is to examine the achievements, contradictions and problems of the relatively fast recovery of agribusiness and the transition to a vibrant, although highly vulnerable, agro-neoliberal economy (more details and complementary analyses will come in subsequent chapters).

Agro-neoliberalism as the redemption of the agribusiness frontier (since the 1990s)

The early 1990s in Brazil were years of great macroeconomic uncertainty (basically due to hyperinflation, structural inefficiencies and declining public sector investment capacity) and acute political instability (related to corruption scandals and the impeachment in 1992 of the first elected president after the long military dictatorship). Similar to other national experiences in South America, Brazilian society was undergoing a period of great turbulence caused by conflicting demands and a lack of response from the state that was associated with the exhaustion of national-developmentalist policies introduced in the 1930s and later boosted by the military governments after 1964. A new constitution, introduced in 1988, recognised and expanded social and political rights, and incorporated provisions for public services (such as universal health, education, social security, etc.), along with details about how these should be delivered. However, this did not serve to resolve mounting economic problems. The solution to the tension between legitimate pressures on the state and a systematic failure to reorganise the economy came in the form of a package of monetary and anti-inflationary measures, known as the 'Real Plan' [*Plano Real*], launched in 1994, and the subsequent election of its main architect, the sociologist Fernando Henrique Cardoso, as president. His administration (1995–2002) was marked by a series of (partial) institutional adjustments aimed at reducing the size of the public sector, modernising production and regulation, and opening the country to globalised markets. As discussed in Chapter 2, the first few years under the Real Plan were a time of serious difficulties for the Brazilian agribusiness sector, particularly because of the temporary strengthening of the national currency and export barriers, and the scarcity of bank credit.

In Mato Grosso, the situation was particularly challenging given that the production of the new agricultural frontier had relied heavily on public funds and federal government incentives. The authorities' answer was to adopt, and eagerly promote, the agro-neoliberal model of agribusiness production from the end of the 1990s onwards. The farming community of Mato Grosso was thus able to negotiate a way out of the impasse caused by the macroeconomic turmoil and, more importantly, the agro-neoliberal agenda was responsible for redeeming the agribusiness frontier and catapulting it to international prominence. In the process, the three dimensions of agro-neoliberalism presented in the previous chapter – that is, novel forms of public–private alliances, sophisticated techno-economic strategies and the containment of critical reactions – evolved consistently together. The agribusiness frontier continued to expand through a dynamic of consolidated and new cultivated areas, as well as an efficient coordination of private and state efforts (Costa, 2016). The mobilisation of the agribusiness community and the pressure it was able to exert on policy-makers became more evident with the foundation of the Association of Soybean and Maize Producers (Aprosoja-MT) in 2005, which was a moment of acute crisis due to increased production costs and losses caused by climatic adversities.[10] In various meetings held by farmers and in public events around Mato Grosso, which were attended during our research, it was clear that Aprosoja-MT is treated by the farmers as their legitimate representation and its activities are described with great pride.[11] It is also common to hear references to the growth of agribusiness activity in Mato Grosso presented as proof that this is 'the Brazil that is doing well' [*o Brazil que dá certo*]. Expressions like this work as a totalising narrative that is repeatedly used by politicians and agribusiness groups to explain practically everything that is considered positive in the region, even the surprising success of the small football team Luverdense, from the city of Lucas do Rio Verde, in the national championships since 2013.

The agricultural federation FAMATO echoes these claims of achievement and excellence, arguing that the

> participation of the 'agro' in the socioeconomic development of Brazil and Mato Grosso increases every year. More than a leader of sustainable food production, the sector became a regular reference when considering a state that works or when [mentioning] the organisation of a group around common objectives.
>
> (FAMATO, 2014: 9)

Obviously, the triumph of agro-neoliberalism has not only depended on clever marketing strategies and visionary leaders, but has involved a range of complex technological and operational adjustments. In Mato Grosso, this has primarily been associated with the strong 'soyfication' of agribusiness – that is, establishing the soybean as central to the economy (a few other crops are rotated or cultivated in association with soybean, such as cotton, maize and sorghum).[12] According to the producers' association, in 'Mato Grosso, soybeans are synonymous with tech-nology. Mato Grosso producers are renowned for using the most up-to-date technology, from planting to harvesting crops' (Aprosoja-MT, n.d.: 22). Since the 1970s, it has been much more difficult for farmers, even on medium-scale farms, to avoid adopting soybean monocultures rather than cultivating perennial crops, which in theory are more adapted to the bio-climatic conditions of the Amazon. The extraordinary exponential increase in soybean production is shown in Table 3.2. After 1999, Mato Grosso became the main producer of soybean in Brazil, and has increasingly consolidated this position.

Table 3.2 Expansion of the main agricultural activities of Mato Grosso, 1978– 2002

Year	Maize	Soybean	Poultry	Cattle	Pork
1978	100	100	100	100	100
1980	119	1,612	500	135	105
1982	241	5,028	3,649	153	109
1984	266	14,446	3,970	175	116
1986	442	26,428	4,449	176	135
1988	584	37,071	5,325	202	163
1990	517	42,161	7,585	233	194
1992	638	50,113	8,242	262	164
1994	972	73,185	12,144	325	178
1996	1,265	69,238	16,052	399	130
1998	792	99,437	17,453	431	143
2000	1,194	120,711	18,131	487	157
2002	1,932	160,987	21,736	571	194

Adapted from Pessoa and Pereira (2006), based on various sources.
Presented in relative terms: year 1978 = 100

Soybean production (see Figure 3.3) accelerated in Mato Grosso during the 2000s commodities boom, and because of the appreciation of the American dollar after the 1999 devaluation of the real (currency devaluation generated notable domestic price increases, even in years of fairly stable world prices). For instance, the price of soybean (US$ per metric ton) in June (the month of reference in Brazil) was 186.75 in 2000, 254.74 in 2005, 552.47 in 2008 and 560.05 in 2013.[13] In the growing season 2015–2016, Mato Grosso cultivated 9.20 million hectares of soybean, and this was expected to increase to 9.23 million hectares in 2016–2017 (IMEA, 2016b). Table 3.3 presents production data from three of the most significant agribusiness municipalities in Mato Grosso.

The encroachment of soybean in Mato Grosso, and also other areas of agricultural frontier in neighbouring states, has been an extension of the profitable agribusiness model previously adopted in the south of Brazil, which included mechanisation, agro-chemical inputs, commercialisation through cooperatives and commodity exports (Ozório de Almeida and Santos, 1990). It also required the selection of crop varieties adapted to the acidic soils of Mato Grosso and better management practices for preserving nutrients in the soil. Soybean and the other few crops grown by agribusiness farmers in Mato Grosso are very capital-intensive and normally cultivated on large-scale farms of between 2,000 and 5,000 hectares, with an increasing number of extremely large enterprises that make use of both

Figure 3.3 Soybean field in early December
Source: Author

Table 3.3 Agribusiness production per municipality (maize and soybean)

	Sorriso		Sinop		Lucas do Rio Verde	
	2004	2013	2004	2013	2004	2013
Maize						
area harvested (ha)	101,000	413,900	17,526	62,631	100,290	180,440
production (ton)	334,800	2,657,940	53,228	353,287	332,030	1,207,980
production value (10³ US$)	20,952	270,366	3,005	35,936	23,349	127,891
Soybean						
area harvested (ha)	540,867	616,900	84,495	131,134	209,237	238,474
production (ton)	1,688,120	1,926,930	243,395	385,023	528,142	699,434
production value (10³ US$)	341,980	632,433	48,417	125,763	108,056	269,452

Source: IBGE (www.cidades.ibge.gov.br)
Based on the exchange rate at May 2004 (1US$ = R$3.100) and May 2013 (1US$ = R$2.035)

owned and rented land (Oliveira and Hecht, 2016). According to Werner (2011), 3.35 per cent of the landowners in the state control 61.57 per cent of the land (in many cases without adequate land titles) while small-scale farmers only own 6.86 per cent (the national average is 33.92 per cent). An important consequence is that the richest 10 per cent of the population of Mato Grosso, largely formed of members of the agribusiness sector, retain 53 per cent of the annual income (according to the government agency SEPLAN, quoted in Frederico, 2008).

The expansion and consolidation of soybean and a few other associated monoculture crops in Mato Grosso have been directly connected with a grow-ing political space for market-based solutions, something that was greatly facilitated by the election of state governors aligned with the federal agenda of neoliberalising reforms. The two main personalities involved were governors Dante de Oliveira (1995–2002) and Blairo Maggi (2003–2010). Dante was elected as a member of the populist party PDT, but soon migrated to the party of President Cardoso (PSDB) and eagerly adopted, at the regional level, the same objectives of privatisation, insertion into globalised markets and rationalisation of the public sector (including important elements of ecological modernisation and flexible environmental regulation). Dante articulated a persuasive discourse of state renovation and the need to remove the old rural oligarchy from control of the state administration (evidently, this was never achieved). Some of the main facilities owned by the Mato Grosso government were privatised, such as CEMAT (electricity), CASEMAT (warehousing and storage), BEMAT (bank) and SANEMAT (water and sanitation). The government introduced an import-ant tax waiver programme [*renúncia fiscal*] called FUNDEI-PRODEI (despite the sustained rhetoric of public deficit and fiscal crisis), which greatly benefited agroindustry. At the same time, the environmental regulator (FEMA-MT) incorporated the agenda of ecological modernisation and economic incentives to conservation, which was quickly appropriated by the agribusiness sector and was highly instrumental in the greening of soybean production. Much more than an economic phenomenon, the adjustment introduced by Dante de Oliveira was a socio-political process that was presented as a necessary and unavoidable agenda of institutional reforms and the search for efficiency and modernisation.

The sector that benefited most from the public policy reforms was agribusiness, which assumed direct control of the public administration of Mato Grosso with the election of Blairo Maggi in 2002. His term in office further consolidated the powerful demands of the agribusiness sector, encouraging novel production technologies and making it impossible for the environmental regulator to act independently. For the industry, Maggi's political manifesto represented the best possible incarnation of the agro-neoliberal platform, and crucially helped to naturalise agribusiness as the economic locomotive of the state. The more recent administrations of Silval Barbosa (2010–2014) and Pedro Taques (since 2015) essentially maintained the same direction in terms of public policy and retained the crucial influence of agribusiness on decision-making – for instance, Carlos Fávaro, Vice-Governor since 2015, is also Vice-President of the Brazilian Soybean Producers Association (Aprosoja Brasil) and a former president of Aprosoja-MT. Fávaro is not only Taques's deputy, but has also been secretary of the environment since 2016 (although there have been widespread rumours that the de facto secretary is a lawyer associated with the former governor Maggi). The strong and convincing naturalisation of agribusiness has been greatly facilitated by a narrow public debate, superficial democracy and acquiescent media. Time spent in Mato Grosso in recent years has demonstrated to us that almost the entire academic community is greatly sympathetic and accepts, almost uncritically, the course of events.

There exists a remarkable paradox behind ideological calls for 'less state and more markets', given that in practice farmers in Mato Grosso do not actually want to be too distanced from the state apparatus. On one hand, there is still a tendency to blame the government for any large or small adversities (while most of the success of agribusiness is attributed to the 'bravery' of the private sector). Notwithstanding the fact that agribusiness farmers in Mato Grosso are deep in the pockets of transnational corporations – which finance production and buy most of the goods produced – farmers paradoxically call on the state to correct market failures and, in bad years, to provide bailout funds (Peine, 2010). On the other hand, this long tradition of antagonism and protest has been largely replaced by systematic attempts to capture the state both directly and indirectly: directly, with the election of Blairo Maggi as state governor and many other agribusiness leaders to the senate or the house of deputies; they also have significant representation in the agriculture ministries (e.g. Neri Geller and Maggi himself);[14] indirectly, with the industry's hegemonic influence on policy-making and the suppression of other economic alternatives for Mato Grosso. In an interview, Blairo Maggi's cousin, Eraí Maggi Scheffer – who owns 36 farms and succeeded Blairo as the greatest individual producer of soybean in the world (it seems that the senator is now more interested in heavy infrastructure, logistical and financial businesses) – affirmed that arguments and clashes with elected politicians are no longer an issue. On the contrary, according to Scheffer, the political leaders now understand the significance and demands of agribusiness farmers and are able to respond. In his words:

> Mato Grosso used to be a problem for Brazil, but now it is proved that Mato Grosso [. . .] is a great solution for Brazil and to the world [in terms of food production]. Today, we are no longer the *ugly duckling* [emphasis in the original] and we also demonstrate that we can produce and have good productivity.
>
> (Agro Olhar, 2014)

The assertion that agribusiness is a mature sector, however, hides a much more complicated relationship of trust and suspicion with the state apparatus. As in other parts of the world where agro-neoliberalism thrives, Mato Grosso farmers consistently expect special treatment from government agencies, including the cancelling of debts with public banks and other concessions, especially in years of bad weather or low prices. The same state that is described as inefficient and restrictive (because of environmental and labour regulation, for example) is asked to intervene as provider and protector against the intrinsic vulnerabilities of agribusiness. While agribusiness farmers presume a constant stream of dispensations and safeguards, the sector has repeatedly attacked the federal government for insufficient investment in transportation and roads, and exerted sustained pressure for the privatisation of existing and new infrastructure projects. As a result, 851 kilometres of federal motorway BR-163 (which crosses the main production areas in Mato Grosso) were transferred in 2013 to a private operator (Odebrecht, a company which has since been heavily involved in a huge corruption scandal – see Chapter 7), following the public-private collaborative strategies of President Dilma's administration. Figure 3.4 has evidences of the privatised management of this motorway. The agribusiness corporation Amaggi – a leading Brazilian company with significant international presence that is owned and commanded by Blairo Maggi's family – also, since 1997, operates a navigation system in the Madeira River (between Porto Velho in Rondônia and Itacoatiara in Amazonas and along the Amazon River).[15] During the time of our fieldwork, the public debate was dominated by the prospect of increasing navigation along the Tapajós River (another major tributary of the Amazon); this came into effect in 2014 and could become an important low-cost alternative for the export of soybean through northern ports.

Comparable to the privatisation of infrastructure, TNCs have increasingly financed production to compensate for the reduction in the subsidised credit offered by public banks. This is the most evident manifestation of the financialisation tendency that pervades agricultural production in Brazil and South America today. TNCs typically help with basic inputs (fertiliser, pesticides, etc.) and later receive repayment in kind (sacks of soybean or other crops delivered during the harvest season). Not by chance, the interest rate adopted by TNCs is approximately double

Figure 3.4 Road sign informing the privatisation of the motorway BR-163, under the administration of Odebrecht

Source: Author

the rate charged by public banks, while they receive payment in kind precisely when market prices are lowest. This represents a triple gain for the TNCs, as they secure a reliable supply of grains, charge inflated interest rates and also pocket the difference in price between the harvest period and the off-season (a premium derived from their ability to store the grains during the rainy season and sell them later when prices increase). Curiously, despite the harsh terms set by TNCs, agribusiness farmers tend to accept the legitimacy of corporations as a fait accompli and normally focus their criticism on the state and its inability to understand their needs. A large-scale farmer argued during a visit that:

> I have a good interaction with the 'tradings' [transnational corporations, or TNCs], they help with inputs and in some years with credit, but it is expensive. But we lack viable options, we can't really diversify. [. . .] In the end, the government is always guilty, because they pay little attention to our problems.
>
> (Interview in Sorriso, December 2014)

It is curious that the language used in publications and campaigns by the farming community of Mato Grosso is often quite aggressive, indicating the eagerness of agribusiness farmers to fight a continuous battle for recognition and state concessions, while at the same time maintaining a relatively cosy relationship with TNCs. There are several layers of contradiction here. It is common to see farmers complaining about the price of transporting grains to the international ports in the southeast of Brazil (around R$330 or US$140/ton); however, these alleged high transportation costs have not affected profitability or the perennial search for new, more distant production areas. The proliferation of plantation farms, mainly dedicated to the cultivation of soybean, is normally explained by the availability of new technologies, such as GMOs and better machinery, good market prices and the competence of the farmers, but probably the most important factor is the super-exploitation of the labour-force and maximisation of surplus value extraction. In addition, rising costs and logistical difficulties have been partly overcome through the combination of cheap land (acquired during the first period of the agribusiness frontier), abundant natural resources and, especially, exploited labour. It should be noted that even though agribusiness farms pay higher median wages than other comparable economic sectors, the labour-to-capital ratio is markedly low. In this regard, it can be seen at the bottom of Table 3.4 that the rate of cropland area per employee increased significantly between 1970 and 2006.

Labour accounts for less than 3 per cent of agricultural production costs, while seed, fertiliser and agrochemicals – generally sold by representatives of transnational companies – represent 60.61 per cent of the total costs (figures are from the production season 2015/16, as expanded in Table 3.5). Because of heavy machinery, it is now possible to cultivate very large tracts of land (many thousands of hectares) with a handful of permanent and temporary workers. This is obviously part of the extraction of surplus value and mitigates the increasing tendency to acquire capital in the form of additional farmland. On average, because of the use of capital-intensive, sophisticated machines, only one employee is needed to cultivate around 200 hectares of crops. This is an undisputable demonstration of the neoliberalising trends of agribusiness in the region, which aims to produce more and more food, energy and raw materials using less and less labour (as discussed by Moore, 2015).

Table 3.4 Evolution of production and labour intensity in Mato Grosso, 1970–2006

	1970	1975	1980	1985	1995	2006
Crop production (ha)	753 749	501 267	1 553 248	2 129 443	2 951 745	6 865 763
Pastures (ha)	31 588 303	11 243 468	14 779 703	16 404 370	21 452 061	22 809 021
Employees (persons)	373 039	263 179	318 570	359 221	326 767	362 895
Tractors (number)	4 386	2 643	11 156	19 534	32 752	40 657
Crop land (ha)/ employee	2.0	1.9	4.9	5.9	9.0	18.9

Source: IBGE Agriculture Census (2006): original table 1.3.25

Table 3.5 Soybean production costs in the state of Mato Grosso

	2010/11	2011/12	2012/13	2013/14	2014/2015	2015/2016	2016/2017**
Main inputs (R$)*	768.38	811.56	968.34	1,192.56	1,492.78	2,071.42	1,786.93
Labour (R$)	25.08	24.54	44.36	64.36	78.56	92.67	92.67
Total costs (variable + fixed) (R$)	1,483.70	1,635.82	1,908.09	2,347.47	2,422.49	3,417.44	3,152.85
Annual rate of inflation (%)							
(2010)	5.91						
(2011)	6.50						
(2012)	5.84						
(2013)	5.91						
(2014)	6.41						
(2015)	10.67						
	, , ,						
Main inputs/total costs (%)	51.79	49.61	50.75	50.80	61.62	60.61	56.68
Labour/total costs (%)	1.69	1.50	2.32	2.74	3.24	2.71	2.94

Source: IMEA (bulletins of 4 April 2014; 20 October 2014; 14 October 2015; 22 August 2016)/Central Bank of Brazil (for the rate of inflation)
R$ = Brazilian currency 'real'
* Main inputs = seeds, fertiliser and agrochemicals
** Provisional figures

Connected with the flexible labour market and increasing exploitation of the labour force (including the use of a large number of temporary employees at critical moments in the production season), there are frequent cases of violence and conflicts related to access to land and resources. Mato Grosso was the state with the second highest level of rural violence in Brazil in 2014 (a trend that has persisted for many years), with 30 serious land-related incidents involving 1,618 families, as well as six cases of water-related conflicts (CPT, 2015). Land disputes involving indigenous groups were identified in some of our interviews with agribusiness leaders as a major problem and a great challenge for the next few years. The controversy is related to Indian rights, which supposedly take priority over the rights of farmers and third parties, although it is not easy to enforce the legislation when disputes involve the expensive farms irregularly established on indigenous land. It is possible to verify that both farmers and indigenous groups have been defrauded by state agencies' failure to properly and legally oversee colonisation and land titling, which has resulted in a situation of perennial tensions. The problem is more acute because most Indians in Mato Grosso today are well aware of the value of soybean lands and are increasingly seeking to secure the recognition of their ancestral rights in areas of intensive production.

A distressing element of the rapid expansion of agribusiness is the physical abuse of employees and even cases of forced labour. If paid labour, according to a Marxist perspective, is intrinsically violent, as the capitalist expropriates part of the value produced by the employer, in the case of the frontier of development in the Amazon there have been repeated situations of ultra-violence due to appalling labour conditions and abusive contracts (Guimarães Neto, 2014). Another disturbing phenomenon, which vividly connects violence across centuries and geographies, is the re-emergence of slavery in rural areas, where those displaced by the advance of modern agriculture or attracted to the region from poverty-ridden areas are then retained to carry out arduous tasks with no pay; this coercion is made possible by the workers' isolation and reference to supposed debts, among other means (Figueira and Prado, 2011). Mato Grosso has been denounced as one of the areas of Brazil with the highest levels of concealed, but recurrent, cases of slavery, which seriously undermines the prevalent claim that agribusiness is responsible for the advance of modern production technologies (Théry *et al.*, 2011). In 2013, the Ministry of Labour and Employment listed 61 properties in Mato Grosso in the national database of slavery cases, including soybean farms, cattle ranches and timber companies (Diário de Cuiabá, 2013). Slavery-like situations were found even on the properties of the most powerful and well-connected farmers, such as those belonging to Eraí Maggi Scheffer (where 41 people were liberated after a government inspection); their connections with powerful elites raise significant obstacles to the prosecution of these farmers (Folha de São Paulo, 2008).

Despite concrete evidence of exploitation and violence, the agribusiness sector has demonstrated a remarkable ability to dilute and deny its responsibility for mounting negative socio-ecological impacts. As in other parts of Latin America, while neoliberalised agriculture makes abundant use of fossil fuels, biotechnology and agrochemicals, it has tried to respond to environmental concerns and customer expectations, but always on its own terms. In Mato Grosso, the response has come in the form of a belated fondness on the part of farmers for the agenda of sustainability and ecological modernisation. The agribusiness sector has even created its own environmental NGO, called 'Green Action' [*Ação Verde*], which has taken a very active part in the discussion of new regulation and occupied seats in public forums (Galvão, 2008). The association of soybean producers has published a bilingual booklet, *On the Road to Sustainability*, which emphasises the environmental consciousness of soybean producers, citing in particular the concentration of production in savannah areas (rather than in the Amazon forest) and the adoption of integrated technologies. According to the association, 'there is a strong correlation between soybean yield and macro socio-environmental indicators, such as the Human Development Index (HDI). The ten cities with the largest soybean production have HDI rates above the state and the country averages' (Aprosoja-MT, n.d.: 11). In our interviews, Aprosoja-MT's spokespersons made frequent reference to the 'green passport' of agribusiness in Mato Grosso, essentially based on the adoption of no-tillage technology and gains of productivity (supposedly eliminating the need for new production areas).

In this way, the agribusiness community has tried to reinvent itself as an environmentally sensitive sector, deeply concerned about the impact of its activity on the well-being of wider society. However, although agribusiness farmers proudly insist that Mato Grosso still maintains large areas of original vegetation, this tends to be because these areas are remote and would not be cost-effective locations for soybean production. Every year this frontier of cost-effectiveness moves, with technological improvements and increases in land prices in the consolidated zones, meaning that new production areas are constantly opening. The situation embodies the Jevons Paradox, where use of a resource becomes increasingly efficient, but increasing demand for the same resource leads to a greater rate of consumption: higher agricultural productivity in Mato Grosso has increased, rather than decreased, rural land use. Between 2001 and 2004 alone, more than 540,000 hectares of forest were directly converted into cropland without the more conventional implementation of pastures as an intermediary step (Morton *et al.*, 2006). Notwithstanding constant increases in the use of resources – land, water and energy in particular – concepts like sustainability and flexible regulation have been used by sector representatives to confer an image of righteousness on modern, intensive agriculture practices:

> Our agriculture cannot be considered anything but sustainable. Sustainability is profitable: we don't do things to gain foreign recognition, but only because of the economic results. [. . .] We do it despite lots of production difficulties [that we face]: too much regulation, the [legal] requirement to set aside part of our property uncultivated [between 20 and 50 per cent, depending on the location] [. . .] But this again demonstrates that we are sustainable.
>
> (Interview with an Aprosoja-MT director,
> Cuiabá, June 2013)

The surprising 'environmental turn' of the agribusiness sector has been accompanied by a search for national and, crucially, international recognition in terms of ecological modernisation. In a talk during a workshop at the Wilson Center in Washington, DC on 4 December 2008, then Governor Blairo Maggi provided a textbook defence of Mato Grosso's ecological prerogatives.[16] As mentioned above, he is the director of the family business Amaggi, established by his father a few decades earlier, when the clan moved from the south of Brazil to Mato Grosso; the former governor is now the owner of one of the largest soybean companies in the world (responsible for around 5 per cent of the total amount of soybean produced in Brazil, and increasingly involved in large public infrastructure, transnational trade and financial services). According to various interviews conducted in Cuiabá in May 2014, during his time as governor Maggi repeatedly claimed to be running the state administration as a business enterprise, and played a key role in the consolidation of agribusiness (including new legislation instituting the transfer of public funds to support Aprosoja-MT, making it the strongest and most active representation of soybean producers in the country). At the Wilson Center, Maggi used his training as an agronomist to explain how technology helps to protect the environment. Although Maggi was awarded the sarcastic 'Golden Chainsaw' trophy by Greenpeace in 2005, as the Brazilian who had contributed most to the destruction of the Amazon rainforest, in Washington the governor talked about the risks of anthropogenic climate change and the need to act 'not because of the environmentalists, but because the scientists are now telling us the urgency and relevance of such issues'.

The most evocative part of Maggi's intervention during the workshop was his passionate defence of market-friendly solutions, especially the role of payment for ecosystem services, carbons markets and the Reducing Emissions from Deforestation and Forest Degradation (REDD) scheme advanced by the United Nations. 'We must find a way to ensure that forests are more valuable standing than destroyed,' said Maggi (Wilson Center, 2009: 2). He stressed the urgency of creating such a mechanism: 'Global warming has been scientifically proven; we no longer have the right to ignore climate change.' The appropriation of environmental claims to serve business and political interests is also evident in Maggi's trajectory as a congressman. After becoming a senator in 2010, Maggi was one of the main advocates for the reform of the Forest Code. The reform was approved in 2012 after lengthy controversy, and specific deregulations demanded by the agribusiness sector were defined in 2014. The aim of the reform was to flexibilise the previous requirement to maintain a certain percentage of natural vegetation on rural land. The reform means that it is now possible to compensate for deforestation on a rural property with another forested area elsewhere, which in practice 'creates' more cropland. The rationalisation of socio-environmental regulation has followed sectoral economic interests and the logic of agro-neoliberal polices (Ioris *et al.*, 2014). It reveals the 'agro' being transformed and reshaped according to a powerful business rationality, which, as argued by Oliveira (2003), reproduces and invigorates outdated features from previous stages of the long trajectory of the Brazilian capitalism.

Taken as a whole, agro-neoliberalism 'resolved' (at least from the perspective of national development) some of the main problems created during the advance of the agribusiness frontier in the 1970s. Its main novelty lies in the fact that agro-neoliberalism, unlike the vast programmes introduced by the military presidents, is normally associated with an image of efficiency, competence and autonomy from government. The exponential growth of soybean production in Mato Grosso since the 1990s is portrayed as the fulfilment of the predicted success of the agribusiness frontier and uncontested proof that the sector is able to take control of its own future now that government intervention seems less critical. This supposed originality, rationality and efficiency of Mato Grosso's agro-neoliberalism is normally contrasted with the repeated shortcomings of the regional economy since the 19th century, beginning with the repercussions of the 1892 Land Act, the March towards the West and the technocracy of the generals. Neoliberalised agribusiness can, finally, be presented as the undisputed redemption of the agricultural frontier. For the leaders of agribusiness, Mato Grosso has a natural vocation towards intensive agroindustry and nothing else will do. When an operator turns on a tractor or any other farm machine, he or she is not only earning a living or producing commodities to be exported, but also an anonymous, minuscule chapter of a much wider narrative is being further and further enriched. However, it is quite unfortunate that regional development and a large proportion of the national economy are also increasingly locked into the extravagant, but highly unequal, society of agribusiness.

Reinventing old practices at the vanguards of agro-neoliberalism

This chapter has briefly discussed the historical and geographical past of Mato Grosso, the introduction of the March towards the West, the intensification of agribusiness during the military dictatorship post-1964 and the transition to a post-developmentalist, agro-neoliberal model of agribusiness production since the 1990s. Based on the empirical evidence, it can be concluded that this transition evolved according to the three main patterns of agro-neoliberalism – namely, new mechanisms of public–private interaction, novel forms of socio-ecological exploitation and coordinated suppression of reactions and alternatives. The relevance of one or more of these three dimensions at any given moment depends on concrete politico-economic and socio-spatial circumstances and is also contingent upon place-specific conditions (Ioris, 2017). All this corroborates the observation of McMichael (2000) that the neoliberalisation of agriculture attempts to legitimise global integration through the deployment of the historic identification of agriculture with specific places and national processes. The specific case of Mato Grosso illustrates how agro-neoliberalism flourishes in a context of market-centred solutions and regulatory flexibility, but also that it demands novel forms of government support and relies on some of the oldest political traditions (e.g. aggressive manipulation of party politics, lack of transparency, deceitful claims of progress and enduring racism). The image of success is reaffirmed daily by sector representatives and endorsed by the national government in its effort to gain political support and maintain the export revenues generated by agribusiness. The result is a nuanced and highly contested situation that connects, often in unexpected ways, different scales, sectors and public policies articulated around the role played by agro-neoliberalism.

Moreover, taking into account the complex combination of achievements and failures, it is possible to verify that the true extent of agro-neoliberalism's success is highly questionable. Agro-neoliberalism, as the most recent phase of the model of agribusiness introduced in the 1970s, flourished in Mato Grosso not only because of abundant land, water, technology and the enthusiasm of southern pioneers, but because farmers were free to produce drastic socio-ecological transformations without the constraints of the rule of law and the demands of organised labour and informed civil society (which were present in the more economically advanced areas of the country). While the neoliberalised agribusiness sector has succeeded in crafting a positive image of technological and economic success, the federal government and the wider business community have become highly dependent on the export of primary commodities (to safeguard the national currency and avoid trade deficits, for example). The economic hypertrophy of agribusiness in Brazil has also resulted in a situation where rural leaders are disproportionately influential in politics, particularly in the national congress and the Ministry of Agriculture, where they attempt to advance conservative agendas and secure further concessions from the government. Agro-neoliberalism evolves not only through these efforts, but also through further modification to the structure and rationale of the state. As part of this turbulent and controversial process, new production areas are constantly being incorporated, with the employment of old and new practices of socio-environmental management and political legitimisation. It is particularly in agribusiness frontier areas such as Mato Grosso that the rationale of agro-neoliberalism is used to combine populist and neo-developmentalist traditions in order to disguise mounting impacts and inequalities. When facing criticism from other social forces in the country, the agribusiness sector reacts with a pre-established rhetoric of heroism and entrepreneurialism that, in the end, serves the corporations and national politicians more than the farmers themselves. This is similar to what happened to small producers in the United States, who were once considered the backbone of democracy but are no longer at the heart of national politics.

Crucially, in frontier development areas, neoliberalised agribusiness reveals its most profound abilities, contradictions and, ultimately, failures. It constitutes a favourable arena for rehearsing the flexible mechanisms of accumulation and regulation required by neoliberalised activities, while at the same time this frontier is shaped by market freedom, low moral standards and associated forms of violence. The peculiar dialectics taking place at the frontier, including processes of transnationalisation, violence and mystification, are firmly mediated by structures inherited from the past, which create a complex pattern, spatially and temporally heterogeneous. José de Souza Martins (2009) argues that this is a human frontier shaped by the false dichotomy between civilisation and non-civilisation, because it constitutes a degraded but comprehensive reality, one of the most brutal periods of economic development in Brazil. The frontier of development in Mato Grosso is in this case a real 'territory of death' and the place where the most inhuman archaisms are reborn; it is 'exactly the opposite of what the imagined idea of a "frontier" proclaims' (Martins, 2009: 13–14). Agro-neoliberalism has been especially successful at the agricultural frontier because it is in itself an economic, ecological and ethical frontier, in which interpersonal and intersectoral relations have a particular configuration and impose undemocratic measures due to the primacy of production and the emphasis on rapid capital accumulation. Our final observation in this chapter is that such complex interplay between general trends and place-specific interactions remains a fertile field of work and continues to demand appropriate scholarly attention.

Notes

1 Teles Pires, shared between Mato Grosso and Pará, is a forming tributary of the Tapajós River, a main affluent of the Amazon.
2 Cr$ is the symbol of the cruzeiro, the currency then in use in Brazil.
3 *Grilagem* is the grabbing of land through the simulation of land ownership and land occupation, making use of various mechanisms of deception and violence; the name derives from the forgery of documents, by means including shutting them in drawers with crickets (*grilos*) (once the insects die, they release a toxic substance that stains the papers, making them look old).
4 The jurisdiction of national development agencies in the state of Mato Grosso overlapped and covered both savannahs [*cerrado*] and forests (if for nothing else, because it is very difficult to establish the exact limits of these two biomes).
5 Agribusiness production in Mato Grosso historically occupied mainly savannah [*cerrado*] ecosystems, but it has also increasingly expanded over forested areas in more recent years.
6 One of the few exceptions is the existence of consolidated, medium-scale properties (of about 200 hectares) around the main urban centres, as in the case of Sorriso; these are properties that remained from the initial process of colonisation (i.e. the land was acquired relatively cheaply) and managed to survive due to low debts and production diversification.
7 Colonist is derived from the Portuguese word *colono* that is used to describe migrants to the agricultural frontier (it is related to the fact that, in the 19th century, European migrants received a plot of land in the south of Brazil called *colônia*).
8 The expression 'small-scale farmer' is used in this book as closely related to 'family farmer' or 'subsistence farmer'. The last two expressions are, however, highly problematic, given that it is almost certain that most of the farmers identified are not merely 'subsistence' farmers, while the term 'family farmer' is inappropriate in this context because many large-scale commercial farmers who moved from southern Brazil to Mato Grosso designate themselves as 'family farmers' even though they are core and key components of the agro-neoliberal sector and process. This includes massive corporate entities such as Amaggi, which remains a family-owned company.
9 In the municipality of Sinop, a biofuel project was implemented in the late 1970s to convert manioc into ethanol, but this failed miserably due to high costs and poor management.

10 Commodity prices eventually increased again after 2007, but it is important to note that there was a significant reduction in cultivated area during the 2005–2007 crisis (cf. Mueller, 2012), which demonstrates the high level of vulnerability in the agricultural frontier.

11 It was possible to verify the association's high level of organisation and preparedness in a special meeting with managers and specialists in the headquarters of Aprosoja-MT, in Cuiabá, in June 2013.

12 Soybean is a plant native to Asia that was introduced to the Americas at the beginning of the 1900s, first in the United States and a few decades later in Brazil. Soybean is certainly an extraordinary crop, easy to mechanise in the vast, flat farms of Mato Grosso, with a growing international market and suited to numerous agroindustrial uses. However, despite the crop's positive agronomic properties, extensive monocultures cultivated over long periods of time (soybean has been dominant in Mato Grosso for almost 40 years) are highly insecure due to sanitary and market risks. Although the environmental history of Brazil has many examples of misfortune associated with reliance on a single commodity, such as sugar, rubber, cocoa, coffee, etc., the agribusiness frontier of Mato Grosso seems to be following a similar pattern, where euphoria is likely to be replaced by widespread pain.

13 According to the CBOT-CME Group at www.cmegroup.com (accessed 8 July 2016).

14 Maggi was elected to the senate in 2010 and eventually replaced Senator Kátia Abreu in May 2016 as Minister of Agriculture in the Michel Temer government that replaced President Dilma's administration. Ms Abreu's predecessor was Neri Geller, also from Mato Grosso and, like Blairo Maggi, born in Brazil's southernmost state, Rio Grande do Sul.

15 Connecting the Madeira River with Mato Grosso is a plan that dates back the time of the Portuguese governments, repeatedly mentioned in official documents since the 18th century.

16 This is even more remarkable considering what Maggi said during his time as governor: 'To me, a 40 percent increase in deforestation doesn't mean anything at all, and I don't feel the slightest guilt over what we are doing here. [. . .] It's no secret that I want to build roads and expand agricultural production; the people voted for that, so I don't see the problem' (*The New York Times*, 2003).

References

Agro Olhar. 2014. 'Não Somos Mais um Patinho Feio', Declara Eraí Maggi sobre a Importância de MT. Available at: www.olhardireto.com.br/agro/noticias/exibir.asp?noticia=nao-somos-mais-um-patinho-feio-declara-erai-maggi-sobre-a-importancia-de-mt&edt=23&id=17568 (accessed 2 November 2014).

Aprosoja-MT (Mato Grosso's Association of Soybean and Maize Producers). n.d. *Mato Grosso, Brazil: On the Road to Sustainability*. Cuiabá.

Arruda, Z.A. 2009. As 'Agrocidades' e as Interfaces entre o Mundo Rural e Urbano: Repercussões Socioespaciais do Agronegócio no Território Mato-grossense. In: *Novas Territorialidades nas Cidades Mato-Grossenses*, Romancini, S.R. (ed.). EdUFMT: Cuiabá, pp. 175–198.

Barrozo, J.C. 2010. A Questão Agrária em Mato Grosso: A Persistência da Grande Propriedade. In: *Mato Grosso: A (Re)Ocupação da Terra na Fronteira Amazônica (Século XX)*, Barrozo, J.C. (ed.). Oikos: São Leopoldo, pp. 11–27.

Branford, S. and Glock, O. 1985. *The Last Frontier: Fighting over Land in the Amazon*. Zed Books: London.

Cabeza de Vaca, A.N. 1922 [1542]. *Naufragios y Comentarios*. Calpe: Madrid.

Cardoso, F.H. and Müller, G. 1977. *Amazônia: Expansão do Capitalismo*. 2nd edition. Brasiliense: São Paulo.

Costa, M.V.V. 2016. O Processo de Construção da Nova Fronteira do Capital na BR-163 Mato-Grossense. In: *As Novas Fronteiras do Agronegócio: Transformações Territoriais em Mato Grosso*, Bernardes, J.A., Buhler, E.A. and Costa, M.V.V. (eds). Lamparina: Rio de Janeiro, pp. 33–52.

Couto e Silva, G. 1981 [1967]. *Conjuntura Política Nacional: O Poder Executivo & Geopolítica do Brasil*. 3rd edition. José Olympio: Rio de Janeiro.

CPT. 2015. *Conflitos no Campo 2014*. CPT: Goiânia.

Diário de Cuiabá. 2013. 61 Fazendas Estão Lista Suja do MTE. Available at: www. diariodecuiaba.com.br/detalhe.php?cod=424512 (published 17 January 2013).

FAMATO. 2014. *Projeto Pensar Mato Grosso*. FAMATO: Cuiabá.

Figueira, R.R. and Prado, A.A. (eds). 2011. *Olhares sobre a Escravidão Contemporânea: Novas Contribuições e Críticas*. EdUFMT: Cuiabá.

Folha de São Paulo. 2008. Primo de Maggi Utiliza Trabalho Degradante. Available at: www1.folha.uol.com.br/fsp/brasil/fc2501200816.htm (published 28 January 2008).

Frederico, S. 2008. O Novo Tempo do Cerrado. Unpublished Ph.D. thesis. USP: São Paulo.

Furtado, P.J. 2010. Nova Mutum, MT: Colonização Particular, Migração Sulista e Cultura 'Gaúcha'. In: Barrozo, J.E. (ed.), *Mato Grosso: A (Re)Ocupação da Terra na Fronteira Amazônica Século XX)*. EdUFMT: Cuiabá, pp. 170–197.

Galvão, M.R.C.C. 2008. A Natureza na Representação Social dos Produtores de Soja em Mato Grosso. M.Sc. dissertation. UFRRJ: Rio de Janeiro.

Graham, D.H., Gauthier, H. and Mendonça de Barros, J.R. 1987. Thirty Years of Agricultural Growth in Brazil: Crop Performance, Regional Profile, and Recent Policy Review. *Economic Development and Cultural Change*, 36(1), 1–34.

Guimarães Neto, R.B. 2014. Violência e Trabalho na Amazônia: Narrativa Historiográfica. *Territórios e Fronteiras*, 7(1), 27–46.

Hecht, S. and Cockburn, A. 1989. *The Fate of the Forest: Developers, Destroyers and Defenders of the Amazon*. Verso: London and New York.

Heredia, B., Palmeira, M. and Leite, S.P. 2010. Sociedade e Economia do 'Agronegócio' no Brasil. *Revista Brasileira de Ciências Sociais*, 25, 159–196.

Ianni, O. 1981. *A Luta pela Terra: História Social da Terra e da Luta pela Terra numa Área da Amazônia*. 3rd edition. Vozes: Petrópolis.

IMEA. 2016a. *Agronegócio no Brasil e em Mato Grosso*. Cuiabá.

IMEA. 2016b. *Primeira Estimativa da Safra de Soja – 2016/17*. Bulletin May 2016. IMEA: Cuiabá.

Ioris, A.A.R. 2012. *Tropical Wetland Management: The South-American Pantanal and the International Experience*. Ashgate: Farnham, Surrey.

Ioris, A.A.R. 2013. Rethinking Brazil's Pantanal Wetland: Beyond Narrow Development and Conservation Debates. *Journal of Environment and Development*, 22(3), 239–260.

Ioris, A.A.R. 2017. Places of Agribusiness: Displacement, Replacement, and Misplacement in Mato Grosso, Brazil. *Geographical Review*. DOI: 10.1111/gere.12222

Ioris, A.A.R., Irigaray, C.T. and Girard, P. 2014. Institutional Responses to Climate Change: Opportunities and Barriers for Adaptation in the Pantanal and the Upper Paraguay River Basin. *Climatic Change*, 127(1), 139–151.

Lambert, J.P. 1970. *Os Dois Brasis*. 6th edition. Companhia Editora Nacional: São Paulo.

Lenharo, A. 1982. *Crise e Mudança na Frente de Colonização*. UFMT: Cuiabá.

Lévi-Strauss, C. 1992 [1955]. *Tristes Tropiques*. Trans. J. Weightman and D. Weightman. Penguin: London.

Lucidio, J.A.B. 2013. 'A Ocidente do Imenso Brasil': As Conquistas dos Rios Paraguai e Guaporé (1680–1750). Unpublished Ph.D. thesis. Universidade Nova de Lisboa: Lisbon.

Martins, J.S. 2009. *Fronteira: A Degradação do Outro nos Confins do Humano*. Contexto: São Paulo.

McMichael, P. 2000. Global Food Politics. In: *Hungry for Profit*, Magdoff, F., Foster, J.B. and Buttel, F.H. (eds). Monthly Review Press: New York, pp. 125–143.

Meyer, H. (ed.). (2015). *Porto dos Gaúchos: Os Primórdios da Colonização da Gleba Arinos, na Amazônia Brasileira*. Entrelinhas: Cuiabá.

Monbeig, P. 1984 [1952]. *Pioneiros e Fazendeiros de São Paulo*. Trans. França, A. and Andrade e Silva, R. Hucitec/Polis: São Paulo.

Moore, J.W. 2015. *Capitalism in the Web of Life*. Verso: London and New York.

Moreno, G. 2007. *Terra e Poder em Mato Grosso: Política e Mecanismos de Burla 1892–1992*. Entrelinhas/EdUFMT: Cuiabá.

Morton, D.C., DeFries, R.S., Shimabukuro, Y.E., Anderson, L.O., Arai, E., del Bon Espirito-Santo, F., Freitas, R. and Morisette, J. 2006. Cropland Expansion Changes Deforestation Dynamics in the Southern Brazilian Amazon. *PNAS*, 103(39), 14637–14641.

Mueller, C.C. 2012. Regional Development and Agricultural Expansion in Brazil's Legal Amazon: The Case of the Mato Grosso Frontier. In: *The Regional Impact of National Policies: The Case of Brazil*, Baer, W. (ed.). Edward Elgar: Cheltenham, pp. 184–203.

The New York Times. 1970. Brazil is Challenging a Last Frontier. p. 1 (published 7 July 1970).

The New York Times. 2003. Relentless Foe of the Amazon Jungle: Soybeans. Available at: www.nytimes.com/2003/09/17/world/relentless-foe-of-the-amazon-jungle-soybeans.html?emc=eta1 (published 17 September 2003).

Oliveira, A.U. 1989. *Amazônia: Monopólio, Expropriação e Conflitos*. Papirus: Campinas.

Oliveira, A.U. 2005. BR-163 Cuiabá-Santarém: Geopolítica, Grilagem, Violência e Mundialização. In: *Amazônia Revelada: Os Descaminhos ao Longo da BR-163*, Torres, M. (ed.). CNPq: Brasília, pp. 67–183.

Oliveira, F. 2003. *Crítica à Razão Dualista: O Ornitorrinco*. Boitempo: São Paulo.

Oliveira, G. and Hecht, S. 2016. Sacred Groves, Sacrifice Zones and Soy Production: Globalization, Intensification and Neo-nature in South America. *Journal of Peasant Studies*, 43(2), 251–285.

Ozório de Almeida, A.L. and Santos, C.F.V. 1990. *A Colonização Particular na Amazônia nos Anos 80*. Texto para Discussão no. 208. IPEA: Rio de Janeiro.

Padis, P.C. 1981. A Fronteira Agrícola. *Revista de Economia Política*, 1(1), 51–75.

Peine, E.K. 2010. Corporate Mobilization on the Soybean Frontier of Mato Grosso, Brazil. In: *Contesting Development: Critical Struggles for Social Change*, McMichael, P. (ed.), Routledge: New York and London, pp. 132–145.

Pessoa, S. and Pereira, B.D. 2006. Agricultura de Mato Grosso: Agribusiness e Outras Análises. In: *VII Congreso Latinoamericano de Sociología Rural: Exclusión y Resistencia Social*. Quito, Ecuador.

Ricardo, C. 1970. *Marcha para o Oeste*. 4th edition. Livraria José Olympio: Rio de Janeiro.

Santos, J.V.T. 1993. *Matuchos: Exclusão e Luta*. Vozes: Petrópolis.

Schwantes, N. 1989. *Uma Cruz em Terranova*. Scritta: São Paulo.

Silva, M.C. 2012. *O Paiz do Amazonas*. 3rd edition. Editora Valer: Manaus.

Siqueira, E.M. 2002. *História de Mato Grosso: Da Ancestralidade aos Dias Atuais*. Entrelinhas: Cuiabá.

Sorj, B. 1980. *Estado e Classes Sociais na Agricultura Brasileira*. Zahar: Rio de Janeiro.

Souza, E.A. 2013. *O Poder na Fronteira: Hegemonia, Conflitos e Cultura no Norte de Mato Grosso*. EdUFMT: Cuiabá.

Théry, H., Mello Théry, N.A., Girardi, E. and Hato, J. 2011. Géographies du Travail Esclave au Brésil. *Cybergeo: European Journal of Geography*, document 541. Available at: http://cybergeo.revues.org/23818

Webb, W.P. 1952. *The Great Frontier*. University of Texas Press: Austin, TX.

Werner, I. 2011. Do Latifúndio ao Agronegócio: A Concentração de Terras no Brasil. Available at: www.ihu.unisinos.br/entrevistas/45914-do-latifundio-ao-agronegocio-a-concentracao-de-terras-no-brasil-entrevista-especial-com-inacio-werner (published 1 August 2011).

Wilcox, R. 1992. Cattle and Environment in the Pantanal of Mato Grosso, Brazil, 1870–1970. *Agricultural History*, 66(2), 232–256.

Wilson Center. 2009. *Sustainability and Agriculture in the State of Mato Grosso*. Brazil Institute special report. Wilson Center: Washington, DC.

Wolford, W. 2008. Environmental Justice and the Construction of Scale in Brazilian Agriculture. *Society & Natural Resources*, 21(7), 641–655.

4   The rent of agribusiness

Introduction

The expansion of agriculture in Mato Grosso offers a paradigmatic example of the late stages of the 'long Green Revolution' (as defined by Patel, 2013), of the conversion of Amazon forest and savannah vegetation into large-scale farmland (e.g. Laval, 2015; Rausch, 2014; Richards, 2015) and, ultimately, of the encroachment of globalised capitalism upon agriculture (e.g. Goodman and Redclift, 1981; Martins, 2010; Peine, 2010). More importantly, as discussed above, it represents an extremely relevant experience of the advance of agro-neoliberalism through novel forms of public–private association, intensive socio-ecological exploitation and ideological reinforcement of its supposed advantages. As alluded to in the previous chapter, there is a growing literature on Mato Grosso's intense agriculture activity, the history of rural colonisation and the idiosyncrasies of agribusiness entrepreneurship has become available (e.g. Arvor *et al.*, 2013; Desconsi, 2011; Oliveira and Hecht, 2016; Richards *et al.*, 2014; Weinhold *et al.*, 2013). Yet, there is still a clear demand for critical studies that go beyond land use change, the contradictions of productivism and the failures of government interventions, but that focus on other issues such as intersectoral exchanges, racial discrimination, household and personal repercussions and the ideological biases of hegemonic science. Departing from the majority of existing narratives and interpretations, the intention with the present chapter is to question the trajectory of agribusiness in the region from a politico-economic perspective and, in particular, weigh up production versus the economic role of rents. For explanatory purposes, rents are basically considered here as additional sources of income beyond direct production activities; it is ultimately based upon surplus value produced by labour (see more below). The goal of our discussion is to interrogate, from the perspective of rents, the productivist argument commonly presented by the agribusiness sector in support of calls for more favourable public policies and state concessions.

The analytical strategy adopted specifically for this chapter was to examine the significance of rent extraction for the consolidation of commodity production in Mato Grosso, which has been since the 1970s one of the most important frontiers of agricultural expansion in the country (according to Jepson (2006), agricultural frontiers are geographical areas with zero, but imminently positive, rents). Referring back to the overall methodological approach described earlier, the analysis of historical documents was particularly relevant for the present discussion, as it served to consider the importance of rent-forging during the period of frontier expansion (1970s–1980s), while interviews and site observations were particularly helpful to understand the more complex flows of rent in the recent and ongoing phase of neoliberalised agribusiness (since the 1990s) characterised by new public–private strategies, intensified mechanisms of socio-ecological exploitation and the ideological containment of reactions. After revisiting the literature on rent, the next sections will demonstrate that, rather than a pre-given and easily definable concept, rent encapsulates the spatial transformation and the political complexity of new agricultural frontiers. The final part of the chapter is an attempt to summarise the findings and propose a new conceptualisation of the rent of agribusiness.

Agrarian capitalism and rent extraction

The word 'rent' was borrowed from the French and first appeared in writing in England between the 12th and 14th centuries, but over time it has incorporated this multiplicity of meanings associated with privilege and power, such as revenue and income obtained by the owner of a property (such as a separate piece of land), or a tax, toll, tribute or similar charge levied by or paid to a person (according to the *Oxford English Dictionary*, electronic version). In the 18th century, the Physiocrats treated rent in the form of net product or surplus, as the only measure of profit in capitalist production and claimed that landowners, as an unproductive class, should be heavily taxed because their luxurious way of life distorts the income flow (as in Quesnay's famous *Tableau Économique*), a claim later endorsed by the American politico-economist Henry George during his legendary campaign for common resource ownership. The politico-economic concept of rent, despite the controversies it has generated for several centuries, constitutes one of the most invaluable tools to understand old and new features of the capitalist economy and agrarian capitalism in particular (Caligaris, 2014). That is because rent remains 'one of the most powerful and contradictory aspects of the political economy of capitalism' (Swyngedouw, 2012: 314).

Rent is typically understood as all payments based on the fixed nature of resources – that is, 'rent is a distinguished feature of every resource whose price increase does not alter the demand' (Tratnik *et al.*, 2009: 105). It is basically an 'extra' payment for a factor of production – such as land and natural resources – in excess of the cost needed to bring that factor into production. This is classically the case with ground-rent, which is related to payment for using someone else's land (i.e. landowner's). Rent also includes the income gained by those who have privileges or patents, or are beneficiaries of other contrived exclusivity, such as protection due to favourable policies and legislation. In this case, the seeking of rents involves the attempt to increase one's share of existing wealth without creating new wealth. Already for Adam Smith (2008: 217), 'rent is the produce of those powers of nature, the use of which the landlord lends to the farmer'. Smith depicted it as a relational phenomenon, insofar as the rent of food-producing land 'regulates' the rent of other cultivated land. The realisation of the relational and differential basis of rent was later expanded by Ricardo (2004), who argued that ground-rent derived from the incorporation of lower quality land into production. Although Ricardo's analysis is quite schematic, it is possible to learn something here about the opportunistic and exploitative behaviour of landowners in a situation of increasing land scarcity and capricious fertility.

Marx was also intrigued by the function of rent in the relations of production and that he emphasised the socio-political attributes of rent in his frontal critique of the 'sanctity' of private property (without ever producing a comprehensive rent theory). The Marxian approach was to highlight the internal and dialectical relationship between rents and production. According to Lefebvre (1991: 324), Marx recognised the impossibility of reducing capitalist economy to the polarisation between bourgeoisie and proletariat, because landed property and landowners showed no signs of disappearing, nor 'did ground rent suddenly abandon the field to profits and wages'. For Marx, all categories of bourgeois economics, such as wage, rent, exchange, profit, are ultimately derived from the alienation of labour and the conversion of everything into a sellable object (Mészáros, 2005). In the final part of his *opus magnum* (i.e. *Das Kapital*), land and agriculture re-emerge emphatically and Marx delineates the dialectics capital–land–labour as essential to comprehend the reproduction of capitalist relations and, ultimately, the production of the spaces of capitalism. While Ricardo focused on accumulation, Marx shifted his attention to production. According to Marx (1991), 'the monopoly of landed property is a historical precondition for the capitalist mode of production and remains its permanent foundation' (p. 754) and whatever 'the specific form of rent may be, all types have this in common: the appropriation of rent is the economic form in which landed property is realized' (p. 772). Marx significantly extended the concepts of extensive and intensive rents proposed by Ricardo, calling these respectively 'Differential Rent I' (equal amounts of capital invested) and 'Differential Rent II' (unequal investments).

Marx (1991: 772) argued that all ground-rent is essentially surplus-value or 'the product of surplus labour' (i.e. the additional time worked by farmers to pay the rent, beyond the time required to reproduce themselves). According to Harvey (2006), Marx shared the same impression of most political-economists of the time that rent is paid to parasitic landowners, who simultaneously drain on both capitalists and labourers. Ground-rent, thus, should not be confused with profit, which involves productive human action and the appropriation of surplus-value by the capitalist, but is a gain acquired at the expense of the privileged position of the landowner. Marx's main insight was to more directly relate rent to production and profitability (both involving the payment to landowner or not, as in the cases where the producer is the landowner) and, crucially, refer to the ways in which the mobilisation of land and other resources affects the value of commodities and the redistribution of surplus-value (Swyngedouw, 2012).

Rent is not solely the additional time of labour in the agricultural sector, but the superior productivity of the human labour power when performed in lands of different quality – that is, the portion of value capitalised by the landlord in the form of rent.

Marx critically assessed the legacy of the Physiocrats, including early elements of ecological economics as we have it today, and how they perceived rent as the general form of surplus-value, something derived from nature (not resulting merely from social relations) and industrial profit and interest as merely different categories into which rent is divided (Marx, 1963, in Burkett, 2009: 34). Marx concentrated on the historically specific form of landed property rehabilitated by the intervention of capital and capitalism, especially the transformation of surplus profit into ground-rent. To achieve that, Marx considered four types of rents, 'Differential I' and 'II', and 'monopolistic' (associated with the unique character of land or location) and especially 'absolute' rents from the extraction of surplus-value by landlords (related to the value of agricultural products is higher than their price and the fact that agriculture has lower average organic composition of capital compared with industry). Absolute and monopoly rents are more directly related to production costs, while differential rent demonstrates the dynamics of expanding land-use and the connection between production areas. Absolute and differential rents are likewise dialectically related, as the expansion or contraction of production areas determine the magnitude of differential rents available in the agricultural sector.

Rent theory evolved very little over the next half a century or so after Marx's death, a period increasingly dominated by a focus on marginal utility and marginal use of land, basically treating land as merely another form of capital. Some noteworthy exceptions were the work of Lenin, in 1901, on the agrarian question, Hilferding, in 1910, on cartel rents, Schumpeter, in 1934, on entrepreneurial rents and Sraffa, in 1960, on a neo-Ricardian theory of value. The study of rent re-emerged, to some extent, in the 1960s mainly because of rapid increase of land and housing prices in the United States. Neoclassical authors, such as Alonso, in 1964, advanced the concept of rent-paying ability and the allocation of rent across different urban sites, which could lead to the most efficient land-use pattern. Such economists, who operate within the marginalist paradigm, maintain that rent arises when the supply of a factor is inelastic or less than elastic – for example, the supply of land cannot be increased when demand, and its price, rises. As it is well known, mainstream economic theory focuses on market forces (ignoring class-based relations, the sources of revenues, surplus values and their distribution, cf. Lefebvre, 2016; see also Lefebvre, 2009) and assumes that farmland values are determined by the discounted stream of expected income returns (which stands for land rents, in this case); however, farmland values and land rents are only partially explained by agricultural returns, as there are other, non-agricultural attributes that contribute to market values (such as location and natural amenities) and therefore help to increase the value of (differential) land rent (Czyzewski and Matuszczak, 2016).

Haila (1990) correctly observes that this debate has evolved in multiple directions since the 1970s, with the complication that the protagonists have discussed disparate questions. One important concept of this decade was 'rent seeking', related to the unproductive behaviour of some societies or groups due to the introduction of protection systems (tariffs, quotas) and industrial support (licences, permits). Krueger (1974) is the main author here as she argues that the formulation of policies is greatly affected by business players trying to influence the political process to obtain favourable outcomes or avoid unfavourable ones at the expense of the misallocation of resources to wider society. The perverse side of rent- seeking activities is the extra, unsolicited costs on the economy, because it means private gains without increasing production (Schmitz *et al.*, 2002). Costs rise because 'the creation of rents by state intervention and the allocation of rents to political supporters invite other social players to engage in rent seeking' (Ngo, 2009: 40).

While mainstream economists emphasised the relevance of rent as extra production costs, leftist authors, such as David Harvey, have considered rent as part of the contested production of space and the actual, lived injustices of contemporary capitalism. The author found, 'deeply buried within Marx's writings', elements to understand the co-ordinating role of the circulation of capital in search of rent and the resulting spatial reorganisation of activities and the influence on land use (Harvey, 2006: 331). As argued by Harvey, land can be considered 'fixed capital' that circulates – that is, it is fixed but continues to circulate as value while remaining materially located within the confines of the production process as use value – in other words, it circulates through the production of commodities and, crucially, the extraction of rents. Consequently, Marx's theory of ground-rent is inseparable from his theory of capitalist production and reproduction. Marx elaborated on the four types of rent aforementioned as the result of the very evolution of capitalism and the legacy from pre-capitalist, feudal times (as in the case of the legitimacy of large private estates). If the magnitude of rent influences directly the price of land, investments, interventions and state policies affect especially the magnitude of Differential Rent I (Swyngedouw, 2012). At the same time, Differential Rent II is a crucial mechanism for the insertion of agriculture into capitalist relations and it is directly connected with the application of technology (see Friedland *et al.*, 1981) to increase the productivity of agricultural labour and maximise surplus-value. Furthermore, profit (surplus-value) and rent (excess surplus-value appropriated outside production) dialectically complement each other, given that surplus-value is the product of agricultural labour set in motion by the institutionalisation of rent- yielding private property.

Although rent can be a drain on immediate capital accumulation (as it diverts value extracted from the exploitation of labour-power), it plays other very important roles in capitalist relations of production and reproduction. Rent influences the relocation of surplus value and decisions about what and where to invest and produce (in both urban and rural areas). Furthermore, rent provides legitimacy to commodification and private property, regulates capital circulation and accumulation and coordinates investment and the flow of capital across different sectors (Harvey, 2006); rent also shapes conflicts between different land users – for instance, subsistence farming, land for resource exploitation, agribusiness farming and land as financial assets, which require active state coordination and the mediation of land markets (Swyngedouw, 2012). For critical ecological economics, rent-seeking attitudes are important elements to explain the unsustainable use of natural resources and ecosystems, given that rent represents the redistribution of surplus value derived from the monopolisation of nature (Burkett, 2014). Rent is also a worthy concept to clarify the sudden richness of oil-rich countries controlled by a rentier elite (such as Angola, Russia and Saudi Arabia), the inescapable destruction of socio-ecological systems and the conversion of biological flows into commodities (as in the case of the so-called 'ecosystem services'). A rentier activity connects the capitalisation of past rents with the expectation of future rents; in that way, the trajectory of private property evolves together with the assembling of rents through time and the development of politico-institutional guarantees for the collection of future rents. Private property contains past rents, but future rents are the safeguards and justification of private property.

Figure 4.1 summarises the interpretation of ground-rent along the lines of the critical politico-economic tradition; the figure represents the centrality of private rural properties and the exploitation of labour-power and socionature for the extraction of rent, as well as the endorsement of the state apparatus in close political alliance with landowners. Ground-rent is the material advantage obtained by landowners from the exploitation of workers and from the transformation of socio-ecological systems into resources (i.e. essentially, the appropriation of surplus-value), but it incorporates and relies on other institutional mechanisms beyond the mere payment made by a leaseholder (tenant) to the owner of the land (landlord). It is possible because of wider economic, political and ecological conditions and it is an integral component of the general processes of production and reproduction of capital that are historically and geographically situated (Ioris, 2013). Although the landowner is the direct and main beneficiary, the advantages associated with ground-rent are also shared with their political allies through, and with the assistance of the state apparatus. The state plays a key role in the enforcement of labour and environmental regulation, in the organisation of agricultural production and the land market, and in the preservation of economic relations based on private property (Ioris, 2015a). Figure 4.1 is an attempt to respond to the interpretative challenge posed by Lefebvre (2016: 67) that rural sociologists have to work with political economists on 'the theory of *ground rent [rente fancière]*', a concept that is incredibly useful to explain extremely complicated realities 'shaken by contradictory movements' and with 'structures that are disintegrating, mixed with new forms and structures'.

Based on Figure 4.1, we can easily recognise that ground-rent processes have evolved together with the evolution of capitalism, from the early industrial period, to the monopolist phase and, more recently, to the neoliberal policy paradigm.

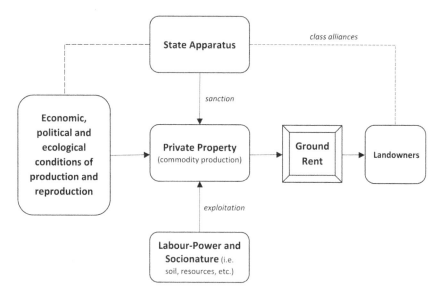

Figure 4.1 Politico-economic representation of ground rent
Source: Author

Moreover, it is still necessary to bring this discussion to 21st century's agrarian dilemmas and, as recommended by Guthman (2002), theorise how rent and surplus-values are translated into meanings. A renovated usage of the rent as an analytical category of agribusiness must necessarily explain where rent comes from, who benefits or loses out, and its part in the production, accumulation and politics of globalised agri-food markets. And it should specifically help to address the difficulty the original Marxist rent theory to convincingly explain the advance of agrarian capitalism – primarily employing absolute rent – and the removal of biophysical obstacles that prevent the increase of surplus-value (Ghosh, 1985; see Marx, 1968: 20–21). In that regard, areas of agricultural frontier such as Mato Grosso offer an experimental opportunity to study the organisation of agrarian capitalism and, crucially, the transition from Keynesian to neoliberalised policies. In the first moment, in the 1970s–1980s, the prospect of rent extraction worked as an incentive for the opening and consolidation of new private properties with the strategic help of the state; later, since the 1990s and under an increasing influence of the private agroindustrial sector, regional agribusiness became highly integrated into the national economy and connected to globalised markets. Over the last four decades, various mechanisms of rent extraction were put in place and these have evolved according to the modernisation of Brazilian capitalism and its current dependency on primary commodity exports (Ioris, 2015b). The persistent relevance of rent extraction in new areas of agriculture-cum-agribusiness in Mato Grosso is analysed next.

Forging rents through the state

As it was considered in previous chapters, Mato Grosso, as most of the Amazon, was for several centuries a subcontinent with countless natural riches but major accessibility and operational difficulties. What is now the territory of Mato Grosso was an area long disputed by the imperial ambitious of Portugal and Spain. The extraction of precious minerals after the discovery of gold in 1719 (Siqueira, 1982) represented a source of high, concentrated rents that entailed the settlement of the colonial frontiers and the organisation of the first towns (Prado Jr., 1977). The 'gold rush' was short-lived and soon Mato Grosso underwent a period of economic and social marginalisation, which only saw some modest improvement after the Paraguayan War (1864–1870) with the gradual revival of production and the commercialisation of rubber, mate leaves, sugar and cattle (Ioris, 2012). After the civil and military uprising led by President Vargas in 1930, national-developmentalist policies followed resolute efforts to fill the 'large voids' in the Brazilian map. A well-orchestrated March towards the West was launched with the mission of contacting and pacifying the indigenous groups (still largely ignored by the state and disconnected from the rest of society). The March towards the West was boosted with the foundation of a new capital Goiânia in the neighbouring state of Goiás, in 1937, and the new national capital, Brasília, in 1960. At the same time, the provincial (state) administration of Mato Grosso was encouraged to put for sale vast areas of 'untouched' land – in effect, rent-income assets inhabited by indigenous peoples – often bought by public and private colonisation schemes and real-estate speculators (Moreno, 2007).

The process took a dramatic turn during the military administrations that ruled the country between 1964 and 1985. The emphasis was then on the Cold War ideology of 'national security' and the promotion of state-led economic development. Initially, the dictatorial government pursued orthodox, liberal policies that primarily favoured the great international capital (Ribeiro, 2016), but soon the regime had to make also increasing concessions to national and international private companies (Branford and Glock, 1985). The conquest of the Amazon was considered a golden geopolitical opportunity and soon the federal government was granting land, providing incentives and boosting the regional infrastructure (i.e. roads, ports, communications, etc.); in addition, poor family farmers and landless groups in the rest of the country could be relocated northwards to placate socio-political turbulences elsewhere in the country (Torres, 2005). Because most of Mato Grosso is contained within what is considered 'Legal Amazon' (an official designation introduced in 1953) – including areas of both forest and *cerrado* (savannah) – it was eligible to take part in the megalomaniac plans of the generals. A large-scale process of land grabbing and socio-ecological transformation was vigorously promoted by the authoritarian state (largely funded by foreign loans and supported by northern governments) in the name of progress and international development. Those who arrived first could, to some extent, occupy the best lands and receive greater support from public agencies, something that Delgado (2012: 111) describes as 'gain of pioneer' (in effect, the appropriation of Differential Rent I). Heavy investments funded by the government were put to work and, as Marx (1973: 252) had long ago observed, capital is the 'presupposition' of modern landed properties.

With the establishment of an official agency (SUDAM) in charge of developing the Amazon in 1966, large farms were opened by business groups established elsewhere in the country, which basically wanted to secure easy money from subsidies, tax exemptions (e.g. on timber), duty-free machinery imports and interest-free loans (which were often forgiven and never paid back, cf. Kohlhepp, 2001).[1] 'The Brazilian capitalism, of patrimonialist tradition, discovered an extremely fertile terrain for development, in which the authoritarian state concentrated resources in order to distribute discretionarily to those privy to the [military] regime' (Tavares and Assis, 1986: 30). Not by chance, during the bloodiest phase of the political repression, the government launched the first and second National Development Plans (respectively in 1972 and 1975) with the primary goal of expanding the agricultural frontier towards the Centre-North of the country (the first plan included the construction of the important motorway BR-163 connecting Cuiabá to Santarém, concluded in 1976, that provided access to the north of Mato Grosso, including the Teles Pires basin). Along the lines of national development plans, specific initiatives mobilised resources for the Centre-West region, as in the case of Plan for the Development of the Cerrado (POLOCENTRO), in 1975, with a US$250 million budget to incorporate new 3.7 million hectares of pasture (1.2 million), cropland (1.8 million) and forest (0.7 million); in practice, the programme reached 2.06 million hectares, which was nonetheless an impressive accomplishment (Müller, 1989). Thousands of projects were approved during the implementation of POLOCENTRO (around one-fifth in Mato Grosso) to assist, primarily, large-scale landowners, who controlled 58 per cent of the projects and were the receivers of 76.5 per cent of the money (Silva, 1985). It was the case that 'the state here takes a "pioneer" role in opening up sectors and areas initially unattractive to certain capitals' (Goodman and Redclift, 1981: 149). In addition, PROTERRA (1971–1979) provided loans with negative interest rates for land purchase, especially for private colonisation, while PROCEDER, since 1976 and financed by the Japanese government, invested in agriculture research and new colonisation projects. Also a sophisticated, nationwide agriculture research network, coordinated by the aforementioned Embrapa, was inaugurated in 1973 and soon developed significant new technologies, particularly focused on the cultivation of the acidic lands of the Centre-West region.

The irony is that such intense national mobilisation was less about agricultural production than other political and socioeconomic goals related to the creation and release of new streams of rents from freshly promoted agribusiness. (It is interesting to note that Malthus, different from Ricardo and Marx, argued that rent contributes to the country's wealth.) Agricultural development opened up a 'speculative front' that had little to do with production, but rather with large landowners greatly benefiting from the intensification of the land market and for the availability of public incentives. Land was rapidly becoming a commodity, regardless of its productivity and of the production of agricultural commodities. As calculated by Almeida (1992), the transference of subsistence farmers to the Amazon was marginally viable (in the sense that paid for the opportunity costs of capital and labour), but the price paid by the small-scale settlers (to buy their land) and by nature (deforestation) was very high and the economic success of the whole process will take time to be confirmed. The secondary importance of production is also demonstrated because the transfer of family farmers to the areas was by and large a failure, at the same time that new business companies were established 'more as land traders than production units. [. . .] The more interesting fact for the new companies was not the low price of the land, but its rapid appreciation' (Sawyer, 1984: 22–23). The value of Amazonian lands increased at 100 per cent per year (in real terms) in the 1970s (with an exponential rise between 1973 and 1975) due to the expectation of future returns and public incentives (Mahar, 1979). The speculative basis of the frontier is related to the fact that the price of land in Brazil is directly related to potential territorial rent and inversely related to the rate of interest, which was relatively low in the period (Rangel, 2000), an important correlation early identified by Marx (1991: 761).

The prospects of easily accessible land and financial support from the government in the new areas of Mato Grosso helped to mitigate social dissatisfaction among poor family farmers in the rest of the country and help to address agrarian problems in the original places. Thousands of poor farmers and landless groups – especially from the three southernmost Brazilian states, mostly descendants of Italian and German migrants who moved to Brazil in the end of the 19th century – were attracted or encouraged to move to the numerous private or public colonisation schemes in Mato Grosso. However, after a few years trying to settle in the agricultural frontier, most of them ended up as employees in the larger farms and, therefore, producers of surplus-value then converted to rent. The whole process confirmed the observation of Mandel about the tendency to reproduce absolute rent in countries such as Brazil, where capitalist agribusiness penetrated belatedly (in Marx, 1991: 68). In that turbulent process, the most central player was (and still is) the state and its power to create properties and unleash rents from new politico-economic arrangements (despite the fact that the state is ignored in most studies on the sociology of agriculture – cf. Buttel *et al.*, 1990). For instance, in the year 1978 alone, there were around 170 separate lines of rural credit available and the national volume of credit reached US$16 billion, roughly the same as the net value of Brazilian agricultural production; most of the operations were concentrated in the centre-south of the country (IBRD, 1979, in Goodman and Redclift, 1981: 144). Pereira (2012: 39) adds that fiscal incentives powerfully increased rent and boosted other production factors, 'among those it is noticeable the process of agrarian concentration'. The new farming land was primarily concentrated in large properties, a pattern that was maintained almost unchanged during the expansion of the frontier and despite the fact that more than 400,00 migrants moved to the state, although excluded from decisions that affected their own interests (Wood and Wilson, 1984): between 1970 and 1996, the total area of properties with less than 100 hectares in Mato Grosso remained the same

(3.3 per cent of the total agriculture area), while the area in properties with more than 1,000 hectares reduced marginally from 85.2 per cent to 82.2 per cent (cf. IBGE, quoted in Ramminger, 2008).

Agriculture and food production were not much more than mere excuses of official plans and political speeches, because the main game was around securing subsidies, concessions and incentives from the state, often through the use of illegal mechanisms (such as false land titles) and the violent removal of any obstacles (such as the presence of squatter-peasants or indigenous groups). The expectation of more rents augments as productivity and profitability increase, creating new incentives for agricultural expansion due to the conversion of pasture and forest into crop fields (Phelps *et al.*, 2013). Rice was the main crop cultivated in Mato Grosso in this period, but the area of production dropped from 780,000 hectares in the 1977–78 season to 404,000 hectares in 1984–85 (Cunha, 2008). Other crops, such as maize, cotton and sugar-cane had comparable poor performances (at the same time, soybean started to expand significantly after 1985, especially because of propitious export opportunities, as discussed in the next section). Those disappointing results were normally attributed to inadequate technologies and, in the 1980s, to declining state funds; nonetheless, rents from Mato Grosso agribusiness, connected with production, played a crucial role in the wider expansion of capitalism in the country (regardless of frustrated production and low productivity in some years). Instead of profits from commodity production, rents were obtained from the newly created properties and then transferred to finance urban-industrial activities in the South and Southeast regions. It involved a process of spatial dislocation as long as the rent from Mato Grosso agribusiness intensified production and accumulation elsewhere in the country (Ioris, 2017). If it is true that the productivity of labour increased (when compared with traditional latifundia), the main goal and the main source of income was not production, but the release of rents that were forged through the creation of the agricultural frontier. The rent-forging mechanism gained momentum and the opening of the new areas continued after the end of the main government programmes; in total, between 1970 and 1990, 35 private enterprises organised 104 settlement projects and agriculture cooperatives that settled 3.9 million hectares of land in Mato Grosso (Jepson *et al.*, 2010).

The new agricultural frontier, as a large spatial phenomenon, was ultimately both rent-forging and rent-dependent. The extraction of ground-rent (related to the appropriation of land and the exploitation of labour-power) was the most immediate goal, but it was organically connected with the appropriation of state incentives, concessions and subsidised loans. In that sense, the alleged success of the frontier was predetermined in advance and it only depended on its simple existence: it was seen as inherently successful by politicians and many others, an entirely new, brave world bequeathed by the military to Brazilian geography. From the perspective of the main economic and political centres, the realisation of the agribusiness frontier depended less on the amount of grain produced or on productivity rates. Moreover, the vitality of the agricultural frontier was severely affected by the macroeconomic turbulence, hyperinflation and exhaustion of public funds throughout the 1980s. The established channels of rent flow could not continue to operate and alternatives were urgently needed. The result was that from the early 1990s, the state assumed a more strategic, indirect role in terms of rent-forging, such as the coordination of the insertion into global markets and looking after logistics – for instance, rural credit funded by the National Treasury was 64 per cent in 1985, 22 per cent in 1994 and only 3.5 per cent in 1996 (and around 8 per cent in 2008). At the same time, soybean became the undisputed king of Brazilian agribusiness and Mato Grosso, the icing on the cake, because of a combination of more favourable exchange rates, the boom of commodity prices (in general terms, between the early 2000s to 2014) and the competent mobilisation of farmers. It means that soybean was the ideal crop to allow the reorientation of the rents obtained from agribusiness, as discussed below with the assistance of the interviews conducted in Mato Grosso.

Consolidating rents through markets

The economic turmoil of the 1980s, which coincided with the end of the initial pattern of agricultural expansion in Mato Grosso, were primarily consequence of the exhaustion of the authoritarian-developmentalist platform introduced by the military dictatorship and its the excessive reliance on international loans. The first period was marked by the production of a new spatial order by concerted state interventions and the mobilisation of a range of social groups to the region, which paved the way for the extraction of agribusiness rents from a web of politico-economics relations created around new rural private properties. Significant rents were extracted from putting land into agriculture, from real-estate speculation and from the siphoning off of government incentives for use elsewhere in the country. However, this model of rent extraction had necessarily to evolve in tandem with the macroeconomic transition to the more flexible mechanisms of production and capital accumulation. Especially with an acute financial crisis initiated in 1985–1986, it was necessary to reorganise the basis of agribusiness. As stated in an interview with a farmer, 'the game now is more on the business and less on the time we spend talking to the manager of the *Banco do Brasil* branch [Brazil's main public bank and historically the main provider of loans to agriculture]' (Sorriso, 5 December 2014).

In the new context, the role and the partnership between the big grain TNCs (Bunge, Cargill, Dreyfus and ADM) and seed and agrochemical TNCs (Monsanto, Syngenta, Basf, Bayer and Dow) became even more strategic, as these were no longer only buying crops, but increasingly financing production and farm infrastructure. Numerous technological adjustments were also put in place, but the prevailing monoculture systems, including the intense use of agrochemicals, digital technology and heavy machinery, were largely maintained. Production became highly specialised on soybean and a few other crops, which further attracted resources away from the production of staples. Soybean-based agribusiness actually provides a good example of the rapid growth of power, influence and control over the supply, processing and trade of food by transnational agribusiness (Bernstein, 2011). TNCs – which in Mato Grosso are called 'tradings', which is a short form of 'input/trading companies' – operate with very low risk and have a strong bargain position, which confirms that when the opportunities for primitive accumulation diminish, capital starts to cannibalise itself through the subordination of some capitalists to others (Harvey, 2006). In the case of Mato Grosso, it involved not only renewed forms of primitive accumulation, but it was first of all a profound reconfiguration of a world considered 'primitive'. Primitive accumulation did not happen only at the genesis of capitalism (in the form of the transitory ownership of land by peasants and squatters), but also when capitalism grows through the creation of new peripheries, which means that primitive accumulation is both structural and genetic (Oliveira, 2003).

Because of the specificities of the Brazilian economy, since the 1990s there has been a growing political relevance of the rents extracted from the renovated agribusiness sector of Mato Grosso to attend macroeconomic demands, and in that process corporations and landowners have also managed to further consolidate their political and economic status. It had basically to do with the heterodox attempts adopted to control inflation and strengthen the currency. After more than a decade with spiralling rates of inflation, in 1994 the federal government introduced an ingenious economic strategy, known as the Real Plan in 1994, which launched a much stronger currency, curbed inflation and paved the road to further reforms. Political support to the Real Plan was further achieved with the facilitation of credit to the general population to consume goods and services (O'Dougherty, 1999). On the other hand, the country started to face serious balance of payment difficulties due to the overvalued currency, deindustrialisation and heavy debt service obligations. With growing public and private deficits, one of the main sources of foreign currency was exactly the export of soybean and a few other primary commodities (Hall *et al.*, 2014). In a situation with challenging macroeconomic adjustment, the rent of agribusiness greatly helped to maintain the Real Plan and fund-growing government expenditures. It was also helped by the introduction of tax exemptions, as the 1996 Kandir Law[2] that removed provincial (state) taxes on the export of primary commodities, such as soybean, under the need to mitigate the growing federal deficit created by the Real Plan (although it has penalised the state administrations). Agribusiness exports became even more attractive when Brazil floated the national currency (real) in 1999, which sent a shock across its economy that set Brazil's soybean boom into motion. This leverage effect of agribusiness rents was facilitated by the favourable market prices in the first decade of the century, which is often described as the 'commodity boom' due to the rising demand (particularly from China). Between 2000 and 2005, the area of soybean production doubled in Mato Grosso (from 3.12 million to 6.20 million hectares, cf. Cunha, 2008) and continued to expand throughout the decade. All that represented a shift from 'big-state' agribusiness to the current 'big-market' agribusiness.

In a context of major political and economic tensions, agribusiness is described as an island of prosperity and the leaders of the sector in Mato Grosso did not hesitate to say that the national and state economy had been 'saved by agribusiness'

(IMEA, 2016). However, agriculture is notoriously cyclical and a few good years are normally followed by a spell of negative returns. In 2005, there was another severe crisis when soy prices dropped, oil and input prices rose, together with high interest rates and credit restrictions. Soybean farmers organised widespread protests, famously in April 2006, and specifically targeted the state for their problems and for market failures – that is, the state failures were perceived as the main cause of their distress (Peine, 2010). The leaders of the farming sector formed strategic, and lasting, political alliances with municipal and state authorities in order to put pressure on the federal administration. As explained in one interview,

> agribusiness was going very well within the fences of the property, but we needed a lot more. The government had to absorb our problems, in one way or another, had to resolve the situation.[. . .] And we still today need a lot from the government, roads and better logistics, for example.
>
> (Interview with a secretary of the municipality of Sorriso, July 2015)

Because of the costs and risks involved, farmers expected to receive at least a baseline agribusiness rent (regardless of the vagaries of the market and the climate) equivalent to their effort to move to the region and their conformity with state calls to create new agricultural areas. As the area with soybean declined from 6.197 million hectares in 2005–2006 to 5.125 in 2006–2007 in Mato Grosso (cf. Cunha, 2008: 18), the government had to intervene in the form of debt renegotiation, new lines of credit and other concessions. In actual fact, in moments like the growing season 2005–2006, the federal state had to act to maintain the rent of agribusiness flowing both to appease the rural sector and also to secure one of its main sources of foreign currency (soybean export).

Soybean production in Mato Grosso reached staggering 28.5 million tons and occupied in 9.2 million hectares in the season 2014–2015 (information provided by IMEA[3]). As in previous decades, production pressures again triggered higher land prices and, consequently, higher agribusiness rents coming from production (absolute rent) and form real estate speculation (i.e. monopoly rent). The Centre-West region saw the highest increase of land prices in the country, 16 per cent per year between 2003 and 2012 (according to the National Confederation of Agriculture and Livestock, CNA).[4] In the best areas of Mato Grosso, the cost can reach 700 bags of 60 kg of soybean grain per hectare or even 1,000 bags (normally, land purchase is calculated in bags). As land values rose, landowners consolidated their claims on land by deforesting or opening their land to increase their property values (Richards, 2015). In a good year, production can leave a profit of 5 bags, which means that it would take 140 years just to pay for the investment; the evident conclusion is that new land is not acquired for production only, but to store accumulated profits (surplus-value) and to gain from price increases.[5] The land market in the region could not be better for the landowners, but it has increasingly squeezed farmers without their own land (i.e. those farmers who by definition pay monopoly rent): 'Land rent is increasingly more expensive, can reach 10 bags per hectare [per year], and the small farmer cannot pay, more to new areas or to the cities' (interview in Sorriso, June 2015). Interestingly, there is an equivalent phenomenon in a similar direction: the pressure on small and medium-size landowners exerted by companies (e.g. Amaggi, Bom Futuro, etc.) that cultivate vast areas (e.g. 30,000 hectares or more) with the application of capital from external investors. 'Now, literally hundreds of thousands of farm units are operated by a handful of companies that manage millions of hectares across South America' (Oliveira and Hecht, 2016: 265). In this last case, although these small number of operators pay rent to the landowners, in return they benefit hugely more from the (almost monopolist) conditions of agribusiness production in Mato Grosso.

It is important to mention that the growth of production and investment were not followed by equivalent gains in productivity; on the contrary, agribusiness remains essentially a rentist activity that expands production due to the incorporation of new areas and the exploitation of labour power. Helfand and Rezende (2004) demonstrated that more than two-thirds of the output growth in Brazilian agriculture, up to the early 2000s, used to come from input growth and not from increases in productivity or technological change; the simple fact that the least productive farmers systematically leave the activity and that the least productive land is often withdrawn from production (when market prices are less favourable) also explained apparent technological gains when there were none (or very little). The situation changed with the biosecurity legislation introduced in 2005 (Law 11,105/2005), which authorised the cultivation of GMO crops; additional legislation approved in the same year included biodiesel in the 'national energy matrix' (Law 11,097/2005) and served as additional incentive for the production of crops such as soybean, cotton and sunflower. The favourable legal and policy landscape, together with good market prices, attracted new soybean growers and helped to increase productivity and, in particular, raise the productivity of the Centre-West region to the national average (Castro *et al.*, 2015). As in other parts of the world, the technology of soybean production has improved with new, high-yield varieties, efficient input use, improved nodulation and nitrogen fixation ability, as well as tolerance to biotic and abiotic stresses. In Mato Grosso, the agribusiness sector even created an independent research facility (called MT Foundation), which competes with the official research structure of Embrapa and the state-owned universities.

On the other hand, it is hard to expect significant additional performance gains over the next few years. The potential levels of productivity obtained at research stations, and by a small number of growers, are difficult to achieve by the vast majority of farmers (Gazzoni, 2010). As noted at Table 4.1, Brazil has expanded the area of production and total output, but yield has been affected (or is at least problematic to maintain, which is a serious issue in other countries as well). Most technological improvements are, in effect, small adjustments in the existing technological package brought to Brazil by foreign companies that sell agrochemicals. Furthermore, bad weather in the Centre-West region may have affected the productivity of 2015–2016, when compared with the previous season, but there is also the impact of new and more resistant diseases and weeds. In our interviews, some farmers mentioned one additional pesticide application every year, which demonstrates the sanitary risks of monoculture farming. Since 2008, Brazil is the champion in terms of pesticide use in the world (Carneiro *et al.*, 2015), which is related to the cultivation of GMO crops and to the growing importance of agribusiness in the country. Therefore, the apparent success of agribusiness is not directly related to production or productivity improvements, but it is first of all derived from the reinforcement of a specific institutional arrangement that in recent years has tried to ameliorate its image, as in the case of the incorporation of the symbolism of sustainability (Lacerda, 2011). Needless to say, in the European Union 'political rents' associated with the adoption of the Common Agricultural Policy (CAP) have been systematically legitimised under food security and environmental protection claims (Spoerer, 2015).

Another perverse side of the more recent phase of agribusiness rent extraction is that TNCs and similarly influential companies became even more active in the financing of production and, later, capture of the agribusiness rents. In a context of very favourable commodity prices in international markets and the need to mitigate the national trade deficit, was the increasing influence of international grain TNCs and the growing role of emerging Brazilian equivalents, as in the case of Amaggi, in terms of commercialisation and funding the production. Such companies own most of the warehouse capacity in Mato Grosso (190 units, capable of storing 5.84 million tonnes) and the four international TNCs control 95 per cent of soybean export and charge interest three times higher than public financing (Recompensa Joseph *et al.*, 2011). In the growing season 2015–2016, the TNCs increased production funding, especially because of easier access to international loans with lower interest rates. Variable costs in Mato Grosso increased by 10 per cent in the production season 2015–2016, compared

Table 4.1 World soybean production: area, production and yield in selected countries and the world total

Country	Area (million hectares)		Production (million metric tonnes)		Yield (metric tonnes per hectare)	
	2014/15	2015/16	2014/15	2015/16	2014/15	2015/16
Brazil	32.10	33.10	97.20	96.50	3.03	2.92
USA	33.42	33.11	106.88	106.93	3.20	3.23
Argentina	19.34	19.45	61.40	56.50	3.17	2.91
Paraguay	3.24	3.40	8.10	8.80	2.50	2.59
China	6.80	6.44	12.15	11.60	1.70	1.80
India	11.09	11.40	8.71	7.00	0.76	0.61
Canada	2.24	2.20	6.05	6.24	2.71	2.83
Russia	1.91	2.08	2.36	2.71	1.24	1.30
World	118.39	119.73	319.72	312.36	2.70	2.61

Source: USDA (2016)
Note: 2015/16 are preliminary results (published in July 2016)

with the previous season and the contribution of TNCs and private banks, in terms of financing, increased from 15 per cent to 28 per cent, while the contribution of public funds declined from 19 per cent to 15 per cent (IMEA, 2015). A main contradiction here is that the risks associated with production, including phytosanitary and market uncertainties, remain basically with the farmers and are only partially mitigated by the state in moments of acute crisis. For instance, since 2011, the prices of agriculture commodities have declined in global markets, at the same time that the costs of production have increased for farmers in Mato Grosso putting the profitability at risk.

The growing dependence of farmers upon credit

> represents the transformation of rent into the form of interest; their receipt of state support signifies rent in the form of a subsidy [. . .] and dependence upon the 'technological treadmill' of seed mechanical and other chemical inputs, represents a system of landed property in which rent potentially accrues to industrial capital despite its separation from ownership of the land.
>
> (Fine, 1994: 532–533)

According to IMEA (Bulletin no. 384, 18 December 2015), in 2015 the production was record in Mato Grosso (9.02 million hectares, 28.08 million ton), but total production costs increased to R$ 2,468.39/ha due to higher input prices; the overall profit in 2014–2015 is lower than in previous years. As observed by an informant:

> More productivity is not enough to cope with rising costs and the harsh demands of the 'tradings' [TNCs]. We have all the risks and their risk [of the TNCs] is minimum. [. . .] The state does not interfere in the relation between farmers and 'tradings', and when interferes on the side of the 'tradings'.
>
> (Interview in Lucas do Rio Verde, December 2014)

In the end, whenever it was possible during the research to have a good and reflective interaction with farmers and other locals involved in agribusiness, it was not difficult to detect a sense of uneasiness intermingled with pride and contentment. Many of those interviewed expressed the view that rent extraction has been a real element of regional development since the early years of public and private colonisation in the early 1970s (as mentioned above, the region has relied on the persistent flow of migrants from the south, as well as workers from other parts of Brazil, in particular from the northeast), but it does not necessarily work in their favour: 'Mato Grosso does not accumulate rent, only produces rent, then it goes elsewhere. A lot of money circulates, farmers deal with a lot of money, but only a small proportion stays here' (interview in Sinop, June 2015).

Taken as a whole, the mechanics of agribusiness rent extraction evolved from the 1970s–1980s to the 2000s–2010s, following an increasingly relevant involvement of national and foreign companies and the ambivalent participation of the state apparatus (highly dependent on foreign currency accrued from commodity exports, but also ready to intervene when there is a risk of collapse due to market instability). Rent not only increased in terms of the amount of money involved (due to significantly higher production), but it is also more asymmetrically distributed and primarily flows to the pockets of the government and large corporations, at the expense of the gain secured by farmers, labourers and local society. In practice, agribusiness necessarily entails a dual role of production and rent extraction. That is why Amin (1987) and others mistake when they claim that the capitalisation of agriculture intensified since the expansion of the imperialist phase of capitalism and the elimination of land rent; in effect, capitalist agriculture is intrinsically rentist and the production and extraction of rents is an integral element of the extraction of surplus-value and accumulation of capital through and in relation to 'agriculture-cum-agribusiness'.

Discussion and conclusions

The previous sections demonstrated that rent extraction has been an important politico-economic phenomenon, related with production, since the establishment of the new agricultural frontier in Mato Grosso in the 1970s. Rent mechanisms were forged by concerted state interventions and have evolved in tandem with the expansion, modernisation and intensification of production. It has also worked as an additional source of income to landowners, agroindustrial companies and the state apparatus (the main rent-collectors) beyond the realm of production and commercialisation, and even represents a safety net against the market and agro-climatic vagaries of agriculture (Ioris, 2016). A comprehensive agrarian transformation was launched by the militarised state primarily to create large-scale properties (as a rule, subsidiaries of companies based in the southeast of the country and instrumental in attracting further government incentives) and to attract peasants and workers to the region (the majority of these would become employees in farms and cities and not be able to maintain their own property). In the first moment, the main provider of rent-extraction conditions was the federal state which triggered flows of ground-rent (as in the form of rising land prices and land speculation, which are obviously directly and indirectly connected with production) and ultimately paved the road for the subsequent consolidation of the rent of agribusiness (as the interconnected, highly politicised rent that is extracted by the stronger groups from the totality of agribusiness activities).

If the agricultural frontier was a region where the level rent was zero, it was soon converted into an entirely new spatial order in which rent extraction was the main economic engine. Such politico-economic arrangement underwent a significant crisis in the 1980s due to the inadequacy of agricultural techniques, low profitability and high vulnerability of the crops then cultivated (as rice, guarana and coffee) and, especially, the exhaustion of government funds. The agribusiness sector in Mato Grosso was then reorganised with the concentration of rural properties, the expansion of soybean and a few other crops (cotton, maize, etc.) and a stronger and more aggressive intervention of TNCs and agroindustries. Since the late 1990s (a few years after the introduction of the macroeconomic Real Plan), the rent of agribusiness became more reliant on strategic alliances between land-owners and private companies – which is certainly not without tensions and disputes – with the endorsement of an increasingly neoliberalised state apparatus. The reason for the support and political leniency towards agribusiness is that the state became increasingly dependent on the rent coming from the sector in the form of exports of primary commodities, which was needed to fund a growing current account deficit. The metabolism of rent-yielding processes in the new agricultural areas of Mato Grosso is summarised in Table 4.2. It should be noted that authors, such as Walker (2014), are wrong when they claim that the first phase was characterised by 'rent capture' in the 1960s–late 1980s, followed by 'global market integration' from the late 1990s. In reality, rent was and remains a decisive element of agribusiness production and agrarian relations in the region.

Building upon the empirical results from Mato Grosso and upon the politico-economic literature, it should be possible to organise our findings around three main conclusions. First, the extraction of rent results from the convergence of different and highly politicised processes. Rent is not merely the payment to the landlord by those who work on agricultural production, but it embraces a range of class-related processes that make possible its extraction. It is essentially the attainment of gains from a situation of unequal power and private (exclusive) ownership of an economically valuable asset. Therefore, rent reflects the ability to mobilise social forces and reconfigure existing social institutions according to privileges accumulated over time and maintained in the course of class struggles. Marx (1988: 55) had early observed that the 'rent of land is established as a result of the *struggle between tenant and landlord*', which is a hostile antagonism that is 'the basis of social organization'. Where the landlord is also the farmer, this tension is transferred to struggles between the agriculture sector and the rest of society.

Second, rent goes beyond the extraction of value from private property only, but more fundamentally it is the appropriation of value from circumstances historically and geographically given for the production and reproduction of capital. Harvey (2009: 170) describes 'class monopoly' rents with respect to the power of landlords over low-income tenants, which is a notion that can be expanded to incorporate the unfavourable position of food consumers and wider society concerning agri-food businesses. In this case, if the labour-force is exploited for the immediate creation of rent, wider society and agri-food customers are also paying rent to companies and transnational corporations (TNCs) because of their power position (something described by Fishman, 2007, as the 'Wal-Mart effect') and their ability to operate as quasi-state agencies. Rent is thus a relational phenomenon between different players and different moments and locations in the process of production and capital circulation. It means that the more imme-diate economic gain derived from ground-rent is only the final result of the thicker configuration of class-based disputes that make rent workable. Third, such contested mechanics of rent extraction also require a sustained, proactive inter-vention of the state in order to control the spaces of production and coordinate such societal forces beyond the market. The apparatus of the state plays a crucial role in the legitimisation and collection of rents derived from the unevenness of

Table 4.2 Evolution of the rent of agribusiness in Mato Grosso

Period	Main features	Prevailing processes	Hegemonic ideologies and driving-forces	Main actions
1970s–early 1980s	Rent-forging agricultural frontier	Unlocking of dormant rents (blocked by previous rural oligarchies) through a spatial reconfiguration	Militarisation of the frontier; national security; centralised power; incentives and subsidies	Occupation of the frontier; migration; deforestation; different support to small-scale farming (i.e. colonisation) and on large-scale farming
Late 1980s–1990s	Transition to an increasingly neoliberalised agribusiness and new sources of rent	Crisis of production; high inflation rates; land as a value-holding asset	Calls for state reforms; mobilization of farming communities	Renegotiation of debts with private banks (e.g. during the in 1986/87 crisis)
2000s–2010s	Consolidation of rent extraction through market interactions	Reorganization of production in order to reinstate and revitalise politico-economic relations that maintain land in production and also secure rents	Rhetoric of efficiency and productivity; stronger influence of agroindustrial companies and market forces; widespread financialization and reliance of the national government	New crops (especially soybean) and technological intensification; public–private alliances; real-estate speculation; federal state retains a safety net, stabilisation role (e.g. during the 2005/06 crisis)

power between landowners, workers and food customers. Large-scale state interventions create a pool of economic rents in the form of subsidies and facilitated permits, while a core part of business strategy is to capture these income-effect rents or at least avoid taking hits to existing asset values (Helm, 2010). At the same time, the state is a political and economic beneficiary of broad agribusiness rents – from commodity production to landowners, and also to companies and TNCs – in the form of strategic alliances, payment of taxes and dynamisation of the economy.

For all those reasons, and because of the intensification, financialisation and integration of agribusiness across multiple activities, more than simply ground-rent, there is today a much wider mechanism of rent extraction from the sector as a whole. The *rent of agribusiness* is not only the convergence of the four components of ground-rent (mentioned above), but it means a qualitative, even ontological, conversion into deeply interconnected flows of rent between land-owners, the apparatus of the state and, crucially, a small number of agri-food companies, including the powerful agroindustrial sector, such as TNCs (see Figure 4.2). Ground-rent continues to play an important role in terms of capital accumulation by landowners, but the 'rent of agribusiness' is a wider and useful concept to capture the complexity of agro-neoliberalism, including the important transfer of rent from agriculture to other economic sectors.[6] The materiality of rent continues to be the exploitation of labour-force and the appropriation of socionature (the main rent-payers), but rent derives from the creation of new private properties and from the organisation of a network between state–landlords–agroindustry that guarantees and intensified the extraction of rent. (It should be noted that the state apparatus continues to be central for the realisation of rent under neoliberalising policies and globalised market transactions.) Figure 4.2 represents this crucial network that guarantees the extraction of the 'rent of agribusiness', as it operates to stabilise production, reduce risks (although in favour of the stronger players) and maximise the extraction of surplus-value from the working force and profits from the consumers of agri-food goods.

More importantly, because of the economic shield offered by rent, agribusiness has been able to flourish and even managed to prevent the prospects of more ecological, less capitalist patterns of food production. The rent of agribusiness provides strong incentives for the maintenance of rural properties and attracts investments in production (which in the end trigger additional rent gains). Rent is therefore not a barrier to agrarian capitalism and agribusiness, but operates as a safeguard mechanism against market instabilities, credit restrictions and bio-climatic risks. It is essentially a cost paid by workers (in the form of surplus-value), by socionature (in the form of deforestation, soil and water degradation, etc.) and the whole society (in the form of profit) to those in control of private rural properties and eventually state agencies and corporations.

Overall, it is possible to conclude that the widespread claim that agribusiness in Mato Grosso constitutes a history of success due to its high productivity and growing production is only partially true. A great deal of the success of agribusiness also derives from the creation of rent extraction opportunities in a context of

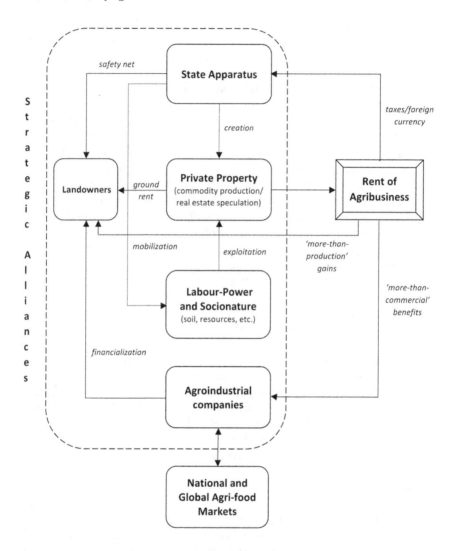

Figure 4.2 Rent of agribusiness in new areas of production
Source: Author

violent spatial reconfiguration. The above analysis demonstrates that rent is not a mere economic instrument or a social institution for private gain, but it essentially provided the baseline conditions necessary to maintain and boost the agribusiness sector. Agribusiness became so vibrant and widely praised in Mato Grosso because it emerged as a rent-forging activity, at the same time that it has always been rent-dependent. In the end, the case study in Mato Grosso shows that the rent of agribusiness is an integral feature of the highly technified, contemporary agriculture and, more importantly, has helped to clear away some of the main obstacles for the powerful advance of capitalist relations in the rural periphery of the Global South.

Notes

1 One main scheme was the investment of 50 per cent of corporate tax liability in Amazon projects (basically, transforming taxes into venture capital).
2 Complementary Law 87/1996, named after the socio-democratic Congressman Antonio Kandir.
3 IMEA is the Mato Grosso Agricultural Economics Institute; it was established in 1998 by the main representative organisations of the agribusiness sector in the state.
4 Published in the magazine *Dinheiro Rural*, no. 103, May 2013 (available at http://dinheirorural.com.br/secao/agronegocios/corrida-pela-terra).
5 The non-agricultural component of land demand is clearly prevalent in Brazil, but land rent markets are seen as underperforming because of unreliable property rights and the lack of effective dispute resolution mechanisms (Assunção and Chiavari, 2014).
6 In a very interesting and provocative article, Grinberg (2013) unambiguously demonstrates the role of agrarian rents, extracted through various forms of state policies and regulatory measures, in sustaining macroeconomic goals and fuelling Import Substitution Industrialisation in Brazil since the 1940s (at least). According to this author, between 1947 and 2008, more than US$1 trillion (R$ 3.460 trillion) were transferred from agriculture to other economic sectors.

References

Almeida, A.L.O. 1992. *Colonização Dirigida na Amazônia*. Série IPEA no. 135. IPEA: Rio de Janeiro.

Amin, S. 1987. *Imperialismo e Desenvolvimento Desigual*. Vértice: São Paulo.

Arvor, D., Dubreuil, V., Simões, M. and Bégué, A. 2013. Mapping and Spatial Analysis of the Soybean Agricultural Frontier in Mato Grosso, Brazil, Using Remote Sensing Data. *GeoJournal*, 78(5), 833–850.

Assunção, J. and Chiavari, J. 2014. *Land Rental Markets in Brazil: A Missed Opportunity*. Climate Policy Initiative: Rio de Janeiro.

Bernstein, H. 2011. A Dinâmica de Classe do Desenvolvimento Agrário na Era da Globalização. *Sociologias*, 27, 51–81.

Branford, S. and Glock, O. 1985. *The Last Frontier: Fighting over Land in the Amazon*. Zed Books: London.

Burkett, P. 2009. *Marxism and Ecological Economics: Toward a Red and Green Political Economy*. Haymarket Books: Chicago.

Burkett, P. 2014. *Marx and Nature: A Red and Green Perspective*. Haymarket Books: Chicago.

Buttel, F.H., Larson, O.F. and Gillespie Jr., G.W. 1990. *The Sociology of Agriculture*. Greenwood Press: New York.

Caligaris, G. 2014. Dos Debates en Torno a la Renta de la Tierra y sus Implicancias para el Análisis de la Acumulación de Capital en la Argentina. *Razón y Revolución*, 27, 59–79.

Carneiro, F.F., Augusto, L.G.S., Rigotto, R.M., Friedrich, K. and Búrigo, A.C. (eds). 2015. *Dossiê ABRASCO. Um Alerta sobre os Impactos dos Agrotóxicos na Saúde*. EPSJV: Rio de Janeiro; Expressão Popular: São Paulo.

Castro, L.S., Almeida, E.S. and Lima, J.E. 2015. A Convergência Espacial da Produtividade de Soja no Brasil: O Caso das Regiões Centro-Oeste e Sul. *Espacios*, 36(21), 20.

Cunha, O.E. 2008. Expansão da Soja em Mato Grosso e Desenvolvimento Econômico no Período de 1995 a 2005. Unpublished M.Sc. dissertation. UFMT: Cuiabá.

Czyzewski, B. and Matuszczak, A. 2016. A New Land Rent Theory for Sustainable Agriculture. *Land Use Policy*, 55, 222–229.

Delgado, G.C. 2012. *Do Capital Financeiro na Agricultura à Economia do Agronegócio*. UFRGS: Porto Alegre.

Desconsi, C. 2011. *A Marcha dos 'Pequenos Proprietários Rurais': Trajetória de Migrantes do Sul do Brasil para o Mato Grosso*. E-Papers: Rio de Janeiro.

Fine, B. 1994. Towards a Political Economy of Food. *Review of International Political Economy*, 1(3), 519–545.

Fishman, C. 2007. *The Wal-Mart effect: How an Out-of-town Superstore became a Superpower*. 2nd edition. Penguin Books: London.

Friedland, W.H., Barton, A.E. and Thomas, R.J. 1981. *Manufacturing Green Gold*. Cambridge University Press: Cambridge.

Gazzoni, D.L. 2010. Produtividade da Soja. *Revista Cultivar*, September issue: 49.

Ghosh, J. 1985. Differential and Absolute Land Rent. *Journal of Peasant Studies*, 13(1), 67–82.

Goodman, D. and Redclift, M. 1981. *From Peasant to Proletariat: Capitalist Development and Agrarian Transitions*. Basil Blackwell: Oxford.

Grinberg, N. 2013. Capital Accumulation and Ground-rent in Brazil: 1953–2008. *International Review of Applied Economics*, 27(4), 449–471.

Guthman, J. 2002. Commodified Meanings, Meaningful Commodities: Re-thinking Production-Consumption Links through the Organic System of Provision. *Sociologia Ruralis*, 42(4), 295–311.

Haila, A. 1990. The Theory of Land Rent at the Crossroads. *Environment and Planning D*, 8, 275–296.

Hall, R.J., Kaveski, I.D.S. and Hein, N. 2014. Análise do Endividamento e o Impacto no Custo da Dívida e Rentabilidade das Empresas do Agronegócio Brasileiro Listadas na BM&FBovespa. *Custos e Agronegócio*, 10(4), 39–59.

Harvey, D. 2006 [1982]. *The Limits to Capital*. 2nd edition. Verso: London and New York.

Harvey, D. 2009. *Social Justice and the City*. Revised edition. University of Georgia Press: Athens and London.

Helfand, S.M. and Rezende, G.C. 2004. The Impact of Sector-specific and Economy-wide Policy Reforms on the Agricultural Sector in Brazil: 1980–98. *Contemporary Economic Policy*, 22(2), 194–212.

Helm, D. 2010. Government Failure, Rent-seeking, and Capture: The Design of Climate Change Policy. *Oxford Review of Economic Policy*, 26(2), 182–196.

IMEA. 2015. *Composição do Funding do Custeio da Soja para Safra 2015/16 em Mato Grosso*. Bulletin December/2015. Cuiabá.

IMEA. 2016. *Conjuntura Econômica*. no. 22, April/2016. Cuiabá.

Ioris, A.A.R. 2012. Reassessing Development: Pantanal's History, Dilemmas and Prospect. In: *Tropical Wetland Management: The South-American Pantanal and the International Experience*, Ioris, A.A.R. (ed.). Ashgate: Farnham, Surrey, pp. 199–222.

Ioris, A.A.R. 2013. The Value of Water Values: Departing from Geography towards an Interdisciplinary Debate. *Geografiska Annaler: Series B, Human Geography*, 95(4), 323–337.

Ioris, A.A.R. 2015a. Theorizing State-environment Relationships: Antinomies of Flexibility and Legitimacy. *Progress in Human Geography*, 39(2), 167–184.

Ioris, A.A.R. 2015b. Cracking the Nut of Agribusiness and Global Food Insecurity: In Search of a Critical Agenda of Research. *Geoforum*, 63, 1–4.

Ioris, A.A.R. 2016. The Politico-ecological Economy of Neoliberal Agribusiness: Displacement, Financialisation and Mystification. *Area*, 48(1), 84–91.

Ioris, A.A.R. 2017. Place-making at the Frontier of Brazilian Agribusiness. *GeoJournal*. DOI 10.1007/s10708–016–9754–7

Jepson, W. 2006. Producing a Modern Agricultural Frontier: Firms and Cooperatives in Eastern Mato Grosso, Brazil. *Economic Geography*, 82(3), 289–316.

Jepson, W., Brannstrom, C. and Filippi, A. 2010. Access Regimes and Regional Land Change in the Brazilian Cerrado, 1972–2002. *Annals of the Association of American Geographers*, 100(1), 87–111.

Kohlhepp, G. 2001. Amazonia 2000: An Evaluation of Three Decades of Regional Planning and Development Programmes in the Brazilian Amazon Region. *Amazoniana*, 16(3–4), 363–395.

Krueger, A.O. 1974. The Political Economy of the Rent-seeking Society. *American Economic Review*, 64(3), 291–303.

Lacerda, E. 2011. Associação Brasileira do Agronegócio (ABAG) e a Institucionalização dos Interesses do Empresariado Rural no Brasil. *Ruris*, 5(1), 183–207.

Laval, E. 2015. Luttes au Sein du Régime Alimentaire Néolibéral: Résistance et Émergence Politique des Producteurs de Soja du Mato Grosso. *Revue Canadienne d'Études du Développement*, 36(3), 296–312.

Lefebvre, H. 1991. *The Production of Space*. Trans. D. Nicholson-Smith. Blackwell: Oxford.

Lefebvre, H. 2009. *State, Space, World: Selected Essays*. Trans. G. Moore, N. Brenner and S. Elden. University of Minnesota Press: Minneapolis, MN.

Lefebvre, H. 2016. The Theory of Ground Rent and Rural Sociology: Contribution to the International Congress of Sociology, Amsterdam, August 1956. *Antipode*, 48(1), 67–73.

Mahar, D.J. 1979. *Frontier Development Policy in Brazil: A Study of Amazonia*. Praeger: New York.

Martins, J.S. 2010. *O Cativeiro da Terra*. 9th edition. Contexto: São Paulo.

Marx, K. 1968 [1862]. *Theories of Surplus-value. Vol. 2*. Trans. R. Simpson. Progress: Moscow.

Marx, K. 1973 [1857–58]. *Grundrisse*. Trans. M. Nicolaus. Penguin: London.

Marx, K. 1988 [1844]. *Economic and Philosophic Manuscripts*. Trans. M. Milligan. Prometheus: Amherst.

Marx, K. 1991. [1894]. *Capital*. Vol. 3. Trans. D. Fernbach. Penguin: London.

Mészáros, I. 2005. *Marx's Theory of Alienation*. Merlin Press: London.

Moreno, G. 2007. *Terra e Poder em Mato Grosso*. EdUFMT/Entrelinhas: Cuiabá.

Müller, G. 1989. *Complexo Agroindustrial e Modernização Agrária*. Hucitec/Educ: São Paulo.

Ngo, T.W. 2009. Rent Seeking under the Licensing State: The Institutional Sources of Economic Corruption in China. In: *Preventing Corruption in Asia: Institutional Design and Policy Capacity*, Gong, T. and Ma, S.K. (eds). Routledge: London and New York, pp. 38–56.

O'Dougherty, M. 1999. The Devalued State and Nation: Neoliberalism and the Moral Economy Discourse of the Brazilian Middle Class, 1986–1994. *Latin American Perspectives*, 26(1), 151–174.

Oliveira, F. 2003. *Crítica à Razão Dualista: O Ornitorrinco*. Boitempo: São Paulo.

Oliveira, G. and Hecht, S. 2016. Sacred Groves, Sacrifice Zones and Soy Production: Globalization, Intensification and Neo-nature in South America. *Journal of Peasant Studies*, 43(2), 251–285.

Patel, R. 2013. The Long Green Revolution. *Journal of Peasant Studies*, 40(1), 1–63.

Peine, E.K. 2010. Corporate Mobilization on the Soybean Frontier of Mato Grosso, Brazil. In: *Contesting Development: Critical Struggles for Social Change*, McMichael, P. (ed.). Routledge: New York and London, pp. 132–145.

Pereira, B.D. 2012. *Agropecuária de Mato Grosso: Velhas Questões de uma Nova Economia.* EdUFMT: Cuiabá.

Phelps, J., Carrasco, L.R., Webb, E.L., Koh, L.P. and Pascual, U. 2013. Agricultural Intensification Escalates Future Conservation Costs. *Proceedings of the National Academy of Sciences*, 110(19), 7601–7606.

Prado Jr., C. 1977. *Formação do Brasil Contemporâneo: Colônia.* 15th edition. Brasiliense: São Paulo.

Ramminger, R. 2008. A Modernização da Agricultura e Indicadores Sociais no Estado de Mato Grosso (1980–2005). Unpublished M.Sc. dissertation. UFMT: Cuiabá.

Rangel, I. 2000. *Questão Agrária, Industrialização e Crise Urbana no Brasil.* 2nd edition. UFRGS: Porto Alegre.

Rausch, L. 2014. Convergent Agrarian Frontiers in the Settlement of Mato Grosso, Brazil. *Historical Geography*, 42, 276–297.

Recompensa Joseph, L.C., Pereira, B.D. and Recompensa Joseph, T.W. (eds). 2011. *Identificando, Mapeando e Analisando Sistemas Produtivos Inovativos e/ou Arranjos Produtivos Locais em Mato Grosso.* EdUFMT: Cuiabá.

Ribeiro, H.S. 2016. *Políticas Territoriais e Colonização numa Área da Amazônia Oriental.* Paco Editorial: Jundiaí.

Ricardo, D. 2004 [1817]. *The Principles of Political Economy and Taxation.* Dover Publications: Mineola.

Richards, P. 2015. What Drives Indirect Land Use Change? How Brazil's Agriculture Sector Influences Frontier Deforestation. *Annals of the Association of American Geographers*, 105(5), 1026–1040.

Richards, P., Walker, R. and Arima, E.Y. 2014. Spatially Complex Land Change: The Indirect Effect of Brazil's Agricultural Sector on Land Use in Amazonia. *Global Environmental Change-Human and Policy Dimensions*, 29, 1–9.

Sawyer, D.R. 1984. Fluxo e Refluxo da Fronteira Agrícola no Brasil: Ensaio de Interpretação Estrutural e Espacial. *Revista Brasileira de Estudos de População*, 1(1–2), 3–34.

Schmitz, A., Furtan, H. and Baylis, K. 2002. *Agricultural Policy, Agribusiness, and Rent-seeking Behavior.* University of Toronto Press: Toronto.

Silva, R.R. 1985. A Expansão da Fronteira Produtiva nos Cerrados. *Fundação João Pinheiro*, 15, 53–61.

Siqueira, E.M. 1982. As Minas de Cuiabá: Primeiros Tempos. *Revista Universidade*, 2(1), 25–32.

Smith, A. 2008. [1776]. *Wealth of Nations.* Selected edition. Oxford University Press: Oxford.

Spoerer, M. 2015. Agricultural Protection and Support in the European Economic Community, 1962–92: Rent-seeking or Welfare Policy. *European Review of Economic History*, 19(2), 195–214.

Swyngedouw, E. 2012. Rent and Landed Property. In: *The Elgar Companion to Marxist Economics*, Fine, B. and Saad-Filho, A. (eds). Edward Elgar: Cheltenham, pp. 310–315.

Tavares, M.C. and Assis, J.C. 1986. *O Grande Salto para o Caos.* 2nd edition. Zahar; Rio de Janeiro.

Torres, M. (ed). 2005. *Amazônia Revelada: Os Descaminhos ao Longo da BR-163.* CNPq: Brasília.

Tratnik, M., Franic, R., Svrznjak, K. and Basic, F. 2009. Land Rents as a Criterion for Regionalization: The Case of Wheat Growing in Croatia. *Land Use Policy*, 26(1), 104–111.

USDA (U.S. Department of Agriculture). 2016. *World Agricultural Production*. Circular WAP 7–16 (July 2016). FAS/Office of Global Analysis/USDA: Washington, DC.

Walker, R. 2014. Sparing Land for Nature in the Brazilian Amazon: Implications from Location Rent Theory. *Geographical Analysis*, 46, 18–36.

Weinhold, D., Killick, E. and Reis, E.J. 2013. Soybeans, Poverty and Inequality in the Brazilian Amazon. *World Development*, 52, 132–143.

Wood, C.H. and Wilson, J. 1984. The Magnitude of Migration to the Brazilian Frontier. In: *Frontier Expansion in Amazonia*, Schmink, M. and Wood, C.H. (eds). University of Florida Press: Gainesville, pp. 142–152.

5 Displacement, replacement and misplacement

Placing Mato Grosso's agribusiness frontier

This chapter deals with the logic of place-making during the expansion of Mato Grosso's agribusiness frontier. It is specifically intended to reconcile contrasting interpretations of place dynamics and the connections between place and other geographical categories, such as landscape, spatial frontiers and agricultural development. The consideration of the vivid political-ecology of place-making is particularly significant in a region where the spatial order is in constant change under the neoliberalising pressures of globalised markets, with local production determined by powerful transnational companies and where the connection between food, rural economy and nutrition is considerably increasingly broken. Curiously, despite the formidable geographical reorganisation in the main areas of agribusiness production in Mato Grosso, there has been only a marginal interest in the spatial configuration of socio-environmental relations and of power disputes imprinted on the production of this agricultural frontier. Most critical authors have dealt with agriculture modernisation mainly through the examination of agrarian issues and farming systems, which misses wider and even more fundamental changes in politico-economic and intersectoral changes. The evolution of agribusiness in relation to place-making has been recognised by only a small number of scholars working on the political-economy of agri-food networks and scalar connections (beyond the more frequent discussion on food deserts, natural resources, organic farms and local food production), for whom agriculture happens in places that are inherently socionatural, at the same time that dynamic socionatural interactions constantly reconfigure territorialised assemblages.

Taking into account this more creative approach, here we will consider agribusiness and place-making as intensely politicised phenomena – that is, processes of simultaneous inclusion and exclusion of individuals and groups that is mediated by the appropriation and transformation of material and immaterial components of reality. The notion of place commonly refers to a particular site or region, with identity of social groups and with the interdependencies with other locations and related scales of social life (Cloke *et al.*, 2005). Nonetheless, together with anthropologists, planners and other scholars, geographers have tried to reinterpret the concept, and merge personal and representative dimensions with collective and socioeconomic properties of places. Places have been explored in relation to the accessibility of certain zones, gender and racial framing, property relations, the sustainability of place-making, resistance of spatial change and place-claiming movements, among other related themes. Places should be seen, thus, as locus of complex socionatural exchange without rigid borders, but connected with other scales of interaction upwards (e.g. national and international spheres of activity) and downwards (e.g. at community, family or personal level). According to Agnew (1987), the different meanings of place can be summarised under the expressions 'place as location' (a point on the Earth's surface), 'sense of place' (subjective feelings) and 'place as locale' (a setting for actions and interactions).

By focusing principally on places, we will be able to challenge the homogenisation of space imposed by the advance of the agribusiness-based economy and reveal a range of socio-spatial contradictions normally ignored because of the alleged lack of socioeconomic alternatives. Neoliberalised agribusiness is certainly not a monolithic entity, but fraught with internal tensions and multiple interests and its strength in Brazil has been the combination of technological innovation, institutional changes and the association between public and private sectors (Ioris, 2017). Unpacking the spatial intricacies of place-making complements the analysis put forward in the previous chapters, as these were particularly acute in the case in the upper Teles Pires River Basin, in the north of Mato Grosso, where vast tracts of rainforest and savannah vegetation were converted, since the 1970s, into places dominated by export-oriented farming. The emphasis on place-making in the Teles Pires is justified here because of the richness of meanings the term conveys, including material and symbolic processes of lived, and constantly recreated, geographies. The current analysis will give special emphasis on how the production of new places combined elements of a hypermodern economic boom with pre-capitalist practices left over from the early conquest of the territory. There was a systematic and well-crafted promise of rationality, progress and welfare underpinning public policies and government actions (Ioris, 2014). However, the founding elements of a supposedly 'new' reality was actually loaded with violence and wrongdoings, as if the Brazilian past, marked by genocide and illegality, 'suddenly explod[ed] in the face of all' (Martins, 2012: 52). Those were all integral components of an astonishing spatial experience articulated around a very specific sense of place in the area, which can be already perceived in the following interview extract:

> When we arrived here, there was no production, because there was no market, only for timber. In practice, we really bought a forest and the land was a sort of bonus, had no [market] value [. . .] And we started to work, worked hard, cut and burn the forest; it was incredible, all those monkeys screaming, and the amount of smoke [. . .] but in time Sinop became what it is today, a place of progress, with a vibrant economy and people who work hard.
>
> (Interview with one of the pioneers, who in 1978 arrived in
> the region, Sinop, June 2015)

It is important to observe that, despite some research carried out in recent years, the literature on Mato Grosso's socio-spatiality has been mainly restricted to landscape ecology and biophysical processes. Whereas the juncture between globalised forces and localised spatial outcomes has been acknowledged by social scientists, we often come across only narrow, fragmented assessments of the multilayered and complex intersections between agri-food systems and place-based interactions. The exception was some research on sustainability, urbanisation and agrarian reform, among other place-related themes (e.g. Arnauld de Sartre *et al.*, 2012; Thypin-Bermeo and Godfrey, 2012; Wittman, 2005), but less has been published about the translation of development goals into the production and the trajectory of places. Likewise, Cleary (1993) recognises the unexpected and multifarious barriers for capitalist relations and the multiple failures of the activities implemented in the Amazon a few years earlier, emphasising that most theoretical frameworks have provided inadequate explanations to complex, non-linear processes of socio-spatial change and to the unexpected advance of capitalist relations of production in the Amazon; however, like most authors, Cleary has limited the analysis to the forest biome and neglected the savannah-forest transition zones.

In order to cope with the complex ontological questions related to place, we can fortunately rely on the geographical sensibilities of the Mato Grosso-born poet Manoel de Barros (1916–2014), considered one of the greatest names of contemporary Brazilian literature. The need to liberate the reality from its pre-arranged configuration and re-create the world permeates Manoel's long and incredibly original artistic construction. Manoel left a vast artistic production fraught with incredible images and lavish verses that basically deal with what is considered secondary or irrelevant (e.g. encounters with stones, birds, insects, horses, the perplexity with organic and decaying matter, the habits of scattered rural families, etc.). From the micro and insignificant, the poet constructs an argument about some of the most universal and unending questions of human existence. His attempt to go beyond the conventional and well-behaved forced him to develop a new language, which he defined as the 'archaic manoelian idio-dialect' [*idioleto manoelês arcaico*]. Manoel was born in the capital of Mato Grosso and spent his first years on the shores of the Paraguay River, where the distances were immense and the time seemed to move very slowly. According to Manoel, his family was then living in a place where there was 'nothing' and where it was necessary to invent the world; therefore, invention was required to 'enlarge' the world (Barros, 2013).

Manoel realised, since his childhood in the 1920s, that the immensity of Mato Grosso was incomplete and, consequently, his world had still to be invented – that is, the intense exchanges with nature and among the small number of inhabitants needed to be complemented with broader social intercourses and connections with wider Brazilian and international society.[1] Manoel's sophisti-cated geographical proposition was that Mato Grosso had yet to be 'invented' – that is, his world had to be created in order to be deciphered, given that it was a world full of unsaid and unarticulated truths. 'What nourished my spirit was not reading. It was inventing. I was raised in the isolated forest. I think that this forced me to broaden my world with my imaginary' (Barros, 2010: 40). Central to Manoel's ontology is the difference between 'invention' and 'lie' – in other words, the sense that invention is diametrically in opposition to falsehood. In what was probably the only public interview ever given by Manoel de Barros – turned into the documentary 'Only Ten Percent is Lying' [*Só Dez por Cento é Mentira*] by the movie director Pedro Cezar, released in 2010[2] – Manoel claims that only 10 per cent of his argument is untrue and 90 per cent is invented. He repeatedly stated that 'all that I didn't invent is false' (Barros, 2013: 319).

Not only Manoel's aesthetics is passionately ecological – in terms of attention to natural features that deserve contemplation, retain exquisite beauty and are central elements of human activity – but the poet has noticeably argued in favour of a new condition for Mato Grosso and its people; these dreams are ultimately a call for a humanist transformation of places. Therefore, his poetry is extremely valuable for the purposes of the present investigation because of his ecological ethics and place-based poetics: a new reality needed to be produced that was not only true, but because it was necessary to unlock the deep structures of existence. Informed by Manoel's dream of a different, more extensive, but also more inclusive geography, the next pages will deal with the dialectics between displacement–replacement, the pervasiveness of misplacement and the place-based prospects for the future. Such a heterodox approach follows the provocative suggestion of Squire (1996) that the interface between geography and literature can uncover multifaceted spatial meanings, particularly through the appreciation of the 'texts of place' rendered by the writer. Before that, and stimulated by Manoel's figurative language, it is necessary to clarify the conceptual framework employed in this chapter and consider three interpretative concerns that need clarification and will enlighten the analysis of place-based changes.

Three main interpretative entanglements

It was indicated above that place-making is a heuristic analytical category to understand the lived space, but also to uncover the discursive and contextual aspects of the agricultural frontier established in Mato Grosso. New areas of production, such as the Teles Pires River Basin, are a locus of intense spatial reworking and relentless experimentation, which stretches from the specific and actually existing to the general and intertemporal. The agricultural frontier is more than just a zone of capitalist transition (as defined by Barney, 2009), but it is a true 'laboratory' or 'smelting' of space with competing tempos and rival spatial rhythms. Because of its intense activity, agribusiness at the frontier is essentially an accelerated mechanism of place-making that is reliant on the rapid conversion of abundant territorial resources (including labour-power) and on the promise of brave new places. The resulting places are still relatively young, in terms of their politico-economic and social-ecological track records, and their ontological novelty encapsulates emerging socio-ecological relations at the intersection between powerful global markets, regional development, widespread disruptions and interpersonal connections. However, instead of merely studying the frontier as a constellation of interconnected places, it is important to scrutinise the politicised genesis of the emerging places and their trajectory under socio-ecological disputes. The nuanced relationships between scales, times and dimensions are normally missed in conventional geographical texts, in which places are simply associated with the local and particular, in contrast with large-scale connections typically related to space. In the tradition of Vidal de la Blache, Fernand Braudel and others, place is taken as a slice, or a portion, of space with specific geographical qualities that are hard to generalise.

Although place is connected to the construction of political thinking and the production of knowledge, questions about place-making cannot be resolved at the level of theory only (Dirlik, 1999). The uniqueness of the agricultural frontier requires a bespoke intellectual device capable of scrutinising the multiple mediations, suspended certainties and disputed rationales. Opportunely, we can find support in alternative approaches that, although not necessarily applied to agricultural areas, lay emphasis on the social practices involved in place-making and on the fluid, dynamic connections between locales, places and other spatial scales (Agnew, 2011). In that regard, there are at least three main interpretative entanglements that require specific attention ahead of our empirical analysis of place dynamics in the north of Mato Grosso. First, we need to acknowledge that, similar to other key geographical concepts, the meaning of place is fraught with ambiguity and openness, which cannot be entirely or definitely removed. In addition, the analytical relevance of place can only be properly appreciated in relation to other connected terms, such as scale, time and, particularly, landscape. Both place and landscape are socio-spatial constructs with no fixed boundaries and, to some extent, the two terms have similar connotations. Nonetheless, while place tends to be more often associated with the existential and particular, landscape are normally related to the appearance of an area (i.e. its image and representation) or as a 'way of seeing' the socio-political processes that shape the landscape (Cosgrove, 1998). 'Landscape is a representation of place, and as such, it is the re-presentation of a relatedness to place, a re-presentation of a mode of 'emplacement' (Malpas, 2011: 7). Landscapes normally encapsulate places, at the same time that places disclose more visibly the politics of landscape features.

Taking an anthropological perspective, Carolino (2010) demonstrates the role of landscape perception, and its materiality, in the lived process of place-making (although she downplays slightly the materiality of places in favour of the supposed embodiment provided by landscapes). Equally, Ingold (2000: 193) submits – against spatial segmentations and human-society dichotomies – that 'the landscape is the world as it is known to those who dwell therein, who inhabit its places and journal along the paths connecting them'. Ingold emphasises that the form of landscape appears detached from the immediate engagement of the agents, at the same time that makes more tangible the pre-constituted social and political entities. Consequently, place-making can be seen as the endowment of locations with meaning through lived experiences, the circulation of narratives and spatialised interactions at different, interconnected scales (from local to national and global), whereas landscape processes are primarily focused on the interrelation between spatial features that are perceived according to the position of the observer and have a stronger representational character. The continuities between place and landscape are prominently helpful here because places in Mato Grosso are intense spots of meaning and interaction, at the same time that the evolution of places results in the highly emblematic and widely mentioned landscapes of agribusiness.

Second, the recognition that there is still significant disagreement about the content and the ramifications of place dynamics. It is well known that the importance of place for critical human geography was greatly reinforced in the 1970s by the work of humanist scholars, who investigated the specific features of individual and group life. Humanist geographers insisted that places are not determined in advance, but are simultaneously performed, sensed and represented. Important is the 'sense of place', as the affective ties between individuals, groups and where they live (Johnston, 1986). Tuan (1976) emphasises people's behaviour, conditions, ideas and feelings in relation to the intricacies of place-making. Such agent-based and phenomenological interpretations were directly concerned with questions about consciousness, experience and intentionality. Intentionality is, thus, an emergent relation with the world and not a pre-given condition of experience (Ash and Simpson, 2016); by the same token, subjective views of place and space influence conscious or unconscious acts (Schutz, 1972). Place-making can be seen, thus, as a relational phenomenon embedded in the activity of politicised, non-territorialised networks in which places are framed (Pierce *et al.*, 2011). Places should be treated relationally in order to better cope with a series of interactions that run 'into' and 'out from' places, such as climate change, labour movements and trade relations (Darling, 2009), and still maintaining a critical engagement with the socio-political ordering of the world, including social, corporate and government organisations (May, 1996). Individuals have multiple attachments to place, and experience it according to their cultural, political and historical circumstances (Pocock, 1981). Places are multifaceted cultural constructions, just as culture is the medium through which socio-spatial changes are experienced, contested and constituted (Cosgrove and Jackson, 1987).

Humanist, and closely related phenomenological, explanations are often intertwined with the arguments of cultural geographers, who contend that the meaning and experience of places also involves cultural questions resulting from a cumulative spiral of signification (Thrift, 1983). Alternative opinions in this debate about the ontological foundations of place-making have come, since the 1980s, from radical scholars associated with Marxist thinking, who challenged the excessive focus on the local and the subjective by humanist colleagues. According to this group of authors, humanists tended to romanticise people's attachment to places and underestimated issues such as inequality and political disputes. Places assume specific attributes under the capitalist mode of production, as capital is able to move quickly and cheaply from place to place, depending 'upon the creation of fixed, secure and largely immobile social and physical infrastructures' (Harvey, 2001: 332). The control of place is essential to secure command over material commodity exchanges and authority over the workforce – for instance, with the threat of moving jobs to other locations. The mobility of capital is even more critical in a globalised world largely shaped by trans-continental trade and exchange of goods and commodities. Therefore, place and space were considered inescapably conquered by capitalism and the two must be treated dialectically within an internally related framework that melts together specificities and generalities (Merrifield, 1993). Equally, disputes over statecraft under capitalism are also shaped by the politics of place and related to the possibilities for political practice by creating particular terrains of conflict, determining the terms of access and influencing subjective experiences of political life (Chouinard, 1990).

Other authors have since then tried to reconcile these two theorisations of place – namely, the more individualistic, agency-centred and the class-based, structure-informed approaches. The synthetic argument is that both agency and structure are mutually constitutive and determine each other at different scales and places. The observer and what is observed are not detached, as suggested by some humanist approaches, but places are designated spaces infused with meanings and resulting from social practices and historicised work. While there is a global and globalised sense of places, the 'global is in the local in the very process of the formation of the local' (Massey, 1994: 120). Consequently, grand narratives about place, and any other spatial formation, exert a highly negative influence, because they obscure the importance of gender, race, caste and age differences and, as a result, lower the possibility for genuine political change (Massey, 1993). The complexity and variegatedness of places definitely require conceptions of abstract power complemented by the politics of everyday life, which should account for interpersonal relations, networks of subjectivity and socioeconomic systems. Swyngedouw (1999) adds that the politicisation of place, as much as the dynamics of social change and the possibilities of political emancipation, are important elements of critical scholarship and have a role in the production of a truly humanising geography. Massey (1993) further argues that geographers need to advocate a 'progressive sense of place' to people – that is, geographers have the moral obligation to show people that place-based actions and understandings make no sense without acknowledging all those things impinging on place from outside. This present study is certainly a concrete attempt to expand such 'progressive' approach to place and place-based interactions at the frontier of agribusiness expansion.

Finally, there is a third interpretative entanglement, linked to the previous two points, but specifically related to the intensity of place change along history. In a situation of dramatic reconfiguration of the spatial order, as in the case of the advance of the agricultural frontier in Mato Grosso, the continuous pheno-menon of place-making assumes a more intricate and, crucially, a clearer political character. These are periods when multiple spatial connections and ramifications across scales have to be rapidly negotiated – and are all normally resisted all the way – which results in configurations of place that are both highly transitory and more subject to socio-political disputes. The intensity of such place transformations corresponds to an extraordinary mechanism of spatial change, which can be described as place-framing and during which political disputes become even more visible and play a more forceful role in socio-spatial dynamics. It is worth remembering that Goffman (1974), quoted in Martin (2003: 733), defines 'framing' as how individuals organise experiences or make sense of localised events. However, for the purpose of our analysis, place-framing refers to a concentrated, transient process of spatial transformation when the socioeconomic and bio-physical features of the existing places are checked and swiftly modified. Latent or silent disagreements that were present during the longer process of place-making can likewise erupt and escalate during the more contested and unstable period of place-framing. The moments of place-framing are therefore critical, decisive phases when the fundamental pillars of the new spatial order are disputed by different groups and sectors that try to influence the direction of place change according to their interests and the wider balance of power.

These three main interpretative connexions only briefly discussed here – respectively, the tensions between representation and experience, between humanist and class-based explanations, and between the intensity of place-making and place-framing – will directly inform our analysis and help to understand the spatial evolution of the agribusiness frontier from the heuristic and highly illuminating perspective of place. We can easily accept that the present analysis has ambitious analytical goals and could have ramified into specific, separate assessments of each of those three tensions. Nonetheless, the aim was to articulate a single conceptual framework for this chapter able to capture place-making as a multidimensional phenomenon (including lived experiences and symbolic representations) that both includes and excludes social groups according to economic, political, racial and cultural differences, and that has an historical evolution that is far from linear (but oscillates between moments of more intense and more discrete transformation). It is worth noting that the focus here is on the meso-scale (the river basin) with insights into the micro-scales of place (towns, farms and neighbourhoods) and connections with the macro-scale (the wider process of agro-neoliberalism). Our research was particularly attentive to the intensification of agribusiness operations, in the form of large-scale crop production and under the influence of transnational corporations selling farming inputs and purchasing production. These are strong evidences of what Woods (2007) describes as the remaking of rural places by the 'differentiated geography of rural globalisation' – that is, the production of a globalised countryside that is only partially or problematically integrated into the wider processes of homogenisation and hybridisation. Inspired by Manuel's ontological proposition about the world to be invented, and enlightened by the three interpretative entanglements, we will now examine the troubling trajectory of places in the Teles Pires River Basin.

Place-framing through the pressures of displacement and replacement

During most colonial and post-colonial Brazilian history, the north of Mato Grosso was considered a universe apart, mostly occupied by 'intractable' tribes and with little connection with the rest of the country (Holanda, 1994). As we have seen in Chapter 3, that began to change in the 1930s with systematic plans of economic and regional integration launched by the national government. The decisive phase of spatial transformation came with the strong resolve of the military presidents – between 1964 and 1985 – to force agriculture development upon the remote corners of the Centre-West and the Amazon regions. (The north of Mato Grosso is exactly at the intersection between these two macro-regions.) National and international companies were attracted to both regions through various forms of fiscal incentives and subsidies to timber and cattle production. At the same time, impoverished small-scale farmers migrated from other Brazilian states in search of a piece of land in public and, mostly, private colonisation projects (Jepson, 2006). Social mobility was notoriously restricted in the Brazilian countryside (Costa Pinto, 1965), but the new agricultural frontier raised the promise of social betterment and the possibility to own a larger rural property. Most new farmers came from the southern states and the majority acquired a piece of land of between 10 and 300 hectares (Santos, 2011). Also the formation of large farms (latifundia) was mostly a novelty in the region, where the majority of agricultural activities had been historically concentrated in small, subsistence farmsteads. In that process, numerous new urban and rural places were produced due to the operation of private and public colonisation companies and the mobilisation of social groups from different parts of the country. Figure 5.1 illustrates the office of the company that promoted the colonisation of Sorriso.

One of the most emblematic experiences was the foundation of the municipality of Sinop – now the main urban settlement in the Teles Pires (130,000 inhabitants, estimated for 2015 by IBGE) – after the acquisition by a company of the same name (*Colonizadora Sinop*) of a property with 645,000 hectares, known as Gleba Celeste. The founder of Sinop, Ênio Pipino, famously declared that Gleba Celeste 'was a green world, sleeping, in the loneliness of the Amazon' (in Souza, 2006: 144) and also that he was 'planting civilisations' and creating a liveable Amazon by opening roads and clearing forests and jungles (Pipino, 1982). The urbanisation of Sinop started in 1972 and the streets were named, ironically, after the species of local trees, just as deforestation advanced rapidly. Timber production was initially the primary commercial activity, but in the 1990s there was a clear decline due to the exhaustion of the forests (in our interviews, it was mentioned that Sinop had more than 500 timber mills in this phase). Colonisation projects like Sinop were aggressively advertised to prospective farmers as an opportunity to restart their lives anew, in a clear mechanism of 'place myth' that was necessary to overcome the negative stereotypes of the new frontier and the widespread images of isolation and hazard (Brannstrom and Neuman, 2009: 125).

Similarly, the town of Sorriso, in the upper Teles Pires catchment, resulted from the violent occupation, in 1972, by private developers of a property that

Figure 5.1 Office of Colonizadora Feliz in the centre of Sorriso
Source: Author

belonged to the American farmer Edmund Zanini, who was defrauded and violently expulsed from the area he had purchased in 1964 (Folha de São Paulo, 2009).[3] Three decades later, Sorriso, located at the edge of the forest and with huge areas of easily cultivable land, is now the main hub of soybean production in the entire country. Dias and Bortoncello (2003) praise Sorriso as a promise of abundance and economic growth that replaced the land of paradise left in the south of Brazil (this is epitomised in the words of the poem 'My Place' in the cover of the book). As in most of the Amazon, the development of Sorriso entailed the superimposition of urban logic and globalisation tendencies over agriculture (Rempel, 2014), which means that the rural places are shaped by the demands of global markets translated and systematised by companies, technicians and businesspeople living and committed to urban life. Less than 30 per cent of the municipality population now lives in the countryside and landowners typically live in the cities and commute every day, only spending more time in the rural property during seedling and harvesting periods.

Examples like Sinop and Sorriso suggest that the first period of place trans-formation in the Teles Pires (manifested as an intense moment of place-framing) was fundamentally characterised by the *displacement* of the existing socio-ecologi-cal features through an intense politics of arrivals and, soon after, unintended departures (see below). New places at the frontier of agricultural expansion were essentially the result of the removal of the original vegetation, the influx of thousands of migrants and the promotion of a gradually more intense production. It was a large-scale process of 'development induced displacement' (Wittman, 2005: 96) in which the transition to a new socio-spatial order was not automatic but happened through the violent dislodgement of those already living in the area and an increasing commodification of nature and its conversion into natural 'resources' (e.g. land, water, timber, bushmeat, etc.). Displacement was not a purely social process, but it involved both the transference of land to the hands of the new farmers who came from other Brazilian regions (at the expense of the livelihood of squatters and indigenous groups) and the conversion of most original ecosystems into pastures and cropland (Gutberlet, 1999). It can be seen that place-making in the Teles Pires initially operated through a mechanism of displacement and selective allocation of land and opportunities. The situation was similar, but in the opposite direction, to the genesis of capitalist farming described by Marx. If in Europe, 'the expropriation of the agricultural producer, of the peasant, from the soil is the basis of the whole process' and the pillar 'of the capitalist mode of production' (Marx, 1976: 876 and 934), what happened in Brazil was the expropriation of the peasants from their original places in the south and the ensuing poverty-induced migration to Mato Grosso.

The vector of displacement continued unabated, as an ongoing phenomenon based upon dispossession and constant movement rather than upon stability, through which different layers of belonging, ties to land and group identity are revealed (Connor, 2012). The wider agenda of regional development obviously intersected with the aspirations and experiences of families and groups involved in, and affected by, the production of new places. That observation is related to the aforesaid second interpretative entanglement, in the sense that both the structure and the agency behind place change are mutually constitutive and determine each other. Globalised market transactions and national development policies have to make allowance for the manifestation of what is specific and unique at the agribusiness frontier in order to overcome the residues of pre-capitalist society. In that sense, Dirlik (1999) is certainly wrong when he affirms that capitalist modernity has rendered places into inconveniences to be dispensed with (either by erasure or by rendering into commodities), while in effect place-making was located at the core of an increasingly globalised agri-food economy. Despite the rapid expansion of the new agricultural frontier, many newcomers struggled to maintain their activity, especially because of the failure to receive the promised support from the government and the lack of market or transportation for their production. Soon after the first phase in the 1970s and early 1980s (characterised by the pressures of displacement), several political and economic constraints limited the ability of the government to keep the doors of the agricultural frontier wide open (in particular the burden of public debt and high inflation in the late 1980s and early 1990s).

It was a turbulent period of reorganisation when not only the small farmers faced difficulties in maintaining their activities in areas of economic frontier; many large property owners and rural companies (*companhias* or *empresas agropecuárias*) failed to cope with the costs of transportation, distant markets, low productivity and, especially, dwindling subsidies and incentives. Capitalised entrepreneurs continue to arrive in the Teles Pires, at the same time that a significant proportion of those who came in search of their own piece of land (*sonho da terra* = dream of land) had actually to leave for other parts of the Amazon and beyond (Souza, 2013), had to find employment in the increasingly large agribusiness farms or even returned to their places of origin in southern Brazilian states: since 1980, migration out of Mato Grosso intensified and the rate even doubled in the 1990s compared to the 1970s (Cunha, 2006). The fact that the frontier was only selectively, and for a relatively short period of time, open was one of the strong indications that at the frontier displacement required its opposite, replacement, in order to produce economic and socio-political meaning. This was particularly evident in the municipality of Lucas do Rio Verde, which initially attracted 203 families of small farmers from the state of Rio Grande do Sul (Oliveira, 2005); after a difficult beginning, just a minority of the original pioneers remained in Lucas do Rio Verde – fewer than 10 per cent – while most lost their properties due to the operational adversities, unfulfilled promises and accumulated debts (Santos, 1993).[4] This experience vividly suggests that the process of displacement could not happen in isolation and, even as the existing features were being displaced, another key trend – *replacement* – was unfolding.

Many of the families drawn to the agribusiness frontier were actually becoming redundant and had to swiftly adapt to a reality fraught with unexpected difficulties. Less productive workers and decapitalised farmers were largely replaced by a small number of skilled machine operators (trained to cope with the rapid automatisation and informatisation of farming procedures) and by a small number of increasingly wealthy landowners in possession of vast rural properties (Mattei, 1998) and who even rent land to maximise the use of their machinery and production capacity. Tragically, some of the newly arrived farmers had been ousted from their birthplaces in disputes with indigenous tribes in the south (as in the case of conflicts between farmers and the Kaingang tribes in the municipality of Tenente Portela in the 1970s) and then were transferred to Mato Grosso by the dictatorial government, only to be expelled again because of the inadequacy of their production. It was a permanent and perverse becoming that undermines the being – the being is the promised becoming that never materialised; in that context, it is curious that poor dispute with poor for forest and land, highly convoluted by the political system. In that process, many of the original small or medium-size farmers lost their land, tried to receive a small plot in agrarian reform projects or transferred their activity to small farmsteads (known as *chácaras*, typically with less than 5 hectares) near to the cities (these are now responsible for a significant part of the food consumed locally, although in our interviews they complained that it was difficult to sell to supermarkets which demand scale and regularity difficult for a small farmer to offer).

To avoid the replacement of those who had been replaced, the municipal authorities of Sorriso and Sinop temporarily operated a form of 'place filter' that prevents the entrance of poor migrants: at the bus station there is a formal check and those unable to demonstrate means or income receive a free ticket back to their homelands. Such form of spatial filter operates in the opposite direction when the same authorities organise farm fairs to attract attention by those willing to do business in the municipality. The same frontier that attracted migrants, as a seductive mirage and promise of a better life to most, began to replace a significant proportion of those initially involved. The impact of replacement pressures can be appreciated in the following interview extract:

> I came to Mato Grosso 29 years ago, lost my initial property because of the banks [*impossibility to pay back the loans*] [. . .] and I am now trying to preserve my small piece of land, only 1.5 hectares large, in Sinop. I sell my milk directly to my clientele; I refuse to give it to the industry because they pay almost nothing. I try to survive, but so much is still lacking. When I go to the hospital, I am really humiliated [. . .] Soybean is not helping us at all and the future is not looking any better [. . .]
> (Interview with small-scale farmer, Sinop, July 2015)

Replacement, as the second moment of place-framing, was not only restricted to the concentration of landed property and the conversion of the weaker farmers into farm labourers. It involved other profound changes in economic and technological trends, including the substitution of the various crops unsuccessfully tried in the 1970s (coffee, cassava, guarana, pepper, rice, etc.) with the overpowering presence, higher profitability and symbolic importance of soybean (predicated on the use of intense agronomic techniques, expensive machinery and profound financialisation of production). Because of the intense interplay between displacement and replacement – under the powerful influence of agribusiness development policies – most of the Teles Pires River Basin become a gigantic 'soyscape' formed by contiguous large-scale farms primarily dedicated to the cultivation of soybean (in succession or rotation with a few other crops). As observed in comparable conditions by Marx (1976: 905), the capitalist farmer results from the enrichment of some individuals who usurped the common land (with the impoverishment of 'the mass of the agriculture folks') and managed to benefit from technological revolutions.

After a moment of great turbulence in the early 1990s, there was a revitalisation of place-framing at the agricultural frontier, helped by currency devaluation in 1999; booming commodity prices in the 2000s; foreign investments in productive, and speculative, ventures; and growing demands for soybeans from Asia. Several large-scale national companies were sold to transnational corporations due to various difficulties associated with market deregulation policies introduced in the 1990s (Wilkinson, 2009), at the same time that a handful of Brazilian corporations benefited directly from generous loans and surreptitious support offered by the federal development bank BNDES during the populist Lula-Dilma administrations (Dieguez, 2015). Farmers in Mato Grosso also became better organised and created, in 1993, a highly effective technological institute, the MT Foundation, responsible for the development of new crop varieties that are more productive and disease resistant. The work of the MT Foundation complemented other technologies traditionally developed by public universities and, especially, Embrapa (the public agriculture research corporation). As a result, both established transnational (Monsanto, ADM, Bunge, Cargill, Dreyfus, etc.) and new, rapidly growing Brazilian transnational corporations (Amaggi, BR Foods, JBS, Marfrig, etc.) have been a decisive contributory factor in terms of business activities and influence behind policy-making.

However, there are also other political and symbolic repercussions of the twin process of displacement and replacement in the Teles Pires. The soybean-based economy was, and continues to be, constantly portrayed by sector representatives as a fine expression of technological efficiency and administrative know-how, which is used as undisputed evidence that rational, high-tech rural development works. The claim of sector representatives is that technified agribusiness replaced the tradition of chaos, incompetence and turbulence typically associated with previous rounds of economic development in the Amazon with a new socio-spatial reality based on rationalism, knowledge and competence (Ioris, 2016). The argument demonstrates what can be described as the 'narcissism' of the agricultural frontier, in which self-constructed declarations of heroism and of unquestionable achievements (mainly by large-scale farmers) serve to fulfil a prophecy of success and the triumph of the new configuration of places brought to the region. The symbolism and rhetoric of the successful frontier plays an important role in the definition of the new agriculture places against other possibilities who are outside (what Massey, 1994, considers the production of selective inclusion and boundaries of exclusion). Furthermore, although 'a great part of the land title in the Brazilian Amazon doesn't pass a serious judicial examination' (Oliveira, 2005: 91), the high productivity of soybean and the impressive expansion of areas under cultivation are used to vindicate the violence, the mistakes and the illegality employed for the creation of the frontier. The good years came to a temporary halt in 2005, when global market prices collapsed and farmers throughout Mato Grosso started a fierce campaign calling for special state support and various forms of concessions (including the postponement of debts and other obligations). The agricultural frontier was established to serve, and continues to attend, primarily, the politico-economic agendas of the self-proclaimed victorious agribusiness players, at the expense of the demands of the majority of the regional population, what results in the widespread sense of misplacement, considered below, but only after an examination of the resulting territorial configuration.

The resulting and widespread sense of misplacement

From the above, it can be inferred that the expansion of the agribusiness sector in the Teles Pires, particularly in the more recent years of aggressive neo-liberalisation, produced urban and rural places of intense economic activity, but was also fraught with differences, tensions and unevenness. It was, and remains, a highly contested and disputed socio-spatial process in which the very configuration of economy and society are still being shaped and are repeatedly affected by the instabilities of agricultural markets and public policy changes. Instead of simply place-making, what prevailed in the Teles Pires was the more politicised process of place-framing, which is demonstrated by the rapid rhythm of changes related to displacement and replacement pressures. The experience of place-framing was also associated with systematic efforts of legitimisation and silent, but important, contestation. On one hand, the high-tech agriculture practised in the Teles Pires secured national and international prestige among agribusiness players and has been widely praised for its productivity, rationality and entre-preneurialism. On the other hand, there are striking contrasts between, for example, the wealthy urban areas and agribusiness farms, and the poverty of urban peripheries and small-scale farms. Poverty is definitely not an easy concept, but the available statistics indicate that around one-third of the population in the cities of the agribusiness frontier suffer from the lack of adequate housing and basic public services (Frederico, 2011). Differences like that are typical of nouveau riche regions, particularly in Latin America, where the accelerated expansion of a lucrative economic sector benefits primarily those with monopoly power over land, resources and markets. However, because of the distinctive origins and the turbulent advance of the agricultural frontier, it seems that there is more than just ostentation and socio-spatial inequality in the Teles Pires. The empirical evidence, primarily from documents, meetings and interviews, suggests that despite signs of progress and opulence, life in the Teles Pires remains in a state of great uncertainty and stiff constraints, particularly to small farmers living in between large estates:

> When it rains we can see the '*veneno*' [literally, 'poison', but actually meaning agrochemicals] coming down the river, destroying our waterbodies, and with the hydropower dams now it is only getting worse. It started with cattle, the cutting of trees, now soybean [. . .] These farmers don't care that we are seeing, that it is affecting our life [. . .] We could do more, but we need more things, more help [from the government].
>
> (Interview with a small-scale farmer, March 2014)

This interview extract exposes a situation in which many social groups are always 'out of place' due to policies and measures that consolidate the agricultural frontier as narrow places of settlement and production (as examined by Prout and Howitt, 2009). One main source of such socio-spatial volatility is the fact that, because of the politico-economic crisis of agribusiness in the early 1990s, the region was hastily and firmly inserted into the circuits of global agri-food markets and neoliberal economic reforms, including the privatisation of roads and the growing funding of production by transnational corporations, instead of the traditional loans from public banks (Ioris, 2015). The regional economy is now largely embedded in trans-spatial flows and international networks through which power is exercised extraterritorially (see Amin, 2004). Public and private life have been affected by those adjustments which, despite renovating the regional economy, reinforced the pattern of socio-ecological exploitation, vulnerability and political subordination. Because of its very nature, places at the agricultural frontier are mostly transient and unstable, particularly in such remote areas in the Amazon that rely on the import and export of the majority of goods consumed and produced locally. Modern farming, which relies on socionatural exploitation and the conversion of land into monoculture, clashes with most of the needs of small farmers and urban social groups, but the compromise is dictated by the reverence and reinforcement of large private properties as the accepted socio-political institution to manage space. Agribusiness-based development demands some sort of spatial control and discursive coordination as a form of useful and practical rationality within the much wider forms of socionatural impacts and, ultimately, the irrationality of globalised markets. Figures 5.2 and 5.3 demonstrate that deforestation continues at alarming rates in the Teles Pires.

The intense periods of place-framing in the Teles Pires – in the 1970s–1980s and then the 1990s–2000s – were both based on a fundamental paradox between the presumption of progress and collective achievement, and the concealment of the fact that most social and economic opportunities are increasingly restricted to a small number of residents. While agribusiness is ubiquitous, not as merely an economic activity but as the holy grail of modernisation and is formally available to all, in reality it is touched by a tiny minority of the population (large landowners

Figure 5.2 Forest area cleared in the previous year
Source: Author

Figure 5.3 Lorry with logs on the way to Sinop
Source: Author

and agro-industrial enterprises). It means that the alleged success of the places framed at the agricultural frontier is insufficient to conceal the mounting contradictions and tensions. As observed by an adviser of the agriculture federation FAMATO (which mainly represents the interests of large-scale farmers), 'there is a lot of technology available today, but it is in the hands of only a few, the big [farmers]' (interview in Lucas do Rio Verde, December 2014). It also confirms the core notion, expressed in the first interpretative entanglement above, that place is fraught with ambiguity, but it is at the same time the mani-festation of historical and geographical particularisms. There are serious concerns in the Teles Pires with, among other issues, the long-term viability of soybean production; the risks of a very narrow economic base; the isolation of the region in relation to input suppliers and soybean buyers; and the hidden agenda of politicians and agribusiness leaders that seem to exclude the many people: 'We live because we are obstinate, because we occupy our space, but I am really concerned about the continuous difficulties. What kind of development is this that leaves us with only a tiny bit of space?' (interview with a small-scale farmer in an agrarian reform project, December 2014).

Those trends affect not only peasants and family farmers, but similarly disturb the situation and the prospects of large-scale farmers:

I arrived here in Sinop 36 years ago; I came with strength and innocence, there was so much to do what I didn't have time to think [about the changes]. The government then needed to maintain territorial sovereignty and used the farmers to occupy the land. People like me agreed, because they wanted more land. Our dream was to have a [rural] property, it was a family dream, something from my grandfather. [. . .] Initially, we had rice, then gradually soybean. It was a great period, the structural problems were still there, but things really improved [in our lives]. We managed to evolve, technologically speaking, productivity increased a lot. What the farmers could have done, we did. But now lots of people are deep into debts, the last decade has been very difficult. Many will leave the sector, I am afraid [. . .] The big companies created a monopoly [. . .] I am anticipating that I myself will also file bankruptcy, maybe next year [. . .] Only those with good savings or excellent credit will remain. Those who can, go into politics. What we really need is more incentives to hard work.

(Interview with a soybean farmer, Sinop, June 2015)

Comments like this suggest that several decades of the spatial dialectics of displacement and replacement actually resulted in a pervasive sentiment of *misplacement*. Despite all the positive images transmitted daily in the local and national media, the economic success of the region seems misplaced, its future is ambiguous and most of the population still struggle to reconcile being and belonging. The fact that misplacement is the dialectical synthesis of the interplay between displacement and replacement taking place in the Teles Pires further reveals the full extent of the colonisation of space by capital. A clear indication of that is that present-day agriculture in the Teles Pires is now decisively associated with the activity of transnational corporations (controlled either by national or international capital, as mentioned above) in charge of selling off farm inputs and controlling credit and foreign trade. More importantly, new places have been framed because of the alleged advantages of the agricultural frontier, whereas these are, in effect, signs of great weaknesses of its narrow production base. Something that is particularly relevant in the Teles Pires is that the unsettling sense of misplacement, which results from dialectics of displacement and replacement, continues to define place-based interactions in the region long after the initial opening of the agricultural frontier. Present-day circumstances, marked by the hegemony of agribusiness at the expense of any other socioeconomic alternative, remain directly based on the original mechanisms of territorial conquest and political control put in practice since the middle of the last century. The violent displacement of the earlier socio-ecological reality was not followed by a condition of spatial stability, but was instead complemented, and magnified, by a never-ending replacement of people, knowledge and social practices.

As in most of the southern and eastern sections of the Amazon region, agribusiness development imposed an urban logic and globalised life styles. Fewer than 30 per cent of the population now reside in the countryside and landowners typically live in the cities and commute every day, only spending more time in the rural property during seeding and harvesting periods (Rempel, 2014). There are sustained and disturbing cases of racial and socioeconomic discrimination against the urban poor, who typically migrated from the northeast or other parts of the Amazon and who are normally non-white migrants (such as the majority of the residents interviewed in the periphery of Sinop and Sorriso, the two main cities in the Teles Pires, respectively in the deprived neighbourhoods of São Domingos and Boa Esperança). See Figures 5.4–5.7, which help to understand the socio-spatial contradictions of the lived places in the Teles Pires River Basin and the growing gap between pockets of affluence and the periphery fraught with poverty and deprivation. Such patterns of inequality and discrimination are certainly not new in the history of Brazil, but were nonetheless brought back and re-created according to the priorities of agribusiness-based regional development. The new places in the Teles Pires are the idiosyncratic result of this balance between innovation and perpetuation achieved through the interplay between displacement and replacement and manifested in the widespread sense of misplacement.

The resulting misplacement has a more disturbing and probably unexpected repercussion, which is the progressive, but concealed, shrinking of space in the Teles Pires. If the physical map of Mato Grosso retains the same area (around 90 million hectares) and the Teles Pires has the same boundaries of 40 years ago,

Figure 5.4 Periphery of Sinop (São Domingos)
Source: Author

Figure 5.5 Periphery of Sorriso (Boa Esperança)
Source: Author

Figure 5.6 Wealthy residence in Sinop
Source: Author

Figure 5.7 Wealthy residences in Sorriso
Source: Author

the social and socio-ecological space has been gradually and awfully reduced year by year. Not only is there a much reduced space, but the totalising strength of agribusiness advances an agriculture model highly divorced from food production concerns (actually, areas of intense plantation activity are by and large food deserts that import the most basic ingredients, such as rice, beans and vegetables, from other Brazilian states) and is responsible for farms that are less efficient, less ecologically complex and highly risky. The regional space has not only been produced, but also wasted, corrupted and ultimately diminished. The fundamental driving-force responsible for such perverse geography is the prioritisation and constant reinforcement of agribusiness not as the best option, but as a normative order. Soyscapes are the outcome of significant investments in land, water and biodiversity management through the mobilisation of heavy machinery, skilled workforce and connections with national and foreign corporations. The never-ending landscapes of soybean are politico-economic and socio-ecological con-structions produced and reinforced at the expense of other places rooted out through violence and mystification. It is therefore a spatial compromise that is both misplaced and *too-much-in-place*. Misplacement derives fundamentally from this excessive and reductionist emphasis on a single direction of place-making – that is, a reality that is too much founded on greatly simplified places and hierarchical social relations.

An imbricated territoriality

A quick inspection of recent maps and remote sense images makes clear that the expansion of agribusiness – under the impact of displacement, replacement and misplacement trends – has produced a peculiar amalgamation of urban, rural and conservation areas organised along Mato Grosso's motorways and secondary roads. However, the territorialised intricacy of the agricultural frontier is much more vibrant and intense than mere spots on a map or colourful bands on a satellite image can convey. The territories of the agricultural frontier are a fusion of emerging spatial configurations, residues of what existed before and imagined spaces that people want to live in. Between 1964 and 2013, it is possible that more than 130,000 families moved to Mato Grosso (Rausch, 2014), resulting in a territorial mosaic directly shaped by the actions of different social groups attempting to expand their influence and secure private gains or, in the case of the weaker players, to survive. Clashes and collaboration around agricultural production directly affect the course of territorialisation and result in the affirmation of certain types of territorialities. As defined by Sack (1986), territoriality is a strategy used by groups and public agencies to exercise power over a portion of space in order to maintain control and systematise activities and services. The territorialisation of agribusi-ness also takes place at the intersection between regional development and state regulation, with interpersonal relations at the scale of farms and locations. A territory is ultimately a political technology that comprises techniques for measuring land, controlling the terrain and promoting socioeconomic agendas (Elden, 2010).[5] Any apparently stable territory is nothing more than a temporary 'territorial fix', and its existence depends on it being accepted internally and externally. In this process, we can find several different types of territories in Mato Grosso.

First, and most notorious, there are the *explicit territories of agribusiness*, containing the large plantation farms that dominate the landscape with the colour of a single crop, most commonly soybean, followed by maize or sorghum cultivated during the remaining rainy season and the dry period (the second crop is called the 'little harvest' [*safrinha*]). The infrastructure of these farms (Figure 5.8), in most cases, includes a large warehouse for machinery and chemical inputs, crop processing plants (to clean and dry grains after harvest), dormitories and refectories for the seasonal workforce and houses for the permanent employees (who normally live on the farm with their families), a house for the farmer (farmers typically live in the cities and only sporadically stay on their farms overnight; it is rare for them to bring their families to the property) and an office for administration. Wealthier farms will have additional buildings such as a small garage, water storage, some animal-production facilities and recreational structures. The fields of production are at various distances from the farm headquarters and will be divided according to machinery and crop rotation needs. In the main production areas, such as the Teles Pires River Basin, the land is typically flat and includes easily mechanisable latosols, which facilitate the use

Figure 5.8 Image of an agribusiness farm in Sorriso
Source: Author

of heavy tractors, self-propelled sprayers and harvest machines. The result is a landscape with vast, continuous production fields occasionally interrupted by the remnants of the original vegetation along the watercourses, in depressions or on hilltops.

A second main category encompasses the *urbanised territories of agribusiness* – that is, the towns and cities of the agricultural frontier that typically developed from the original settlements or the initial nucleuses of private or public colonisation projects. The main cities started as planned towns (the urban nuclei of the colonisation project, which did not anticipate the formation of growing peripheries), and around these, smaller, spontaneous and unplanned towns, with more limited services and mainly a residential function, proliferated. All these settlements are major sites of social activity and capital circulation, and their structure and function depend on development trends and on the cultural composition of the social groups involved. Such towns are described by Elias (2007) as 'agribusiness municipalities', with high levels of urbanisation and a range of specialised services to meet the demands of modern agriculture (including logistics and financial services), but also with significant contrasts between the wealthy centres and growing urban peripheries, home to low-paid workers and the unemployed. Urban planning and urban reproduction in the Teles Pires have been clearly dominated by the interests of large-scale farmers and agribusiness companies, who have been able to influence policy and regulation in order to serve their infrastructure needs and facilitate real-estate speculation (Volochko, 2015). More recently, some municipalities have even been created as a result of the intervention of agribusiness companies, as in the case of Sapezal, officially recognised in 1994, which was a project of the Maggi Group.

These 'agro-towns' operate not only to control agribusiness production but as *loci* for the reproduction of agribusiness society in terms of labour force management, promotion of consumption patterns, banking and financing, etc. (Arruda, 2009). They have attracted and continue to attract two main types of migrant – namely, the professional agents of agribusiness who are well paid and take a direct part in industry activity (such as agronomists, managers, commercial representatives, etc.), and those who travel around in Brazil in search of better economic opportunities and are driven basically by poverty and desperation. This fundamental inequality helps to shape and perpetuate a landscape of urban cleavage and fragmentation. Likewise, farmland rent in the region is directly influenced by urban land rent, in the sense that successful cities increase the value of the surrounding farms. These urban areas nurture pockets of wealth and ostensible affluence that stand amid vast zones of deprivation, overcrowding, pollution and multiple forms of violence in the periphery. Relatively successful indicators, like HDI and GDP per capita, which are regularly praised by the representatives of agribusiness, hide the major inequalities, the housing deficit and the shortage of public services. Local food supply to these towns is declining in importance, and there is a growing reliance on the large supermarkets (Desconsi, 2011), especially in municipalities with intense soybean production, which now import more than 90 per cent of the fruit, vegetables, rice, beans and cassava consumed locally (Schlesinger, 2013). This creates an obvious and uncomfortable paradox whereby large-scale farms produce enormous quantities of grain, but almost no staple food for the regional population.

A third spatial phenomenon in the region are the self-evident and highly conspicuous *hyper-agribusiness territories*, which are structures built for the operation of national and international corporations (Figure 5.9). These units of hyper-agribusiness can be located either in the countryside (along roads and motorways) or on strategic sites in urban areas. This is an increasingly influential territory dominated by large-scale silos and warehouses, side by side with administrative buildings, security facilities and car parks. The affluent and well-designed operational units of the TCNs and associated agro-industries are located at strategic points along the main roads or in key production areas. It is easy to notice these units from a long distance because of the heavy lorries waiting to be served and the groups of drivers chatting or cooking. It is also possible to see small restaurants, bars or tyre shops nearby, aiming to profit from the movement of people and freight. Although normally owned by national business groups (unlike the grain processing plants of the TNCs), large or small abattoirs also employ a significant number of people and attract equivalent movement.

Fourth, there is *the leftover territory* of agribusiness – that is, the other types of rural properties that coexist, either competing or interacting with the core plantation farms. In 2006, the year of the last rural census for which data are

Figure 5.9 Grain processing unit along BR-163 in Lucas do Rio Verde
Source: Author

available, Mato Grosso had 86,167 small-scale farming units, comprising both independent properties and those in agrarian reform projects. Small-scale farming typically involves members of the farmer's family and paid occasional workers. According to the classification used by the federal government, small-scale farming includes properties of up to four regional modules; in the case of Mato Grosso, the module area varies between 30 and 100 hectares. These are farmers who use their land mainly for subsistence, have limited technical assistance and rarely access bank credit because of the difficulty of regularising property documentation. Another type of leftover territory is the vast area occupied by the extensive traditional ranches that historically characterised most of Mato Grosso's agriculture. These are relatively unproductive farms, often dedicated to low-yield cattle raising and a few other low-intensity activities (they sometimes let part of their land to agribusiness farmers). Such extensive properties may be located in more hilly areas, where mechanisation is difficult, or may be situated in core agribusiness areas but waiting for the land price to increase. It should be noted that because the definition of agribusiness in Brazil is so fluid, the difference between unproductive latifundia and agribusiness farms is not clear-cut.

Fifth, there is the *territory of what was there before* – that is, the areas beyond agribusiness (or more-than-agribusiness). These are tracts of the landscape where fragments of the original ecosystems remain – either savannah or forests – normally located in parks, private conservation units or indigenous reservations. Far from any claims to be pristine, it is often the case that such territories are already partially or greatly affected by the construction of roads that cross parks and indigenous reserves, as well as a growing number of hydropower schemes. When compared with the other Amazonian states, Mato Grosso has fewer conservation units and parks, which further demonstrates the power of agribusiness and pressures exerted by the sector on public authorities. The situation is different regarding indigenous reservations, especially because of the vast Xingu National Park, which was established in 1961 (before the agribusiness boom) and is directly associated with the achievements of the Roncador–Xingu Expedition, part of the March towards the West (see Chapter 3). But even the Xingu is increasingly under pressure from agribusiness and the range of transformations associated with urbanisation and road construction. Cases of conflict, abuse and serious violence (including homicides and suicides) are frequent, especially in areas where indigenous land is suitable for agribusiness production.

The hegemony of agribusiness pervades these five schematic territorial units and reinforces a spatial order according to the priorities and symbolism of plantation farms and related economic activities. As argued by Wainwright (2005), hegemony, in the Gramscian sense, is profoundly geographical, as it is constituted on the basis of spatial relations, and such relations become hegemonic as geographies are naturalised as common sense through political and cultural practices. This is epitomised in the idealised figure of the *'gaúcho'*, a term used to refer to natives of the southern state of Rio Grande do Sul, the most well-known group of immigrants to the Teles Pires. Curiously, in Mato Grosso, the meaning of the expression *gaúcho* was extended so that it is now also used to designate those born in the states of Paraná and Santa Catarina (often themselves descendants of individuals from Rio Grande do Sul who moved to the neighbouring states). *Gaúcho* identity is extremely fluid, given that the word was originally used to refer to groups of mestizos involved in the capture and management of cattle in the pampas (as the twin term *gaucho* is normally used in Argentina and Uruguay). Gradually, in Brazil the word became synonymous with anyone who was born in Rio Grande do Sul, including the large urban majority and also small-scale farmers with no connection to cattle ranching. Settlers who migrated from Germany (who arrived in Rio Grande do Sul from 1824 onwards) and Italy (from 1875) in particular formed important contingents of small-scale farmers normally called *colonos* (because they each received a small plot of land, between 24 and 48 hectares, called a *colônia de terra*), whose descendants are now described, and describe themselves, as *gaúchos*.

In just a few generations, the large families of *colonos* (typically with more than ten children) ran out of land, and in the first decades of the 20th century many had to move to other parts of Rio Grande do Sul, described as the new *colônias*, or to Paraná and Santa Catarina. The same processes then happened again, with land becoming increasingly scarce due to the advance of agribusiness and mechanisation from the 1950s onwards. In the early 1970s, land-related conflicts involving impoverished small-scale farmers or landless peasants were serious questions and threatened the legitimacy of the ruling military government. One of the alternatives found by the technocracy was to incorporate these groups into the overall process of the agribusiness frontier in Mato Grosso and other parts of the Amazon region. Curiously, if in the original state of Rio Grande do Sul these small-scale farmers were casually called 'German' [*alemão*] or 'Italian' [*italiano* or *gringo*], in Mato Grosso they all became *gaúchos* and were automatically associated with a socio-cultural infrastructure that was largely foreign to them, but connected with the large-scale cattle ranches of the border region between Rio Grande do Sul, Uruguay and Argentina. The image of the *gaúcho*, which traditionally corresponded to a sort of modern centaur (because of their famous equestrian abilities), served to reshape the identity of small-scale farmers who arrived in Mato Grosso from minifundium areas where cattle have never been raised on a large scale. The irony is that, as a form of alter-ego, the descendants of German and Italian migrants unintentionally adopted in Mato Grosso the symbolism of the original *gaúcho* ranchers, who always assumed a position of superiority and aggressive discrimination against the poor German and Italian families who migrated to Rio Grande do Sul.[6]

The saddest part of this story is that the 'new *gaúchos*' have merged the apparent success of agribusiness, and the fact that now they own much more land, with the arrogance of the 'old *gaúchos*' (i.e. the original cattle ranchers) and many forms of discrimination against the lower income population in Mato Grosso, who are mainly non-white. The 'gauchification' of the landscape of agribusiness and its symbolic association with the supposed racial purity of those who moved from the south of Brazil operates as a disturbing mechanism of segregation that basically transfers the ideology of the frontier region of Brazil–Argentina–Uruguay to the

Figure 5.10 CTG (Gaúcho Tradition Centre) of Sorriso
Source: Author

new agribusiness frontiers of Mato Grosso (and beyond). In its celebration of a heroic past that never actually existed, the artificial and somehow ridiculous purity of *gaúcho* traditions is articulated against the non-white customs and socio-economic rights of those who migrated from the northeast, the original residents of Mato Grosso and even poorer *gaúchos* (who failed to share in the success of agribusiness and are, consequently, less *gaúcho* than the others). This all means that the rigid social hierarchy of the *gaúcho* society established in the 19th century in Rio Grande do Sul has been reconstructed to legitimise the organisation of agribusiness-based society in Mato Grosso, which theoretically provides an abundance of opportunities for all, but in fact makes these available to only a very few.

When thinking about the range of injustices and misunderstandings involved in this strange cultural metamorphosis, one is left with a difficult and troubling question: why did those who were so poor only one generation before, and consequently had to travel more than 2,000 km to secure a larger piece of land, so quickly adopt the unpleasant ideology of the *gaúcho* rancher and so easily absorb the rhetoric of agriculture-cum-agribusiness, neglecting their class origins and their family tradition as small-scale farmers? Is it a purely racial phenomenon, exacerbated by the social stratification that follows intensive agribusiness, or does it reveal otherwise hidden elements of Brazilian society that are brought to the fore at the frontier? These are thorny issues, and any explanation will have to deal with the unequal and anti-ecological basis of agribusiness activity, and with the darkest elements of the advance of modernity in the Amazon.

Conclusion: framing places, emplacing controversies

Due to the convergence of developmentalist policies and the attraction of large contingents of migrants, the northern section of Mato Grosso has become one of the important frontiers of agricultural expansion in recent decades. Instead of a gradual advance of private property and market transactions as in other areas of agricultural frontier, the national government planned and imposed the new places in the Teles Pires upon vast areas and easily mechanisable tablelands since the 1970s. The main conclusion that can be drawn from the specific historico–geographical experience is that it followed a very different trajectory to the humanistic and deeply ecological proposition put forward by Manoel de Barros for his motherland. The poet wished for an 'invention' of Mato Grosso, because it was a world apart, fraught with anachronisms and subject to spatial forces that isolated people into remote communities. Manoel's main intention was to reconfigure those places and realise human potentialities at the same time. But Manoel also warned about a rival pathway, which was qualitatively inferior and would produce a misleading reality based on lies and wrongdoing. From the empirical evidence available, there is plenty of material to infer that Manoel's stipulation was not observed. On the contrary, the geographical typology provided by Manoel – that is, the difference between invention (as something genuine and positive) and falsehood (as inauthentic and dubious) – helps us to realise that the new places in the Teles Pires have been framed through an accumulation of promises and frustrations, instead of the proper invention of the world. That happened through another crucial paradox (in a long sequence of perverse controversies discussed above): what was considered too simple a space was displaced and replaced with an even simpler space, which is only deceptively more sophisticated or more advanced.

Instead of a humanist, progressive invention of places (advocated by Manoel in order to overcome falsehood), place dynamics in the Teles Pires obeyed a distinctive spatial trajectory marked by displacement, replacement and, in the end, misplacement of economy and society. Table 5.1 contains a synthesis of each phase of place-making (manifested in the Teles Pires primarily as periods of the intense phenomenon of place-framing), its main impacts and consequences. What existed before had to be violently displaced through the firm hand of the state and the involvement of a large number of impoverished farmers from the south of Brazil (and also some business enterprises in search of the easy, subsidised government incentives). The region was opened up to public and private colonisation schemes and rent-seeking companies in an intense socio-spatial process boosted by the state through the construction of roads, airfields, storage facilities and the growing expansion of urban settlements. Soon after the

Table 5.1 Three schematic phases of place-making in the Teles Pires River Basin

Place-making period	Main direction of place-making	Fundamental characteristics	Impacts and consequences
1970s–1980s	Displacement	National security and development policies; influx of thousands of migrants to public and private colonisation schemes, as well as to isolated farms.	Violent transformation of socio-ecological features (ecosystems, resources, landscapes, communities, etc.); private appropriation of the commons.
1990s–2030s	Replacement	Macro-economic instabilities and dwindling financial support from the national state; technological change and 'soyfication' of farm production; market obstacles and infrastructure limitations.	Migration out of Mato Grosso and proletarianisation of most farmers (established in the previous phase); forced and turbulent adjustment to the new macro-economic situation and liberalising pressures; concentration of rural properties.
2000s +	Misplacement	Flexibilisation of market transactions and more direct insertion of the regional economy into globalised markets; more strategic and supportive role of the state.	More decisive influence of national and international corporations; further concentration of land and socioeconomic opportunities; increasing inequalities and socio-ecological impacts.

agricultural frontier was considered irreversible, there was an opportunity to accommodate the needs and aspirations of all those initially involved, which clearly reveals the entanglement between structure and agency-shaping new places. Although at first the aim was to occupy areas considered (or made) empty and cope with major structural deficiencies in the best way possible, since the 1980s the main driving force was to replace the promise of land for all and emphasise high-tech, efficient agribusiness production as the only way forward. Instead of making the world bigger, as Manoel wanted, place-framing in the region has been characterised by spatial compression through the accumulation of land and accelerated financialisation of production (particularly under the sphere of influence of multinational corporations and private banks). Another factor is the growing hegemony of globalised agri-food systems, which has further reduced the socioeconomy, agri-food production and interpersonal interactions to the narrow practices and distorted semiotics of agribusiness.

The Teles Pires River Basin now is not only a chain of numerous places that are profoundly interconnected, but the new places also reveal a great deal about tensions related to spatial change and are themselves geographical frontiers between the new spatiality of agribusiness and old, exclusionary practices. Beyond the apparent uniformity of crop fields and the homogeneity of plantation farms there are major social inequalities, the almost forgotten genocide suffered by indigenous groups and the risks of a socioeconomy reliant on almost a single activity (soybean production and export). Although the advocates of agribusiness make optimistic claims about the 'brave new places', they systematically pursue strategies that are inherently partial and leave most of the population and socionature behind. The places dominated by agribusiness in the area are undeniably based on a totalising spatial plan, systematically defended and reinforced by senior public authorities and sector representatives, which has unfortunately excluded many social groups and undermined alternative forms of production and livelihoods.

That leads us to a final observation (which has actually worldwide repercussions): there was nothing inevitable in the process of rural and regional development promoted in the Teles Pires, but at the same time, and considering the long tradition of violent territorial conquest and place-making in Brazil, the problems, conflicts and injustices that characterised its turbulent geographical trajectory were all, more or less, visible from the outset. In other words, very little could have been different in the Teles Pires, considering the bitter lessons from the Brazilian past and the brutal mechanisms of socio-spatial change (chiefly in the form of place-framing). At least a focus on place-based disputes and controversies, as we have carried out in the previous pages of this chapter, can help us to make sense of Mato Grosso's discriminatory and intolerant geography in the making.

Notes

1   The great Brazilian novelist Guimarães Rosa (2001: 139) reinforces the same feelings in a story that takes place in Mato Grosso: 'For us it served any direction, because the Pantanal is a world and each farm a centre.'

2   Information about the documentary can be seen at: www.sodez.com.br. The poet had
    an extremely reserved life and his work was only revealed to the wider public in recent
    decades when some well-known intellectuals started to praise the relevance of Manoel's
    poems.
3   The Zanini family fled Mato Grosso in 1977 and the dispute was only resolved by the
    courts in 2011.
4   With the inauguration of the Canoa Quebrada hydropower plant in 2007 (28 MW
    of capacity), the municipality of Lucas do Rio Verde is now a main agro-industrial
    centre in the region.
5   Interestingly, the word 'territory' (*território* in Portuguese) is widely used nowadays in
    Brazil by academics, activists and policy-makers, as it was possible to record in public
    meetings. The term seems to be particularly popular because it evokes the social and
    dynamic dimensions of spatial arrangements, and it has tended to be used in place of
    the more traditional 'region', 'valley' or 'location'. Nonetheless, the terminology is
    hardly clear, and words often have conflicting meanings.
6   The transfer of *gaúcho* culture to other social and ethnic groups was studied by Furtado
    (2010), who reiterated the conclusion of other authors that *gauchismo* is essentially
    an urban phenomenon, which began in the 1940s in the state capital Porto Alegre
    and aimed to restore and reinvent the rural values of a mystical, idealised past. The
    ideological celebration of the *gaúchos* as hard workers, modernisers and promoters of
    a higher civilisation mainly takes place in social clubs called CTGs (Gaúcho Tradition
    Centres, see Figure 5.10), where the (white) members of the landed elite perform dances
    in folk costume (such as *bombacha* trousers) and enjoy a type of music and cuisine that
    is supposedly authentic, although in effect the whole ritual was fabricated and refers
    only to an idealised version of rural practices. Furthermore, the alleged advantages of
    life on cattle ranches and the fictional image of harmony on the large estates conceal
    a reality of super-exploitation and profound inequalities between male landowners,
    their family members and the wider rural population.

References

Agnew, J.A. 1987. *Place and Politics*. Allen & Unwin: Boston, MA.
Agnew, J.A. 2011. Space and Place. In: *The SAGE Handbook of Geographical Knowledge*.
    Agnew, J.A. and Livingstone, D. (eds). SAGE Publications: London, pp. 316–331.
Amin, A. 2004. Regions Unbound: Towards a New Politics of Place. *Geografiska Annaler*,
    86, 33–44.
Arnauld de Sartre, X., Berdoulay, V. and Lopes, R.S. 2012. Eco-Frontier and Place-Making:
    The Unexpected Transformation of a Sustainable Settlement Project in the Amazon.
    Geopolitics, 17, 578–606.
Arruda, Z.A. 2009. Onde Está o Agro deste Negócio? Transformações Socioespaciais em
    Mato Grosso Decorrentes do Agronegócio. Unpublished Ph.D. thesis. UNICAMP:
    Campinas.
Ash, J. and Simpson, P. 2016. Geography and Post-phenomenology. *Progress in Human
    Geography*, 40(1), 48–66.
Barney, K. 2009. Laos and the Making of a 'Relational' Resource Frontier. *The Geographical
    Journal*, 175, 146–159.
Barros, M. 2010. *Encontros*. Organ. A. Müller. Beco do Azougue: Rio de Janeiro.
Barros, M. 2013. *Poesia Completa*. LeYa: São Paulo.
Brannstrom, C. and Neuman, M. 2009. Inventing the "Magic Valley" of South Texas,
    1905–1941. *Geographical Review*, 99, 123–145.

Carolino, J. 2010. The Social Productivity of Farming: A Case Study on Landscape as a Symbolic Resource for Place-making in Southern Alentejo, Portugal. *Landscape Research*, 35, 655–670.

Chouinard, V. 1990. State Formation and the Politics of Place: The Case of Community Legal Aid Clinics. *Political Geography Quarterly*, 9, 23–38.

Cleary, D. 1993. After the Frontier: Problems with Political Economy in the Modern Brazilian Amazon. *Journal of Latin American Studies*, 25(2), 331–349.

Cloke, P., Crang, P. and Goodwin, M. (eds). 2005. *Introducing Human Geographies*. 2nd edition. Routledge: London and New York.

Connor, T.K. 2012. The Frontier Revisited: Displacement, Land and Identity among Farm Labourers in the Sundays River Valley. *Journal of Contemporary African Studies*, 30(2), 289–311.

Cosgrove, D. 1998. *Social Formation and Symbolic Landscape*. University of Wisconsin Press: Madison, WI.

Cosgrove, D. and Jackson, P. 1987. New Directions in Cultural Geography. *Area*, 19, 95–101.

Costa Pinto, L.A. 1965. *Sociologia e Desenvolvimento*. Civilização Brasileira: Rio de Janeiro.

Cunha, J.M.P. 2006. Dinâmica Migratória e o Processo de Ocupação do Centro-Oeste Brasileiro: O Caso de Mato Grosso. *Revista Brasileira de Estudos de População*, 23, 87–107.

Darling, J. 2009. Thinking Beyond Place: The Responsibilities of a Relational Spatial Politics. *Geography Compass*, 3, 1938–1954.

Desconsi, C. 2011. *A Marcha dos 'Pequenos Proprietários Rurais': Trajetória de Migrantes do Sul do Brasil para o Mato Grosso*. E-Papers: Rio de Janeiro.

Dias, E.A. and Bortoncello, O. 2003. *Resgate Histórico do Município de Sorriso*. Cuiabá.

Dieguez, C. 2015. O Estouro da Boiada: Como o BNDES Ajudou a Transformar a Friboi na Maior Empresa de Carnes do Mundo. *Piauí*, 101, 16–24.

Dirlik, A. 1999. Place-based Imagination, *Review*, 22, 151–187.

Elden, S. 2010. Land, Terrain, Territory. *Progress in Human Geography*, 34(6), 799–817.

Elias, D. 2007. Agricultura e Produção de Espaços Urbanos não Metropolitanos: Notas Teórico-metodológicas. In: *Cidades Média: Espaços em Transição*, Sposito, M.E.B. (ed.). Expressão Popular: São Paulo, pp. 113–138.

Folha de São Paulo. 2009. Justiça de MT Decidirá Destino de Área que Vale mais de R$ 1 bi. Available at: www1.folha.uol.com.br/fsp/dinheiro/fi1209200918.htm (published 12 September 2012).

Frederico, S. 2011. As Cidades do Agronegócio na Fronteira Agrícola Moderna Brasileira. *Caderno Prudentino de Geografia*, 33, 5–23.

Furtado, P.J. 2010. Nova Mutum, MT: Colonização Particular, Migração Sulista e Cultura "Gaúcha". In: Barrozo, J.E. (ed.), *Mato Grosso: A (Re)Ocupação da Terra na Fronteira Amazônica (Século XX)*. EdUFMT: Cuiabá. pp. 170–197.

Guimarães Rosa, J. 2001 [1969]. *Estas Estórias*. 5th edition. Nova Fronteira: Rio de Janeiro.

Gutberlet, J. 1999. Rural Development and Social Exclusion: A Case Study of Sustainability and Distributive Issues in Brazil. *Australian Geographer*, 30(2), 221–237.

Harvey, D. 2001. *Spaces of Capital: Towards a Critical Geography*. Edinburgh University Press: Edinburgh.

Holanda, S.B. 1994. *Caminhos e Fronteiras*. Companhia das Letras: São Paulo.

IBGE. 2015. Database 'Cidades'. Available at: http://ibge.gov.br/cidadesat/xtras/home.php (accessed 1 November 2015).

Ingold, T. 2000. *The Perception of the Environment: Essays in Livelihood, Dwelling and Skill*. Routledge: London and New York.

Ioris, A.A.R. 2014. Environmental Governance at the Core of Statecraft: Unresolved Questions and Inbuilt Tensions. *Geography Compass*, 8(9), 641–652.

Ioris, A.A.R. 2015. Cracking the Nut of Agribusiness and Global Food Insecurity: In Search of a Critical Agenda of Research. *Geoforum*, 63, 1–4.

Ioris, A.A.R. 2016. The Politico-ecological Economy of Neoliberal Agribusiness: Displacement, Financialisation and Mystification. *Area*, 48(1), 84–91.

Ioris, A.A.R. 2017. Encroachment and Entrenchment of Agro-neoliberalism in the Centre-West of Brazil. *Journal of Rural Studies*, 51, 15–27.

Jepson, W. 2006. Private Agricultural Colonization on a Brazilian Frontier, 1970–1980. *Journal of Historical Geography*, 32, 839–863.

Johnston, R.J. 1986. *Philosophy and Human Geography: An Introduction to Contemporary Approaches*. Edward Arnold: Baltimore, MD.

Malpas, J. (ed.). 2011. *The Place of Landscape: Concepts, Contexts, Studies*. MIT Press: Cambridge, MA.

Martin, D.G. 2003. "Place-Framing" as Place-Making: Constituting a Neighborhood for Organizing and Activism. *Annals of the Association of American Geographers*, 93, 730–750.

Martins, J.S. 2012. *A Sociedade Vista do Abismo*. Vozes: Petrópolis.

Marx, K. 1976 [1867]. *Capital: A Critique of Political Economy*. Vol. 1. Trans. B. Fowkes. Penguin: London.

Massey, D. 1993. Power Geometry and a Progressive Sense of Place. In: *Mapping the Futures*, Bird, J., Curtis, B., Putnam, T., Robertson, G. and Tickner L. (eds). Routledge: London, pp. 59–69.

Massey, D. 1994. *Space, Place, Gender*. Polity Press: Cambridge.

Mattei, L. 1998. *A Evolução do Emprego Agrícola no Brasil*. Abet: São Paulo.

May, J. 1996. Globalization and Politics of Place. *Transactions of the Institute of British Geographers*, 21, 194–215.

Merrifield, A. 1993. Place and Space: A Lefebvrian Reconciliation. *Transactions of the Institute of British Geographers*, 18, 516–531.

Oliveira, A.U. 2005. BR-163 Cuiabá-Santarém: Geopolítica, Grilagem, Violência e Mundialização. In: *Amazônia Revelada: Os Descaminhos ao Longo da BR-163*, Torres, M. (ed.). CNPq: Brasília, pp. 67–183.

Pierce, J., Martin, D.G. and Murphy, J.T. 2011. Relational Place-making: The Networked Politics of Place. *Transactions of the Institute of British Geographers*, 36, 54–70.

Pipino, E. 1982. Não há 'Inferno Verde' (interview by O. Ribeiro). *Contato*, 33, 3–6.

Pocock, D.C.D. (ed.).1981. Humanistic Geography and Literature: Essays on the Experience of Place. Croom Helm: London.

Prout, S. and Howitt, R. 2009. Frontier Imaginings and Subversive Indigenous Spatialities. *Journal of Rural Studies*, 25, 396–403.

Rausch, L. 2014. Convergent Agrarian Frontiers in the Settlement of Mato Grosso, Brazil. *Historical Geography*, 42, 276–297.

Rempel, E.T. 2014. *Políticas Públicas Ambientais e seus Nexos com a Educação: Um Estudo no Município de Sinop-MT*. EdUFMT: Cuiabá.

Sack, R.D. 1986. *Human Territoriality: Its Theory and History*. Cambridge University Press: Cambridge.

Santos, J.V.T. 1993. *Matuchos: Exclusão e Luta*. Vozes: Petrópolis.

Santos, L.E.F. 2011. *Raízes da História de Sinop*. Arte Design: Sinop.

Schlesinger, S. 2013. *Dois Casos Sérios em Mato Grosso: A Soja em Lucas do Rio Verde e a Cana-de-açúcar em Barra do Bugres*. FORMAD: Cuiabá.

Schutz, A. 1972. *The Phenomenology of the Social World.* Northwestern University Press: Evanston, IL.

Souza, E.A. 2006. *Sinop: História, Imagens e Relatos.* EdUFMT/FAPEMAT: Cuiabá.

Souza, E.A. 2013. *O Poder na Fronteira: Hegemonia, Conflitos e Cultura no Norte de Mato Grosso.* EdUFMT: Cuiabá.

Squire, S.J. 1996. Landscapes, Places and Geographic Spaces: Texts of Beatrix Potter as Cultural Communication. *GeoJournal,* 38, 75–86.

Swyngedouw, E.A. 1999. Marxism and Historical-geographical Materialism: A Spectre is Haunting Geography. *Scottish Geographical Journal,* 115, 91–102.

Thrift, N. 1983. Literature, the Production of Culture and the Politics of Place. *Antipode,* 15, 12–24.

Thypin-Bermeo, S. and Goodfrey, B.J. 2012. Envisioning Amazonian Frontiers: Place-Making in a Brazilian Boomtown. *Journal of Cultural Geography,* 29, 215–238.

Tuan, Y-F. 1976. Humanistic Geography. *Annals of the Association of American Geographers,* 66, 266–276.

Volochko, D. 2015. Terra, Poder e Capital em Nova Mutum-MT: Elementos para o Debate da Produção do Espaço nas 'Cidades do Agronegócio'. *GEOgraphia (UFF),* 17, 40–67.

Wainwright, J. 2005. The Geographies of Political Ecology. *Environment and Planning A,* 37, 1033–1043.

Wilkinson, J. 2009. The Globalization of Agribusiness and Developing World Food Systems. *Monthly Review,* 61(4).

Wittman, H. 2005. Agrarian Reform and the Production of Locality: Resettlement and Community Building in Mato Grosso, Brazil. *Revista NERA,* 7, 94–111.

Woods, M. 2007. Engaging the Global Countryside: Globalization, Hybridity and the Reconstitution of Rural Place. *Progress in Human Geography,* 31, 485–507.

6 Poverty in rich Amazonian ecosystems
The poverty-making geography of development

The expansion of agribusiness in the Amazon seems to accomplish the old plan to conquer territorial resources since the 16th century and the more recent attempt by the military to occupy and colonise the region. The new frontiers are not only spatial, but also genetic and ecological, given the growing interest in biodiversity and in the socio-ecological features of the regional ecosystems. This chapter goes beyond the existing areas of agribusiness production in the Teles Pires (in the upper Tapajós River Basin) and explores the situation in the rest of the Amazon, particularly in the lower Tapajós River Basin, in the state of Pará, to the north of Mato Grosso, where there is growing interest in soybean production and also where significant investments in river navigation infrastructure were made by official agencies in collaboration with powerful TNCs (Ioris, 2015). According to the company's media releases (Cargill, 2012), the port terminal of Cargill in Santarém was built in 2003, can store 60,000 metric tons and handle about 1.2 million metric tons of grains per year (nearly 95 per cent of the grain arrives in barges from the neighbouring state of Mato Grosso and about 5 per cent already comes from farmers in the west of Pará). See Figures 6.1 and 6.2. In this context of expanding agro-neoliberalism, decisive influence of TNCs and growing soybean production, the intention here is to examine the controversial meanings of poverty and development with a focus on the politico-ecological basis of modernity promises and persistent socioeconomic inequalities. The main aim is to expand our understanding of the meaning and consequences of a poverty-making economy at the borders of an aggressive phenomenon of economic growth. This critical discussion is important because, as pointed out by Santos (2014: viii), there is no global justice without global cognitive justice (as much as 'there is no way of knowing the world better than by anticipating a better world').

Few regions in the world have given rise to so much politico-ecological controversy and have been associated with such high levels of uncertainty as the Amazon. Since the time of Francisco de Orellana (c. 1511–1546), and his epic search for El Dorado, the Amazon has been known for an 'extravagant' geography, immense challenges and, potentially, even greater rewards. The region was considered the archetypical representation of the Garden of Eden by renaissance chroniclers and generations of explorers (Holanda, 2000). Yet, after the economic

Figure 6.1 River grain terminal in Santarém
Source: Author

boom because of a highly profitable rubber production at the turn of the 20th century, there was an inescapable reversal to subsistence agriculture and barter economy (Bunker, 1985). A few decades later, in the post-Second World War period, the Amazon became one of the most disputed frontiers of Western modernity, a process that engulfed, but also re-created, territories, relationships and peoples. Particularly in its Brazilian section – which comprises around 67 per cent of the Amazon – new development-related initiatives were put into effect by the military dictatorship and resulted in an increasing conversion of catchments and localities into hotspots of intense commodity production. The promise of rapid enrichment, often combined with cultural estrangement and sheer fascination, provided once again the rationale for violent conquest, eviction of existing communities and the expropriation of land, resources and livelihoods. Hegemonic relations of production and reproduction deliberately disregarded ecological limits and aggressively incorporate nature into the logic of commodity production exactly because of the money to be made from the privatisation of collective ecosystems and territorial resources (Ioris, 2007). Far from being politically neutral, the product of such changes has been primarily accumulated in the hands of a coalition between traditional elites and emerging business sectors that is endorsed by local and national public authorities. Development is

Figure 6.2 Detail of the loading structure of Santarém's river terminal
Source: Author

justified by the need to overcome poverty, but in the end it reproduces and per-petuates poverty.

Instead of the mere absence of material means, empirical results will show below that poverty is a relational phenomenon that arises from the selectiveness of productive activities and socioeconomic opportunities. Persistent levels of poverty and new structural inequalities are nothing else but the mirror image of development based on short-term gains, lasting negative impacts and commodi-fication of nature. More importantly, poverty constitutes an integral feature of socio-ecological (or socionatural) interactions (after Castree, 2002) which are deeply politicised and encapsulate class-based differences and the balance of power. The interactions between society and (the rest of) socionature bring the imprint of old and new forms of injustice, which are central driving-forces in the constant reshaping, and contestation, of space. For instance, governmental instruments (such as credit, subsidies and the granting of private property) and infrastructure investments (in the form of roads, ports and warehouses) attracted different contingents of people to the Amazon, who have only marginally benefited from the process of development. At the same time, Amazonian biodiversity has been filled with inequalities and asymmetries spreading from local to regional and even international scales of socio-ecological exchange. The reality is that capital, as a dominant social relation, encroaches upon the Amazon to retransform the landscape, generates serious social and environmental impacts, and creates new signifiers according to its own priorities. It doesn't matter if the forested land is crucial for the survival of people and ecosystems, because land (i.e. nature), as capital can be exploited and increased 'just as much as all the other instruments of production.' . . . The tragedy derives from the fact that *'[l]and as capital is no more eternal than any other capital'* (Marx, 1956: 185; emphasis added).

The existence and persistence of poverty is one of the most disturbing contradictions of emerging markets and regions experiencing fast economic growth. Sustained rates of economic development – for example, by the BRICS countries in the last decade – have not been enough to guarantee the amelioration of the living conditions of a large proportion of the low-income population (Gaiha *et al.*, 2012; Goldstein, 2013; Power, 2012). Particularly in a situation of uneven access to resources, rigid social institutions and a highly asymmetric balance of power, the process of development leaves some groups, often the majority of the inhabitants, clearly behind those who are in control of the economy and the apparatus of the state. The problem is even more serious when development is achieved at the expense of the ecological systems that directly support most poor families, as in the case of the recent experience in the Amazon region (Guedes *et al.*, 2012). Livelihoods, forest ecosystems and group identities are all under threat from the consequences of mainstream development and alterations happening at local and regional scales (Bicalho and Hoefle, 2010; Gomes *et al.*, 2012; Hecht, 2011). Development policies have demanded an intensified exploitation of minerals, timber, water, biodiversity, etc., as well as the expansion of plantation farms and the construction of gigantic dams (Diversi, 2014). In particular, the agribusiness sector has converted vast tracts of the Amazon into cattle ranches, soybean farms and sprawling agro-industrial towns, whereas most of the regional population have benefited little from the belated insertion of the Amazon in national and international development agendas (Weinhold *et al.*, 2013).

Despite the multifaceted complexity of poverty and the politicised basis of socio-ecological change, most poverty alleviation schemes today are still based on a normative perspective (Mawdsley, 2007) anchored on the imperative of economic growth (Peck, 2011) and on the need for stable government arrangements (Ferguson, 2007; see also *The Economist*, 2013). Poverty conditions which do not conform to pre-established policy headings tend to be overlooked and subsequently removed from policy networks. This enables politicians and project managers to systematically deny that the prevailing model of development is itself responsible for hardship and destitution, and for the corrosion of existing socioeconomic relations. However, poverty – defined as a condition of unsatisfied material and socio-political needs caused by combined mechanisms of exploitation, alienation and exclusion – cannot be seen as merely the result of bad production practices or the failure of deprived groups to join the process of development (as typically described in official documents and mainstream interpretations). On the contrary, poverty is development-induced scarcity (Yapa, 1993) that is experienced by deprived groups in spatial and socio-ecological terms (Gordillo, 2004). It arises from the selective dismissal of some practices and the emphasis on other economic activities and opportunities situated in specific time and space settings (Lawson *et al.*, 2010). Therefore, it is possible to talk about a poverty-making geography in which the production of space carries on the inequalities and injustices related to the capitalist process of development. In that regard, Marx (1973: 604) argues that only 'in the mode of production based on capital does pauperism appear as the result of labour itself, of the development of the produce force of labour'. In the specific circumstances of the Amazon, poverty has been an integral component of the economic transformation initiated in the latter half of the last century designed for the exploration of territorial resources and the intensified export of goods and commodities. The implementation of national development policies by successive administrations, supported by multilateral agencies and foreign governments, attracted social groups from different regions, who together with those already living in the region have only marginally benefited from economic growth and modernisation.

A related aim of the present chapter is to revisit the conventional blame on economic deficiencies or the inadequacy of existing governance approaches in order to offer a critical interpretation of the complexity of the phenomenon of poverty amid rich ecosystems and abundant natural resources. Making use of case studies carried out in impoverished areas of the eastern Amazon and the experience of several local communities, the discussion will question the wider process of regional development, social welfare and environmental policy-making. The starting point is to understand the Amazon River Basin as a vast territory that is simultaneously social and natural – that is, inherently socionatural. The region is the product of multiple trajectories of both 'society' and 'nature' co-evolving together in permanent interrelation and in constant transformation (it is worth mentioning, for example, the ancestral practice of lagoon construction by indigenous groups to regulate the flow and flooding of Amazonian rivers). These are deeply contested relationships, in which the interactions between society and (the rest of) socionature bring the imprint of old and new forms of injustice and reshape landscapes according to the balance of political power. Poverty and affluence are metabolised through the appropriation and change of forest ecosystems and of also the regional space. Before moving to the examination of the empirical results and main findings of the research, the following section will first describe the study areas and the methodological and interpretative approaches employed specifically for this chapter.

Study areas, methodological and analytical approach

The current examination of the causes and reactions to poverty is based on qualitative geographical research conducted between 2010 and 2011 in the state of Pará (around the city of Santarém), which is at the frontier of regional development and has a tense history of deforestation, population migration and multiple forms of conflict. Land disputes, violence and scarcity result from power struggles over the region's abundant resources (Simmons, 2004). Socio-ecological tensions have been particularly relevant in relation to activities such as agribusiness production, cattle ranching, dam construction and rapid urban growth. As in other parts of Brazil, poverty has declined in Pará in recent years due to national economic expansion and, crucially, compensatory cash transfer mechanisms introduced by the federal government (IPEA, 2010). However, peasants and small farmers have benefited comparatively much less from the overall process of development (Steward, 2007). In order to reduce absolute poverty (i.e. per capita income of less than one half of minimum legal salary) and eradicate extreme poverty (i.e. less than one quarter), Pará would have to reduce poverty by 2.2 per centper year between 2009 and 2016 (IPEA, 2010). Likewise, official statistics show a decline in poverty in Santarém from 59.50 per cent (in 1991) to 31.07 per cent (in 2010), but inequality (in terms of the Gini coefficient) increased in the same period (PNUD, 2013).

The investigation that underpins this chapter combined various sources of data and complementary research strategies to allow the reinterpretation of poverty from a political economy and, more specifically, a political ecology perspective. It involved the systematic examination of the interconnections between the condition of socionatural systems and the everyday experiences of hardship, collaboration and resistance by the communities under study. The study followed a participatory action research approach – that is, using collaborative and engaged research oriented towards social change (Kindon *et al.*, 2010). Research methods included 64 semi-structured interviews conducted between October and December 2010, participant observation and a regional workshops (attended by academics, civil servants, development officers, community representatives and NGO activists). It particularly entailed sustained interaction with residents in the extractive reserve (RESEX) near Santarém (this is a type of conservation unit where subsistence and extractive practices are allowed and encouraged; the RESEX was established after persistent political campaigning and contains more than 20,000 residents and 72 communities, of which around a third were visited during the research). Figure 6.3 shows one of those communities. Interview questions were organised under six main themes: life trajectory, understanding poverty, relationship with the forest, impact of government and anti-poverty programmes, political mobilisation and coping strategies. As well as qualitative data, regional and national statistics, secondary data and spatial information were considered to inform the understanding of the heterogeneity in the land-use patterns and in the adaptation capacity of farmers, peasants and forest dwellers.

A decisive element of the research was the commitment to give voice to forest-dependent poor in order to articulate their concerns over degradation and deforestation. Likewise, the project intended to bring together forest-dependent poor, policy-makers, NGOs and other social groups to jointly identify key issues pertaining to the case study areas. This inclusive approach was informed by a range of geographical and non-geographical reinterpretations of the complexity and the

Figure 6.3 Farming and extractive community along the Tapajós River
Source: Author

ramifications of poverty. Poverty-related issues are certainly highly heterogeneous and required an adequate treatment able to uncover the variegated practices, needs and experiences of disadvantaged people (Shubin, 2010) and material conditions had to be analysed according to specific spatial arrangements, cultural knowledge, skills and social values (Appadurai, 2002; Lin and Harris, 2010; Robinson and Oppenheim, 1998). Poverty was then reinterpreted in relation to the reciprocal relations among historical, ecological and social processes under the influence of new rounds of capital accumulation (after Lawson *et al.*, 2010). The research also called for new theoretical and methodological strategies able to embrace the human and the more-than-human dimensions of poverty, as well as the materiality and the symbolism of poverty. Nonetheless, as observed by Bakker (2010), the socionatural configuration of the world (including the human and the more-than-human dimensions of a unified, dynamic reality) is still difficult to handle with the frameworks normally used. In the present study, the response was to place the relationships between people, things and processes as central to the analysis. The research findings, examined next, derived from the application of this relational agenda. In the final part, the conclusions will be focused around the political reactions to poverty as a process that is also necessarily socio-ecological.

Development as hegemony over socionature

Development is a highly complex phenomenon that, particularly in such as huge region, cannot be interpreted in black or white terms, but one should be able to recognise specific advances and setbacks associated with the development as a lived geographical experience. Nonetheless, most academic examinations so far have been very insular and lacked a more thorough historico–geographical perspective of the process of development in the Amazon, especially failing to link the politics of economic growth with its myriad effects at different scales and across society and the rests of socionature (e.g. Barrett *et al.*, 2011; Minang and van Noordwijk, 2013; Vadez *et al.*, 2008). The importance of the multiple and complex relationships between society and the rest of socionature is often missed in these analyses of development. In other words, the process of development does not rely on the separate, discrete control of people and territorial resources, understood as individual or unconnected relationships. On the contrary, regional development in the Amazon has been promoted from a perspective of hegemony over the entirety of socionature (including the human and the more-than-human dimensions) and always with the purpose of commanding and containing socionatural change. The exercise of hegemony is considered here in the Gramscian sense, as a geographical project that transforms spatial divides from the standpoint of the stronger sectors of society (Kipfer, 2012). Socionatural hegemony is primarily achieved through ideological, discursive and material practices of the state and of strong socioeconomic groups, which lead to the appropriation and transformation of socionatural relationships according to their own priorities and interests.

It means that development in the Amazon is an intrinsically politico-ecological phenomenon that requires renewed forms of authority over multiscale socionatural interactions in a way that has allowed the imposition of rules and property relations across far-flung areas. Ever since the early days of European colonisation, the Amazon region has been connected to global markets through the joint appropriation of territorial resources (Ioris, 2007), the transformation of ecosystems (Aldrich *et al.*, 2012) and the violence exerted against indigenous inhabitants (Vadjunec *et al.*, 2009). Economic activity intensified significantly since the 1960s, when a series of national development programmes were adopted by the Brazilian military dictatorship as part of the reaction against social reforms (Hecht, 2005). The Amazon was then seen as an economic frontier and a suitable destination for poor peasants and landless farmers causing 'problems' elsewhere in the country (Kirby *et al.*, 2006). The intention was to replicate the technological, institutional and economic dimensions of the mainstream model of international development put forward in the post-Second World War decades (Peet and Hartwick, 2009). Even more than before, the accumulation of wealth in the recent past relied on the dissolution of cultural and ethnical identities, and the reduction of socio-ecological complexity to the sphere of market transactions. From being a remote land of exuberant biological formations that fascinated explorers for many centuries, the Amazon was brought to the centre of national and transnational development policies. And further integration of the region with the rest of the national economy has increasingly required and perpetuated the hegemonic control of socionatural systems.

Therefore, in contrast to the critique often raised by most NGOs and environmental groups, the Amazonian process of development is not inherently anti-ecological or against the forest (i.e. in the sense that it necessarily demands the destruction of forest ecosystems and the replacement with radically different landscapes). On the contrary, development directly depends on territorial resources and rich ecosystems, and it is the availability of land and labour that directly fuels the expectations of rapid capital accumulation by cattle ranchers, agribusiness, miners, loggers, construction companies, dam operators, etc. (Weinhold *et al.*, 2013). The most fundamental contradictions of development are not simply ecological, but entirely socionatural – that is, the process of development demands the double and simultaneous control and exploitation of the human and non-human dimensions of the Amazon region. The most important consequence is that poverty and socio-political exclusion is maintained by hegemonic socionatural practices. With the advance of development, Amazonian ecosystems are increasingly transformed according to new economic activities that mobilise resources and people for the accumulation and export of capital, despite socio-ecological tensions and poverty trends. The region is now firmly at the edge of the advance of Western modernity over new territories, peoples and ecosystems previously beyond the reach of mass markets. This process has renewed tensions related to the dispute for land between large and small farmers, as well as between peasants, farmers and Indian groups.

The same governments that introduce environmental legislation and establish nature reserves constantly formulate economic incentives and construct roads and infrastructure that lead to further land concentration and aggravate land conflicts (Simmons *et al.*, 2007). In that process, socionatural relations have been brutally altered (in material and symbolic terms) and the devastating impacts of development become evident – for example, in the growing erosion of communal practices and complex relationships with forest ecosystems. The perverse consequences of the political hegemony established over socionature became evident, for example, in discussions with residents of the extractive reserve in Pará during visits and workshops. The locals argued that their life improved after the establishment of the already mentioned RESEX, given that it reduced the pressure of neighbouring timber and mining companies. It means that, to some extent, in the space of the reserve the hegemony of development is temporarily contained and the locals have better opportunities to sustain meaningful socionatural relationships. However, as claimed by several residents, these recent victories seem increasingly secondary when considering the still strong and mounting pressures of the economic development agenda, which may affect the existence of the extractive reserve in the long term.

The exercise of hegemony, especially following external politico-economic priorities championed by the national states, is a highly contradictory process (Ioris, 2014). Because development is pursued from a hegemonic perspective of power and the pursuit of immediate results, it is fraught with socionatural contradictions that, inevitably, end up affecting the socionatural basis of economic growth. The conventional platform of development is commonly endorsed for the Amazon on the assumption that the region has almost inexhaustible territorial resources that can be easily converted into profits, taxes and prestige, while ignoring that scarcity and abundance are relative and highly contested terms in the Amazon (Schmink and Wood, 1992). The same process of development that creates a mirage of abundance is responsible for a sudden generation of scarcity, particularly through the seizure of large tracts of land by cattle ranchers and agribusiness farmers (Hecht, 2005). The result is the absurdity of a growing scarcity of water in recent years in the middle of the largest river basin in the world, as experienced by local residents:

> We need plenty of things here. Water, we need water. Because before [. . .] now in the summer, this thing with a very long, hot summer. Look where the water is, over there, almost over the other side.
> (Interview with a RESEX resident, female, retired)

Or the lack of wood in the largest rainforest:

> Today for us to use the wood, there isn't much. It's hard to find wood. Not much wood and what there is, is very green. They have taken the best part. So what I do is cut out a few fields, but not big ones. If you compare what they take out and what we do. And also I regret what happened further up the river. That timber merchant that cuts down so much wood. We see the ferries go pass.
> (Interview with a RESEX resident, male)

The contradictory exercise of hegemony over socionature for the purposes of development has influenced not only economic trends and the allocation of resources, but even affected contemporary environmental conservation policies aimed at mitigating the impacts of development activities such as cattle ranching, soybean production and mining. The official reaction to those problems comes in the form of regulatory controls and incentives that end up reinforcing anthropocentric world-views, as in the particular case of market-based solutions such as the payment for ecosystem services (PES), which is one of the main policy instruments advertised and offered to the Amazon population by the Brazilian government. In our discussions, it was evident that community leaders and NGO members are aware of the intention to adopt PES schemes as a central policy tool. PES is certainly a key concept of environmental management currently, especially because it seems to convey the idea that ecosystems are socially valuable and in ways that may not be immediately intuited (Daily, 1997). In the Amazon, PES has been increasingly advocated as an alternative to slash-and-burn agriculture by compensating farmers for including forest conservation that guarantees water provision, carbon sequestration and biodiversity (Ioris, 2010).

In theory, PES could provide the necessary bridge between the ecological and social dimensions of Latin American ecosystems (*The Economist*, 2014). In practice, however, this is an instrument that reproduces the dichotomy between nature and society promoted through Western economy, technology and planning (as analysed by Worster, 1994). The notion of ecosystem services entails a profound depoliticisation of both social demands (which are described as homogeneous across groups and automatically justified – that is, without considerations of the patterns of consumption and distribution of goods and services) and of ecological conservation (given that the impact on ecosystems, which reduces the provision of ecosystem services, is typically described as the result of human action in abstract, with no acknowledgement of asymmetric responsibilities).

PES implies an emphasis on the notion of 'services' supposedly provided to humans and, consequently, directly excludes the possibility of a more integrative, relational perspective (Boelens *et al.*, 2014). In other words, humans are portrayed at the receiving end of services available to satisfy socioeconomic needs. The adoption of PES schemes works through the denial of the socionatural ontology that is the product of long-term interactions between humans and non-humans. In practice, market-based responses are an adjunct of the private appropriation of the commons and of the expansion of development institutions over socionatural systems (Lansing, 2013). As a result, ecosystems are detached from their long process of socionatural evolution and become the static and passive providers of services. Attempt to impose environmental conservation strategies through the language of money, as in the case of PES, could only produce short-lived results and reinforce the same hegemony that produced socionatural degradation in the first place (Van Hecken and Bastiaensen, 2010). The commodification of such 'ecosystem services' is part of the new social order based on successive abstractions and is comparable to the capitalist transformation by which individual human labour becomes social labour (Robertson, 2012), whereas in actuality the poor rely on the local ecosystems not because of the supposed 'services' that they provide, but because ecosystems are part of their survival strategies. The everyday life in the Amazon involves the creation of a very complex set of relations, in which peoples actively reconstruct their identities and help to reshape the physical and political landscape throughout the region (Vadjunec *et al.*, 2009).

From the above, it is not difficult to recognise that the hegemonic process of development in the Amazon has favoured certain politico-economic goals and aimed to remove what is perceived by most politicians as obsolete, inadequate and out of place. Even inventive responses to mounting environmental degradation, as in the case of PES, normally operate within the same epistemic framework and rely on the control of socionatural relationships. From the perspective of those with the lion's share of regional development – mining and construction companies, and especially the agribusiness sector – the poor should associate themselves with an ongoing, already defined process of economic growth and modernisation (Pacheco, 2006). The demands of low-income groups, the request that ecosystems are preserved or restored, and pleas for more transparent and inclusive public administration are considered 'inconvenient' distractions to mainstream development plans (e.g. the discourse of Senator Kátia Abreu, President of the National Confederation of Agriculture and Livestock, in 2013). Furthermore, it is highly significant that the denial to the poor of any decisive role corresponds to the beleaguered place of forest ecosystems in regional development strategies. Development in the Amazon is, therefore, a politico-ecological project that happens through the imposition of a hegemonic rationality of economic growth and private accumulation over both society and the rest of socionature. This corresponds to the expected political passivity of the poor in the process of development as promoted around the world (Gray and Moseley, 2005), which is typically informed by Malthusian ideas about the rights and the treatment of the destitute (Empson, 2009). Because poverty is the most perennial materiality of development, any effort to alleviate poverty *through* development is inevitably undermined and ends up reinforcing the perverse situation of hegemony over socionature, as discussed next.

The materiality of development undermining the possibility of poverty alleviation

Because development is reliant on the perpetuation of hegemony over socio-natural relations, old and new government approaches to poverty reduction in Brazil have revealed a perennial incompatibility with the material, cultural and political demands of the wider sectors of the Amazon society and their unique socionatural condition. In a situation of fierce hegemony over socionature required for the purposes of regional development, poverty alleviation is promoted by government and multilateral programmes *in spite of* the forest and not considered *in relation to* forest ecosystems. There is in place a systematic attempt by develop-ment policy-makers and practitioners to rescue impoverished social groups and incorporate them – as subordinate players – in economic activities imposed from the outside on the Amazonian ecosystems. Most poverty alleviation approaches place the forest in a distant position from people, which is certainly not unrelated to the intentional depoliticisation of low-income groups vis-à-vis mainstream economic development goals. On the contrary, the ideological separation of local residents from their socionatural condition that characterised most public schemes is an integral part of the political intention to reinforce hegemony. From the perspective of public agencies, the best case scenario that the poor can hope for is a combination of government concessions and sub-ordinate participation in aggregate economic results. This operates in striking contrast to the largely communal and socionatural world-view of the locals (including elements of cross-generational benefits and responsibilities), for example:

> We are working here on a small project with plants so we can reforest the areas that have already been damaged. These are projects that start but don't have that support [from public agencies]. *Even the trees are the owners of the*

land, you know? So, the project starts and they say, look here are some plants, now get on with it. [. . .] They leave you on your own. So we have to get on with planting and looking after everything [. . .] *We know it's not so much for us, it's more the environment that will gain from this. But then other people will gain something from this, after we rebuild what man has destroyed. But until it has all come back, we won't be around anymore.* But we want to plant, to help out so that future generations when they come past here they can see that a lot of people at least.

(Interview with a RESEX resident, male; emphasis added)

Also, the following statement from someone living in a rural community in the Amazon indicates the paradox of poverty amid a situation of rich ecosystems and abundant resources and, in particular, the distance between the approaches taken by the public sector and grassroots demands:

Even in this poverty that we live in, the forest gives us lots of things. A lot of the riches that are there we can use. We can pick the fruit [. . .] but there is a problem with poverty, as they say, which is the government's plans. Our government doesn't look out for us, and these 'capitalists' don't help us. So that really affects us because we need a lot of things in our region because we suffer, but not because of the forest, more because of our health, education, which we need here. Because we need help in the area of health and education. If the government paid us more attention [. . .] we are not poor, we just have a low income. If the government paid more attention we could improve things. And get better in the future, because the government is really [. . .]

(Interview with a RESEX resident, female)

The incomprehensibility of the unique socionatural reality of the Amazon, and how it plays a fundamental role in the life of humans, was long ago demonstrated by the words of Cunha (2005: 4) when, after an official and historically important expedition to the borders between Bolivia, Peru and Brazil in 1909, claimed that 'man, there, is still an impertinent intruder'. In more recent decades, poverty is still seen by public offices and international agencies as something predetermined in advance and unconnected with the daily socionatural interactions with forest ecosystems. Official polices regularly ignore that human actions happen within ecosystems and are shaped by the accumulated interactions and past experiences between humans and non-humans. For instance, whereas subsistence farmers and forest dwellers are frequently led to clear land and explore the forest in order to survive (Coomes *et al.*, 2011), their socionatural condition and technological approaches are perceived as the simultaneous expression of the richness of the forest and the need to exert self-restraint, as evident in this statement:

Because you know we weren't born to eat that much game and fish. God didn't give it to us to eat it that much. [. . .] The poor don't get by [only] if they don't want to. But the forest gives them everything, and comforts them with its warm embrace.

(Interview with a RESEX resident, male)

The latter quotation makes direct reference to the socionatural configuration of the world, whose long-term existence depends, first of all, on a responsible and self-restrained interaction with socionature. In many interviews it was declared that, rather than any artificial uncoupling, humans and non-humans are co-constituted and constantly re-create each other through inter-reliant socionatural relationships. This means a rejection of the conventional split between nature and society in favour of a hybrid configuration of the world that considers it simultaneously natural and social. By contrast, policies aimed at promoting development through forest and land management have largely failed because of the ideological and procedural separation of the natural and social elements of socionatural systems. Even supposedly improved responses – such as the recommendations of UNEP (2003) that poverty reduction should happen through the sustainable management of ecosystems that is related to participative freedom, economic facilities, social opportunities, transparency and ecological security – remain largely embedded in the same ideological framework characterised by the passivity of socionature. That is evident when the discourse of sustainable forest management is hijacked by loggers, farmers and development agents to mould forestry governance and dictate how community-owned forest should be managed (Medina *et al.*, 2009).

The muddling of sustainable development policies pervades not only poverty-alleviation interventions, but also the formulation of legislation aimed at ecological conservation. At the time of this research, Brazil had a populist administration (under presidents Lula and Dilma, who governed the country between 2003 and 2016) that insisted on the importance of a sustainable development of the Amazon but paradoxically promoted a growing exploitation of resources and intensive agribusiness. The government endorsed the need to address poverty and promote development while at the same time preserving ecological systems. It was possible to observe during the fieldwork that those living in the forest try to develop multiple strategies to escape poverty, but this is also constantly undermined by their growing connection and dependency on urban markets in the regional towns and cities. An emblematic example of renewed hegemony undermining poverty alleviation is the Sustainable Amazon Plan (PAS in Portuguese) launched by the Brazilian government in 2008 with ambitious targets but suffering from the old vices of centralisation, populism and subordination to market rules (Souza and Filippi, 2010). Although the motto of the administration of President Dilma Rousseff since 2011 was *País Rico é País sem Pobreza* (A Rich Country is a Country without Poverty), the main reactions to poverty led by the Brazilian government are a series of short-lived mitigation schemes. Likewise, conditional cash transfer schemes (conditional because they require beneficiaries to fulfil specified conditions in order to continue receiving grants) were introduced in Brazil – called *Bolsa Família* – in order to help to alleviate poverty. The *Bolsa Família* programme entails a family allowance in the form of financial aid to poor families, provided that infants attend school and are vaccinated.

Another programme was launched in 2011 for those working in extractive activities in the Brazilian Amazon (called Green Stipend) and promises around US$150 per month per family. Initiatives such as these may help to momentarily address the depth of poverty (at least while the government can fund it), but are part of the new heterogeneity of the post-neoliberal era that combines liberalised economics, behavioural changes and bolder social interventions (Ballard, 2013). In the lower Tapajós River Basin, *Bolsa Família* certainly increased the purchase capacity of people who previously had no regular source of income. Even so, it was possible to detect a clear criticism of the financial dependency and subtle discrimination promoted by the same programme:

> Although I receive it [*Bolsa Família*], I am against this family benefit. I would like the government to create public policies that benefited us as small farmers. A credit that is de-bureaucratised!! So we can have access to this credit [. . .]. For example, you receive R$150 a month [US$70], but that is only really enough for the children's school materials. There are no other public policies in our favour.
>
> (Interview with a RESEX resident, female)

The main problem of most communities continues to be the question of land tenure that limits the ability of the poor to improve their activities and escape poverty. But the action of national governments strongly favours the establishment and reproduction of large estates and an export based economy (e.g. soybean production). The apparently positive experiences of rubber tappers in the Brazilian state of Acre and of other similar extractive industries (as the artisan production of many types of craft goods in the RESEX near Santarém) have suggested the existence of viable economic alternatives to the conventional pathway of deforestation and production. At the same time, however, these are usually small-scale solutions that produce only sporadic gains to the community:

> If people would come and buy our crafts [. . .] Or whatever we have to sell, because it's not just crafts, it is flour, tapioca [. . .]. It would be good if, from time to time, a group of tourists could come and buy things. Because sometimes they come just for leisure. Sometimes they ask questions about things here, sometimes they look around but they don't actually buy anything [. . .]
>
> (Interview with a RESEX resident, female)

However, the crucial problem with these localised and fragmented alternatives to the hegemonic process of development is that, on their own, they are unable to interrupt the overarching trend of poverty and marginalisation. These are certainly noteworthy initiatives informed by the discourse of sustainable development (enthusiastically supported by organisations and cooperatives in the Santarém) but have been largely valued by the customers for their exotic appearance and its connection with a vague desire for sustainability. For instance, the experience of several communities highlights the gap between the actual management of the forest by those living close to the forest and the agroforestry approach incentivised by the national government. In our discussions, many complained that agroforestry systems require significant capital and specialised technologies that are beyond the reach of subsistence farmers. Examples like this show the codification of inequality and poverty into the environmental change associated with the very process of development in the Amazon. Overall, poverty is not only inbuilt in the prevailing model of economic growth, but it represents the most persistent materiality of the hegemony over socionature that pervades development. In the end, public policies have played a key role in justifying the obstacles to address poverty inbuilt in the process of development. This combination of factors suggests that overcoming the imprint of poverty on ecosystem entails a fundamentally socio-ecological reaction from the local to the regional and national scales of political interaction, which will bring us to the concluding part of this analysis.

Socio-ecological reactions to poverty-making

The previous pages dealt with the peculiar, somehow paradoxical, situation of rich Amazonian ecosystems rife with poverty and under the pressure to develop rapidly and become more connected to other economic regions. The starting point was the recognition that poverty in the region is a situation of unfulfilled material and socio-political needs that directly derives from combined mechanisms of exploitation, alienation and exclusion associated with the perverse model of regional development. In order to unpack this complexity, fieldwork research was carried out in emblematic areas of the Brazilian Amazon and followed an innovative politico-ecological approach that emphasised the ontological interdependencies between the human and more-than-human dimensions of an integral reality. That proved to be an adequate entry point into a socionatural, and highly politicised, condition. The assessment of empirical results, informed by the academic and non-academic literature and making use of socioeconomic data, led to two main themes that represent main contributions to the academic literature. First, mainstream development has depended on the exercise of hegemony over the entirety of socionature (i.e. more than simply the exploitation of nature and the control of society, development requires coordinated socionatural transformations under the sphere of influence of politico-ecological hegemony). Second, while poverty is the most widespread and perennial materiality of development (i.e. the discernible mismatch between ephemeral economic gains and the lasting legacy of poverty due to socionatural degradation), the exercise of hegemony over socionature undermines the possibility of both poverty alleviation and environmental conservation. Those two fundamental, and synergistically connected, processes form the basis of a poverty-making geography that permeated the transformation of the Amazon region in recent decades.

While some government initiatives and international collaboration have brought positive results to individuals and communities, as a whole, investments and assistance programmes failed to produce the desired outcomes in terms of addressing poverty through the valorisation of the socionatural features of the Amazon. Efforts to alleviate poverty and sustain the forest are normally hampered by an overly simplistic representation of economic development and of the multiple scales across which drivers of poverty and environmental degradation operate. Likewise, approaches to forest management adopted under the canon of environmental governance have offered narrow, formalised solutions (e.g. payment for ecosystem services), which may be relevant to farmers and commercial land managers but are less relevant to the poor (Nebel *et al.*, 2005). Such programmes are also blighted by limited structure and coherence, so that the lack of cross-institutional communication, gaps in implementation and fragmented delivery aggravates deforestation and perpetuated poverty. The poor are systematically stereotyped and assumed to be culturally backward and incapable of escaping poverty on their own. Their socio-ecological knowledge is mistrusted and their rights to economic activity are constrained by the political-economic shaping of environmental management.

Yet, for those suffering the consequences of development, poverty is never a single phenomenon but reflects the corrosion of socionature and the manifestations of other shortages and deprivations (including lack of real democracy and scarce social opportunities). Instead of a mere material condition, poverty is closely related with alienation, as significantly stated in one interview, 'to be poor doesn't mean lack of money, but poor in the sense of, closing your eyes' (RESEX male resident). Different from the alleged passivity portrayed by official schemes and wider poverty alleviation policies, subaltern groups are able to perceive and rise up against the negative trends of development from within their socioecological condition, as famously happened in the 1980s with the *seringueiro* (rubber tapper) movement led by Chico Mendes. The daily struggles for survival and political representation help to produce a variegated social space in which the connections between the forest and local communities provide the basis of survival and group identity (Adams *et al.*, 2009). More importantly, rather than a reduction of the poor to a static condition of poverty, the everyday life in the Amazon involves a very complex set of relations that allow them to critically reflect and creatively resist through their close connection with forest ecosystems. Considering that the advance of development is the main source of socionatural transformation and that it has the imprint of poverty-making, the reaction needs to be positioned as a socio-ecological phenomenon in which the experience and the familiarity with the forest are of decisive assistance.

As argued by Santos (2010), the recognition that their knowledge and practices are socio-ecological is a crucial element of their political empowerment and opens new perspectives for justice and socioeconomic development. In many interviews, people specifically stated that the forest offers opportunities and provides for development, but that the help offered by the forest requires working, and working with, ecosystems. Beyond the rhetoric of development and mainstream poverty alleviation schemes, working the forest and with the forest are the main forms of getting by or escaping more acute conditions of deprivation. It is exactly the socionatural identification of the poor that presents the possibility of political autonomy and the interruption of the long trend of poverty. Instead of the easy, largely urban, discourse of environmentalists about protecting the forest, the alternative ethics of the poor are based on physical effort and appropriate knowledge. This form of grassroots environmental ethics is put into practice through the constant and almost daily reworking of the forest, in a perennial practice that incorporates the condition of poverty into socionatural relations:

> Well, I think that I was already born poor. They have already taken everything they could from me. The society has been built in this way for many years now. [. . .] I think that the forest is a companion to those who live in it. But that's not enough, the forest offers an important part of our life and the government offers nothing.
>
> (Interview with a RESEX resident, male)

Reworking the forest and with the forest – for example, producing subsistence food, artisanal artefacts and other objects that can be sold in local markets – constitute the most concrete alternative to the anti-commons trends of main-stream development. The impasse of development and poverty-making is only overcome with substantive solutions that can be found through a contextual, place-based approach to resources and social relations (Yapa, 1996). Through a persistent engagement with people living in and near the forest, this research project highlighted that forest communities in the Amazon cleverly associate the value of the forest with the value of their own labour, in a way that both spheres of value are inextricably linked. Their condition of poverty is the outcome of a powerful hegemony being applied simultaneously to both them and the forest (which exist as a unified socionatural category), but it does not diminish the value people attach to their community life. At the same time, it will never be possible to overcome poverty without confronting the hegemonic forces – in alliance with other groups in the region and elsewhere – that persistently undervalue the socionatural whole and accumulates capital from fragmented elements of socionature (e.g. mineral resources, timber, water storage and electricity generation, plantation farms, etc.). The mere preservation of socio-natural relationships will never be enough to escape poverty if the hidden hand of hegemony maintains its control over socionature for the purpose of an exclusionary development. On the contrary, the reduction of poverty in the rich ecosystems of the Amazon is necessarily a political project across different scales and social movements.

For the forest-dependent poor, their association with the Amazon ecosystems is in itself the main political answer to the perverse poverty-making geography. Significant tracts of the Amazon are now landscapes of impoverishment, large territories where deprived groups formally own or occupy pieces of land in order to practise subsistence or semi-commercial agriculture. In such impoverished areas, it is exactly the close connection with the forest (or what is left of it) that constitute a very important safeguard mechanism against famine and economic uncertainties. It should be remembered that, after the collapse of the rubber production promoted by Henry Ford in the lower Tapajós River Basin (known as the Fordlandia Estate, which had its operations closed in 1945) the poor were able to subsist due to their connections with the ecosystems as a form of residence to the crisis of capitalist activity in the Amazon after the Second World War (Grandin, 2010). The experience of local communities along rivers or roads, around the borders of large estates and in extractive reserves constitutes important, ingenious socionatural activity where viable alternatives to hegemonic and unjust development can emerge. The marginalisation is therefore relative and, for many forest-dependent communities, the best form of hope is to reaffirm their socionatural condition and establish strategic alliances across multiple scales. Their (multiple and legitimate) demands don't start from a state of hopeless destitution, but from a position of strength provided by their interaction with the forest and with other comparable groups in the Amazon region and in other parts of the planet.

References

Abreu, K. 2013. *Abram Alas para o Agro.* Available at: www1.folha.uol.com.br/fsp/mercado/94015-abram-alas-para-o-agro.shtml (published 16 February 2013).

Adams, C., Murrieta, R.S.S., Neves, W.A. and Harris, M. (eds). 2009. *Amazon Peasant Societies in a Changing Environment.* Springer: New York.

Aldrich, S., Walker, R., Simmons, C., Caldas, M. and Perz, S. 2012. Contentious Land Change in the Amazon's Arc of Deforestation. *Annals of the Association of American Geographers*, 102(1), 103–128.

Appadurai, A. 2002. Deep Democracy: Urban Governmentality and the Horizon of Politics. *Public Culture*, 14(1), 21–27.

Bakker, K. 2010. The Limits of 'Neoliberal Natures': Debating Green Neoliberalism. *Progress in Human Geography*, 34(6), 715–735.

Ballard, R. 2013. Geographies of Development II: Cash Transfers and the Reinvention of Development for the Poor. *Progress in Human Geography*, 37(6), 811–821.

Barrett, C.B., Travis, A.J. and Dasgupta, P. 2011. On Biodiversity Conservation and Poverty Traps. *Proceedings of the National Academy of Sciences of the United States of America*, 108(34), 13907–13912.

Bicalho, A.M.S.M. and Hoefle, S.W. 2010. Economic Development, Social Identity and Community Empowerment in the Central and Western Amazon. *Geographical Research*, 48(3), 281–296.

Boelens, R., Hoogesteger, J. and Rodriguez de Francisco, J.C. 2014. Commoditizing Water Territories: The Clash between Andean Water Rights Cultures and Payment for Environmental Services Policies. *Capitalism Nature Socialism*, 25(3), 84–102.

Bunker, S.G. 1985. *Underdeveloping the Amazon: Extraction, Unequal Exchange, and the Failure of the Modern State.* Chicago University Press: Chicago and London.

Cargill. 2012. Cargill's Santarém Port Terminal Gets Operating Permit. Available at: www.cargill.com/news/releases/2012/NA3065493.jsp (published 6 August 2012).

Castree, N. 2002. False Antitheses? Marxism, Nature and Actor-networks. *Antipode*, 34(1), 111–146.

Coomes, O.T., Takasaki, Y. and Rhemtulla, J.M. 2011. Land-use Poverty Traps Identified in Shifting Cultivation Systems Shape Long-term Tropical Forest Cover. *Proceedings of the National Academy of Sciences of the United States of America*, 108(34), 13925–13930.

Cunha, E.R.P. 2005 [1909]. *À Margem da História*. Academia Brasileira de Letras: Rio de Janeiro.

Daily, G. 1997. *Nature's Services: Societal Dependence on Natural Ecosystems*. Island Press: Washington, DC.

Diversi, M. 2014. Damming the Amazon: The Postcolonial March of the Wicked West. *Cultural Studies – Critical Methodologies*, 14(3), 242–246.

The Economist. 2013. Poverty, Geography and the Double Dilemma. Available at: www.economist.com/blogs/feastandfamine/2013/06/aid-agencies-future (published 1 June 2013).

The Economist. 2014. A Clearing in the Trees, edition no. 8901, 54–56 (published 23 August 2014).

Empson, M. 2009. *Marxism and Ecology: Capitalism, Socialism and the Future of the Planet*. SWP: London.

Ferguson, J. 2007. Formalities of Poverty: Thinking about Social Assistance in Neoliberal South Africa. *African Studies Review*, 50(2), 71–86.

Gaiha, R., Imai, K.S., Thapa, G. and Kang, W. 2012. Fiscal Stimulus, Agricultural Growth and Poverty in Asia. *World Economy*, 35(6), 713–739.

Goldstein, A. 2013. The Political Economy of Global Business: The Case of the BRICs. *Global Policy*, 4(2), 162–172.

Gomes, C.V.A., Vadjunec, J.M. and Perz, S.G. 2012. Rubber Tapper Identities: Political-economic Dynamics, Livelihood Shifts, and Environmental Implications in a Changing Amazon. *Geoforum*, 43(2), 260–271.

Gordillo, G.R. 2004. *Landscapes of Devil: Tensions of Place and Memory in the Argentinean Chaco*. Duke University Press: Durham, NC and London.

Grandin, G. 2010. *Fordlandia: The Rise and Fall of Henry Ford's Forgotten Jungle City*. Icon Books: London.

Gray, L.C. and Moseley, W.G. 2005. A Geographical Perspective on Poverty-environment Interactions. *Geographical Journal*, 171(1), 9–23.

Guedes, G.R., Brondízio, E.S., Barbieri, A.F., Anne, R., Penna-Firme, R. and D'Antona, A.O. 2012. Poverty and Inequality in the Rural Brazilian Amazon: A Multidimensional Approach. *Human Ecology*, 40(1), 41–57.

Hecht, S.B. 2005. Soybeans, Development and Conservation on the Amazon Frontier. *Development and Change*, 36(2), 375–404.

Hecht, S.B. 2011. The New Amazon Geographies: Insurgent Citizenship, "Amazon Nation" and the Politics of Environmentalisms. *Journal of Cultural Geography*, 28(1), 203–223.

Holanda, S.B. 2000. *Visão do Paraíso*. Brasiliense: São Paulo.

Ioris A.A.R. 2007. The Troubled Waters of Brazil: Nature Commodification and Social Exclusion. *Capitalism Nature Socialism*, 18(1), 28–50.

Ioris, A.A.R. 2010. The Political Nexus between Water and Economics in Brazil: A Critique of Recent Policy Reforms. *Review of Radical Political Economics*, 42(2), 231–250.

Ioris, A.A.R. 2014. *The Political Ecology of the State: The Basis and the Evolution of Environmental Statehood. Routledge Studies in Political Ecology*. Routledge: London.

Ioris, A.A.R. 2015. The Production of Poverty and the Poverty of Production in the Amazon: Reflections from those at the Sharp End of Development. *Capitalism Nature Socialism*, 26(4), 176–192.

IPEA (Institute for Applied Economic Research). 2010. Dimensão, Evolução e Projeção da Pobreza por Região e por Estado no Brasil. *Comunicados do Ipea* 58. Instituto de Pesquisa Econômica Aplicada: Brasília.

Kindon, S., Pain, R. and Kesby, M. (eds). 2010. *Participatory Action Research: Approaches and Methods*. Routledge: London and New York.

Kipfer, S. 2012. City, Country, Hegemony: Antonio Gramsci's Spatial Historicism in Gramsci: Space, Nature, Politics. In: *Gramsci: Space, Nature, Politics*, Ekers, M., Hart, G., Kipfer, S. and Loftus, A. (eds). Wiley: Chichester, pp. 83–103.

Kirby, K.R., Laurance, W.F., Albernaz, A.K., Schroth, G., Fearnside, P.M., Bergen, S., Venticinque, E.M. and da Costa, C. 2006. The Future of Deforestation in the Brazilian Amazon. *Futures*, 38(4), 432–453.

Lansing, D.M. 2013. Understanding Linkages between Ecosystem Service Payments, Forest Plantations, and Export Agriculture. *Geoforum*, 47, 103–112.

Lawson, V., Jarosz, L. and Bonds, A. 2010. Articulations of Place, Poverty, and Race: Dumping Grounds and Unseen Grounds in the Rural American Northwest. *Annals of the Association of American Geographers*, 100(3), 655–677.

Lin, A.C. and Harris, D.R. 2010. *The Colors of Poverty: Why Racial and Ethnic Disparities Exist*. Russell Sage Foundation Publications: New York.

Marx, K. 1956 [1847]. *The Poverty of Philosophy*. Lawrence & Wishart: Moscow.

Marx, K. 1973 [1857–1858]. *Grundrisse: Foundations of the Critique of Political Economy*. Trans. M. Nicolaus. Penguin: London.

Mawdsley, E. 2007. The Millennium Challenge Account: Neo-liberalism, Poverty and Security. *Review of International Political Economy*, 14(3), 487–509.

Medina, G., Pokorny, B. and Campbell, B.M. 2009. Community Forest Management for Timber Extraction in the Amazon Frontier. *International Forestry Review*, 11(3), 408–420.

Minang, P.A. and van Noordwijk, M. 2013. Design Challenges for Achieving Reduced Emissions from Deforestation and Forest Degradation through Conservation: Leveraging Multiple Paradigms at the Tropical Forest Margins. *Land Use Policy*, 31, 61–70.

Nebel, G., Quevedo, L., Bredahl Jacobsen, J. and Helles, F. 2005. Development and Economic Significance of Forest Certification: The Case of FSC in Bolivia. *Forest Policy and Economics*, 7(2), 175–186.

Pacheco, P. 2006. Agricultural Expansion and Deforestation in Lowland Bolivia: The Import Substitution versus the Structural Adjustment Model. *Land Use Policy*, 23, 205–225.

Peck, J. 2011. Global Policy Models, Globalizing Poverty Management: International Convergence or Fast-policy Integration? *Geography Compass*, 5(4), 165–181.

Peet, R. and Hartwick, E. 2009. *Theories of Development: Contentions, Arguments, Alternatives*. Guilford Press: New York and London.

PNUD (United Nations Development Programme). 2013. *Atlas do Desenvolvimento Humano no Brasil*. Programa das Nações Unidas para o Desenvolvimento/Instituto de Pesquisa Econômica Aplicada/Fundação João Pinheiro: Brasília.

Power, M. 2012. Angola 2025: The Future of the "World's Richest Poor Country" as Seen through a Chinese Rear-view Mirror. *Antipode*, 44(3), 993–1014.

Robertson, M. 2012. Measurement and Alienation: Making a World of Ecosystem Services. *Transactions of the Institute of British Geographers*, 37(3), 386–401.

Robinson, P. and Oppenheim, C. 1998. *Social Exclusion Indicators: A Submission to the Social Exclusion Unit*. Institute for Public Policy Research: London.

Santos, B.S. 2010. *Descolonizar el Saber, Reinventar el Poder*. Trilce: Montevideo.

Santos, B.S. 2014. *Epistemologies of the South: Justice against Epistemicide*. Paradigm Publishers: Boulder, CO and London.

Schmink, M. and Wood, C.H. 1992. *Contested Frontiers in Amazonia*. Columbia University Press: New York.

Shubin, S. 2010. Cultural Exclusion and Rural Poverty in Ireland and Russia. *Transactions of the Institute of British Geographers*, 35(4), 555–570.

Simmons, C.S., Walker, R.T., Arima, E.Y., Aldrich, S.P. and Caldas, M.M. 2007. The Amazon Land War in the South of Pará. *Annals of the Association of American Geographers*, 97(3), 567–592.

Souza, A.L. and Filippi, E.E. 2010. O Programa Amazônia Sustentável: Novas e Velhas Estratégias de Inserção Continental. *Amazônia – Ciência & Desenvolvimento*, 6, 191–210.

Steward, C. 2007. From Colonization to "Environmental Soy": A Case Study of Environmental and Socio-economic Valuation in the Amazon Soy Frontier. *Agriculture and Human Values*, 24, 107–122.

UNEP (United Nations Environment Programme). 2003. *Poverty and Ecosystems: A Conceptual Framework*, Twenty-second Session of the Governing Council/Global Ministerial Environment Forum. United Nations Environment Programme: Nairobi.

Vadez, V., Reyes-García, V., Huanca, T. and Leonard, W.R. 2008. Cash Cropping, Farm Technologies, and Deforestation: What are the Connections? A Model with Empirical Data from the Bolivian Amazon. *Human Organization*, 67(4), 384–396.

Vadjunec, J.M., Gomes, C.V.A. and Ludewigs, T. 2009. Land-use/Land-cover Change among Rubber Tappers in the Chico Mendes Extractive Reserve, Acre, Brazil. *Journal of Land Use Science*, 4(4), 249–274.

Van Hecken, G. and Bastiaensen, J. 2010. Payments for Ecosystem Services: Justified or Not? A Political View. *Environmental Science and Policy*, 13(8), 785–792.

Weinhold, D., Killick, E. and Reis, E.J. 2013. Soybeans, Poverty and Inequality in the Brazilian Amazon. *World Development*, 52, 132–143.

Worster, D. 1994. *Nature's Economy: A History of Ecological Ideas*. Cambridge University Press: Cambridge.

Yapa, L. 1993. What are Improved Seeds? An Epistemology of the Green Revolution. *Economic Geography*, 69(3), 254–273.

Yapa, L. 1996. What Causes Poverty?: A Postmodern View. *Annals of the Association of American Geographers*, 86(4), 707–728.

7 Conclusions

Fields of empty grains

We have reached the end of a journey through some of the main features and failures of contemporary agribusiness and its growing neoliberalisation. There should be no illusions that the topic has been exhausted. On the contrary, this book is just the beginning of a critical assessment of the intricate trajectory of agro-neoliberalism in Brazil and, in particular, the disputes in and around the apparatus of the national state. Due to the country's vast agricultural production and its sizeable influence on globalised markets, the Brazilian experience has major academic and socio-political implications beyond the country's borders. There is a lot more to investigate from a politico-ecological perspective in order to further grasp the complexity of an agriculture practised almost exclusively for the market (i.e. agriculture-cum-agribusiness) and the opportunities and constraints caused by neoliberalising strategies (in particular, novel financing mechanisms and more flexible patterns of capital accumulation and policy-making). One of the main motivations for this present analysis was the virtual absence of research on the wider contradictory features of neoliberalised agribusiness beyond agrarian and environmental issues. In that regard, the previous chapters already dealt with the politics of the transition to agro-neoliberalism, the fallacy of production gains on account of the continued importance of rents, the production of places and the widespread sense of misplacement, and the meanings of poverty and wealth in locations that are rapidly being brought into the sphere of influence of soybean-based agribusiness. This is only a small list of the multiple connections between the economic and technological dimensions of agro-neoliberalism and the associated impacts at household, farm and regional level.

A key conclusion of our investigation is that the achievements of neoliberalised agribusiness in areas like Mato Grosso are uneven, unstable and transient, and that they are offset by a legacy of socio-ecological degradation and a highly hierarchical social order fraught with injustices perpetrated against the region's original inhabitants as well as poor migrants who have moved to the Amazon since the 1970s. Another result is that these questions are normally dismissed in mainstream academic and non-academic texts because the neoliberalised agribusiness sector has captured the public imagination in Brazil with repeated claims of efficiency and success, reinforced by the euphoria of soaring trade balance surpluses and even predictions of another record production in 2017 (based primarily on monumental soybean harvests). In a period of great national difficulties due to several years of economic contraction, high unemployment and widespread debt, agribusiness often seems to be the only source of positive news. The salience of agribusiness is maximised by the specific historical and geographical circumstances in which neoliberalism unfolds in the country. The political system, dominated by parochial interests and the patrimonialist control of the state, has demonstrated a profound inability to respond to conflicting civil society demands and has failed to move the economy out of the long stalemate caused by disputes over the neoliberalising reforms themselves (such as policies based on astronomical interest rates, growing public deficits, fiscal concessions to corporations, oligopolistic banks and fraudulent utility privatisations), the need to maintain direct state investments, and some mitigatory measures such as the *Bolsa Família* conditional cash transfer scheme. Since 2014, with the end of the commodity boom and mounting public deficits, the national economy has been in serious disarray and some of the main sources of foreign currency exchange have buckled. In this challenging context, and thanks to the international demand for Brazilian agro-industrial goods, the agribusiness sector has shrewdly managed to reaffirm its image of modernity and efficiency, notwithstanding evidence of widespread negative socio-ecological impacts and limits to the maintenance of current rates of growth.

Despite the fact that most of the chemical, digital and mechanical technology used by agribusiness farmers is imported, and foreign companies control large shares of inputs and trade, the sector rejects any criticism and consistently claims great achievements on behalf of Brazilian society. The leaders of agribusiness in Brazil, including powerful organisations such as CNA, ABAG and FIESP, and their congressional representatives organised as the Parliamentary Farming and Cattle Raising Front (FPA), together with sympathetic academics, civil servants and the mainstream media, have managed to convince most of the general public that neoliberalised agribusiness is now the main locomotive of the economy and, regionally, the redeemer of the agricultural frontier opened in the Amazon and the Centre-West four decades ago. It is emblematic of the highly protective barriers placed around agribusiness that the sector successfully rebuffed, in a highly coordinated fashion, even oblique references to the degradation of indigenous lands in a song written by the Imperatriz Leopoldinense samba school for the 2017 carnival of Rio de Janeiro. It is astonishing that although the lyrics of the song make no direct reference to agribusiness or farmers, just mentioning the forests of Xingu, one of the main indigenous reserves in the country, was enough to provoke a stream of fierce protest and condemnation. The outrage felt on the sector's behalf contrasts with the crude reality of continuous environmental degradation, particularly in the north of Mato Grosso and around the Xingu park; remote sensing data released in 2016 showed that, despite claims that agribusiness growth in Mato Grosso and other states is now 'decoupled' from deforestation, *cerrado* (savannah) and forest ecosystems continue to be destroyed, both legally and illegally (Folha de São Paulo, 2017).

The acclaimed triumph of neoliberalised agribusiness in Brazil hides a systematic attempt to conceal structural risks and uncertainties. One main vulnerability which obviously threatens the prospects and profitability of export-oriented agribusiness is market volatility due to exchange rate fluctuation and the vagaries of Asian and international sales; this has been aggravated in recent years by growing production costs due to the expanding use of agrochemicals, land speculation, higher interest rates and transportation deficiencies. Furthermore, it is worth noting that the apparent success of Brazilian agribusiness is a direct consequence of monumental mistakes made in other sectoral policies by national and state governments. This is particularly exemplified by the industrial sector, which has declined significantly due to neoliberalising policies and lost most of the prominence accrued since the 1930s. This sector of the national economy traditionally depended on substantial state support, which was eroded by the advance of neoliberalism, and now struggles to compete with Chinese imports; in recent years, its overall participation in the economy has returned to the levels of the 1950s (Ioris and Ioris, 2013). Those controversial trends were examined in the first chapters of the book, and analysis then concentrated on the emblematic situation of Mato Grosso, considering the disturbing paradox of escalating agricultural production but less food. Although the agribusiness sector celebrates growing commodity production and agroindustrial exports, particularly soybean and processed meat, the country continues to rely on imports for some of the most basic ingredients of the Brazilian daily diet, such as wheat, rice, maize and beans. One of the main reasons for this discrepancy is the fact that a large proportion of the staple food produced in Brazil comes from small-scale family farming, which is not by any means a policy priority.[1]

It is evident that the influence of large-scale farmers has always been decisive in the national political game (we can make reference to the power of coffee, rubber and cocoa 'barons' in the first century of Brazilian history), but during the governments of Lula and Dilma (2003–2016), particularly after 2006, there were signs of a spurious and largely unexpected convergence between the agribusiness sector and national-developmentalist politicians, an alliance that was allegedly needed to secure a congressional majority for advancing the government's legislative and regulatory agendas. In practice, the neoliberalisation of agribusiness was intentionally associated with the reassertion of populist agendas. This constitutes yet another curious paradox of the hegemony of agribusiness in Brazil, that is, the highly neoliberalised sector, under growing influence of financialisation, globalisation and transnational corporations, has flourished even more under the support, and through the vulnerabilities, of leftist presidents. At the same time, because of its macroeconomic influence, the expansion of neoliberalised agribusiness to new production areas such as Mato Grosso has revived the expansionist and speculative plans of the military governments (1964–1985) and reasserted some of the more violent features of Brazil's colonial past, such as slavery-like labour relations, massive socio-ecological degradation, new rounds of primitive accumulation and intense attacks on the land of the remaining indigenous tribes. It is on the frontiers of the advance of agro-neoliberalism that this peculiar conflict of interests and these clashes of rights can be more heuristically appreciated. As already mentioned above, Busch (2014) rightly declares that neoliberalism is mythical, as it is ultimately based on myths about state and market, even though its power and disruptive impacts are real.

The material and symbolic complexity of agro-neoliberalism provides fertile ground for further academic work, but this will require from the scientific community the capacity to creatively connect the abstract face of neoliberalism with the concrete and lived reality of rural and regional changes. Nonetheless, supporters and detractors alike have probably exaggerated the distinctiveness of neoliberalised agriculture, paying too much attention to certain specific features while disregarding the wider economic history of capitalism and the political alliances between those advocating agro-neoliberalism and other capitalists and landowners who have prospered since pre-neoliberal periods. The advance of neoliberalised agribusiness in Brazil is essentially the embodiment of both the most progressive and the most regressive elements of capitalism in the country's history. This hybrid situation represents clear evidence of the perennial and always partial process of modernisation, as if the spectre of the new (to paraphrase Marx) needed the help of what is already obsolete to function. The obsolete is an integral part of neoliberal modernity, which is constantly re-creating the world according to its own values. When confronting political resistance from other sectors, agribusiness players most often react with a pre-established rhetoric of heroism and entrepreneurialism, although this mostly serves the goals of transnational corporations and national politicians rather than the farmers themselves.

What has happened in Brazil over the last two decades helps to demonstrate that agro-neoliberalism is not merely an economic phenomenon or even the superimposition of economic agendas on to other sectors of social and political life. The main dimension of agro-neoliberalism is certainly economic, given that it is fundamentally an attempt to revitalise the economy and create new opportunities for socio-ecological exploitation and capital accumulation; moreover, agro-neoliberalised production has major interdependencies and synergies with the reform of the state apparatus, with social interactions and disputes across different scales, and with the affirmation of certain technological, ethical and political practices. Agro-neoliberalism is a multidimensional process that has reiterated and expanded the economic, social and cultural basis of capitalist agriculture (agriculture-cum-agribusiness) according to a market-centred rationality. The main promoter of market-based alternatives has been the state itself, which has happened through the reconfiguration of its strategic and pragmatic connections with private business, landowners and their political representatives. In this process, producers, consumers, traders and civil servants have increasingly accepted, and helped to reinforce, the alleged advantages of agro-neoliberal reasoning, even when the negative impacts of market forces have caused great distress (as in the case of drastic price oscillations, spurious trade barriers or unfair competition). For example, in 2005, when a sudden drop in the international price of soybean coincided with a significant expansion in the production area in Mato Grosso, the reaction of the farming community was initially to plead for

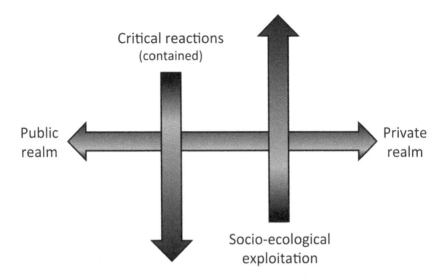

Figure 7.1 Conceptual framework of agro-neoliberalism
Source: Author

special government support (the postponement of debts, extraordinary funding schemes, etc.), and then to reassert the same trend of financialisation, alliances with TNCs and wider insertion into global markets.

In order to navigate these local, national and international intricacies, a schematic conceptual framework was introduced in Chapter 2, which identified the three main features of agro-neoliberalism – that is, renewed public–private alliances, novel techno-economic strategies that intensify socio-ecological exploitation, and the containment of critical reactions. The association between these three main driving-forces is represented in Figure 7.1.

The asymmetries and uncertainties of the neoliberalised Brazilian agri-food sector are directly and indirectly related to the instabilities of the contemporary economy, characterised by global speculation, major geographical inequalities, renewed forms of exploitation and wasteful patterns of production and consumption. Never before has so much food been produced and so much land been used for farming, but while a significant proportion of the global population struggles to maintain minimum levels of nutrition, a comparable percentage suffer from the consequences of obesity and record amounts of foodstuffs are wasted each day (Heasman and Lang, 2004). Still, food and agriculture problems can often go unnoticed in a world dominated by many other concerns and, more importantly, due to the false sense of food security offered by intensive technologies and extensive global trade. Particularly in the Global North and among high-income groups in the Global South, food is easily affordable and even taken for granted, despite the fact that food supply depends on the effective functioning of a highly vulnerable distribution network controlled by a small number of transnational companies and supermarket chains. Although local food production remains an important segment of agriculture in the Global South (particularly practised by family farming and peasant communities), there has been a displacement of traditional crops by high-price fruits, vegetables and agro-industrial products. Southern countries have likewise expanded the export of luxury, niche products to northern markets (e.g. out-of-season or exotic fruits and vegetables), as well as the cultivation of biofuel under the influence of northern environmental agendas, at the expense of staple food and undermining individual and collective rights.

It is thus possible to conclude that neoliberalised agribusiness not only encapsulates the old and new contradictions of capitalist agriculture, but that it is also characterised by structural and systemic *corruption*. This has many implications, some more evident and others less apparent. As is well known, the recent history of Brazilian politics has been greatly tainted by appalling corruption scandals involving contractors, construction companies and senior politicians. These include the crimes now being investigated by Operation Car Wash [*Operação Lava Jato*],[2] as well as others related to the hosting of the 2014 World Cup Football and the 2016 Olympic Games, and many other shocking cases of public money mismanagement. National corruption has been mirrored in numerous scandals implicating the political elites of Mato Grosso, which even led to the imprisonment of the previous governor Silval Barbosa and other prominent individuals in 2015. In recent years, it has become quite common to see articles in the national newspapers implicating the grandees of Mato Grosso politics and their close advisers. For instance, it was reported that in January 2017 a judge ordered the removal of a member of Mato Grosso's Audit Office (TCE), Sérgio Ricardo de Almeida, who was accused of paying R$4 million (around US$1.5 million) to obtain his seat; the same judge ruled that Blairo Maggi, the Minister of Agriculture, and several other key politicians and public authorities were also involved, and determined the terms of their arrest. At the time of our fieldwork in 2014, Maggi was under criminal investigation by the federal police, suspected of having used illegal sources to fund his senate election campaign in 2010. Travelling around Mato Grosso, it is never difficult to collect a long list of appalling stories, which almost always end with no one being convicted, or even prosecuted, for any crime. One of the most worrying of those cases was the collapse of the cooperative of Lucas do Rio Verde (Cooperlucas), reported by the Public Prosecutor's Office [*Ministério Público*] in 2007, in which more than R$200 million (US$110 million) disappeared, with the direct involvement of the city's mayor and its richest farmer, Otaviano Pivetta, among several others.

Corruption scandals like these certainly help to sell newspapers and attract large media audiences (especially given that arrests, court decisions and details of the lives of corrupt personalities and dishonest civil servants are increasingly covered live on television and radio), as well as provoking public debate and forcing political leaders to introduce better control systems. However, considering the continuous stream of cases and the growing sums involved, it is difficult to foresee any significant improvement in the near future in the handling of public assets or the pattern of state interactions with contactors. The main consequence of extensive media attention is not the containment of corruption, but rather its banalisation. As Lazar (2005: 212) puts it, corruption is everywhere and nowhere, 'it is always somewhere else perpetrated by someone else'. More importantly, the frequent scandals involving public authorities using their positions of power as a means to steal money, particularly in agricultural frontier areas like Mato Grosso, are facilitated by, and help to maintain, the highly unequal society typical of areas dominated by agribusiness. The rapid and overwhelming success of agribusiness has led to significant pressures on the state apparatus and on mechanisms of environmental, fiscal and labour control. The economic and social relevance of the sector acts as a catalyst for repeated requests for state favours and an agri-business-friendly rule of law. In this crucial sense, neoliberalised agribusiness is ultimately corrupt, first and foremost because it derives from, but also helps to reinstate, conservative elites and class-based hegemony. Corruption should be seen as more than simply the mishandling of public assets and the taking of bribes in exchange for state favours; the most important form of corruption is the misappropriation of collective resources and socioeconomic opportunities that eventually results in the marginalisation of most of the population from the potential benefits of development.

The difficulty in perceiving the widespread and ingrained corruption that characterises and fosters agro-neoliberalism is largely due to the corruption of corruption theory. The existing literature on corruption is largely unable to explain the more systemic and multilayered substance of corruption. For many centuries, political thinkers have grappled with the problem, from Aristotle, Polybius and Machiavelli to British, French and American authors in the 18th and 19th centuries; there is a long tradition of discussing the basis and repercussions of corruption habits. Nonetheless, although this is a word that has existed for more than 600 years in the English language (having been incorporated from the French in 1340, according to the *Oxford English Dictionary*), it is only in the last twenty years, under market globalisation, that the international development community has begun to consider corruption a major threat to economic stability and business transactions. Since the early 1990s, with the end of the Cold War and the expansion of global trade, key national governments and multilateral agencies have introduced detailed mechanisms to identify and contain corruption. Curiously, until a few decades ago, corruption was even seen as a positive factor (or a necessary evil) that could speed up economic growth in situations where the rule of law was uncertain and major institutional barriers were in place (e.g. Huntington, 1968). This sort of reasoning was prevalent during the opening of the new agricultural frontier in the Amazon, and particularly in Mato Grosso, when corruption was considered an integral part of attracting new farmers and companies to the region. Corruption was not normally perceived as a destructive influence, but rather as a productive driving force, at least from the perspective of those in power who were benefiting from it, either directly or indirectly, and those with other hidden agendas. This tolerant attitude changed significantly as international organisations gradually converged around an 'anti-corruption consensus' which closely followed the liberal-rationalist approach and public choice theory (Gephart 2009). Klitgaard (1988) went as far as to introduce an algebraic formula that synthesises rationalist thinking around the issue: 'corruption equals monopoly plus discretion minus accountability'.

Things evolved in more recent decades with the perception that corruption was basically undermining the prospects of market operations and the legitimacy of neoliberal agendas. Corruption has now come to be seen by powerful organisations and national governments alike as evidence of macroeconomic malfunctioning, and is commonly linked to protectionism and the hyper-trophy of the state. According to the neoliberal canon, the source of corruption is the excessive sensitivities, inefficiencies and vulnerabilities of the state. The state is typically defined as a managerial organisation whose main weakness is its responsivity to political pressures, as if it were possible to have a complete separation between public and private categories (Bratsis, 2003). The contemporary anti-corruption discourse is increasingly associated with the supposed failures of conventional government practices – that is, too much power concentrated in the hands of unscrupulous officers together with a lack of transparency and the concealment of rent-seeking behaviours. For instance, for the World Bank (2007) the reduction of corruption has a disciplinary function, informed by moralist rationale aimed at promoting accountability and fiscal discipline. More than a criminal or ethical question, graft and bribery are condemned because they represent an obstacle to development and, in particular, to the mobilisation of natural resources (Kolstad and Wiig, 2009). The crux of the matter, according to those calling for market freedom and globalised transactions, is the negative impact of corruption on investments and on the interests of transnational corporations and business sectors. It was not a coincidence that in 2003 the United Nations formalised its Convention against Corruption (known as the Mérida Convention) in an effort to contain the alleged far-reaching impacts of corruption on democracy, economic development and the rule of law.

Probably the most representative player in this narrow anti-corruption crusade has been the NGO Transparency International (with operational and ideological associations with the World Bank), which has campaigned for institutional reforms in southern countries to curb corruption practices and facilitate business transactions. Corruption indicators, such as the annual corruption perceptions index (CPI) produced by Transparency International, have been highly influential in this debate. However, technocratic measurements like this typically relegate the countries perceived as being most corrupt to a position of discrimination and force them to adopt drastic reforms that are in practice untenable (Andersson and Heywood, 2009). Such rationalist and neo-colonialist treatment of corruption has been criticised as an adjunct of the expansion of neoliberal platforms and the promotion of market globalisation. The conventional discourse normally conceals the promiscuous association between neoliberalism and neopopulism that happens through often contradictory forces that guide individuals to misuse their power (Weyland, 1998). More importantly, mainstream authors and organisations have deliberately ignored the fact that the recent dismantling of previous developmental structures and the endorsement of the minimal state model may actually have stimulated corrupt behaviours (Murphy, 2011). Brown and Cloke (2011) denounce the simplistic scapegoating of the public sector as the source of corruption, which constitutes an ideological distortion of the nature and role of the state apparatus whereby the blame is systematically placed on unscrupulous politicians (the bribe-takers), without sufficient focus on the interference of national and international enterprises (the bribe-givers). These authors further observe that mainstream interpretations of corruption serve as a convenient excuse for the failure of recent pro-market economic reforms and the connivance of northern governments.

Critical scholars have likewise denounced the depoliticisation and decontextualisation of corruption through simplistic calls for efficiency, business accountability and technocratic improvements. Instead of recognising corruption as a social construct, a value-ridden concept that has cultural, historical and geographical specificities, it has been repeatedly described as a generalised problem with the same characteristics anywhere in the developing world, 'from Nigeria to Bulgaria' (Ivanov, 2007). Such a flat ontology of corruption, as if the problem had the same universal features regardless of the local context, reduces potential solutions to adjustments in the legislation and public sector procedures that would favour, primarily, wider business interests. Another related distortion is the supposed manifest distinction between the ethical behaviour of businesspeople in northern and southern countries. Regions like Britain and Scandinavia are too easily portrayed as role models for honesty and good governance, while the presence of corruption in the Global South is alleged to be endemic and a serious internal factor contributing to the erosion of democracy and justice (Bukovansky, 2006). It is lost in translation here that corruption in developing countries is also boosted and reproduced by the continuation of illegitimate wealth and hegemonic power in other parts of the world. As much as markets and information flows are globalised, so is corruption. In other words, the presumed low levels of corruption in Scandinavia or in the United Kingdom can only be sustained – even at rhetorical and symbolical levels – by persistent high levels of corruption in Africa, Asia and Latin America. As pointed out by Hardt and Negri (2000: 389), 'corruption is everywhere' because it is a general process of decomposition and mutation that 'is the cornerstone and keystone of domination'.

Moralist campaigns launched by policy-makers and conservative academics weaken the meaning of corruption and, as a result, occlude related demands for citizenship, social inclusion and fair public policies that depend on global interactions. The main goal of the prevailing anti-corruption crusade is to remove commercial excesses and safeguard business profitability, rather than considering the fact that corruption emanates from processes of gains and privileges located in wider social relations (Bracking, 2007). There is a case, therefore, for a more comprehensive epistemology, able to embrace the multiple sources and perennial reinforcement of corruption at local, national and international levels through the advance of agro-neoliberalism. More important than static definitions of corruption is to try to understand what the concept means in practice, what it does to disadvantaged and marginalised people (Bracking, 2009). This entails a radically different conceptualisation of corruption, not as a mere deformation of public services and policies, but as the institutionalisation of mechanisms of exclusion and concentration of socio-political and economic opportunities (Ioris, 2015). The corrupted basis of agro-neoliberalism needs to be considered as a historico-geographical phenomenon with contemporary manifestations and manifold causes. Instead of narrow interpretations that primarily serve business interests, corruption must be treated as a deeply politicised and intrinsically socio-ecological phenomenon that occurs under specific circumstances and aggravates existing patterns of inequality and exclusion. The most decisive aspect of the corruption associated with agro-neoliberalism is that it reflects the more fundamental, and intrinsic, corruption of capitalism. As Murphy (2011: 127) rightly emphasises, there is an organic relationship between corruption and capitalism, insofar as 'capitalism itself is the pathogen for corruption'.

The experience and consequences of corruption are certainly not the same in different locations and historical periods, but what is universal and pervasive is the corrupting influence of capitalist relations of production and reproduction. Capitalism has corrupted agriculture (essentially, due to production for exchange, the double exploitation of labour and nature, and the drive for growth) and the advance of agro-neoliberal rationality has represented a renovation and intensification of long-term corrupting trends (including intensive production not to feed the world but to supply globalised markets, the incorporation of risky technologies that magnify socio-ecological impacts, the grabbing and concentration of land and territorial resources, and the financial dependency of farmers and the financialisaton of agriculture). The easy escalation of corrupted agro-neoliberalism benefits from pre-existing socioeconomic inequalities inherited from earlier developmentalist, Keynesian models of agriculture, but agro-neoliberalism itself now contributes to the reinforcement of corruption in other areas of social and economic activity. Even when corruption seems to disappear, it flourishes and persists in the social tissue of highly unequal societies, only to resurface in an intense fashion when politico-institutional circumstances are more favourable. In the case of Mato Grosso, a critical examination of the metabolism of corruption needs to comprehensively address political manipulation and ideological claims as some of the most prominent features of the advance of neoliberalised agribusiness. Corruption remains an active driving force and represents a robust, intergenerational social institution that helps to explain the perverse geography of agribusiness in Mato Grosso and elsewhere in Brazil. There is a fundamental paradox here, which needs to be properly examined: the increasing interest in tackling corruption is justified as an important requirement for promoting market interactions and, essentially, securing the success of agro-neoliberalising strategies; however, the more corruption is confronted supposedly to benefit agro-neoliberalism, the higher the level of corruption becomes (because agro-neoliberalism is itself inherently corrupt).

The powerful and comprehensive influence of the corruption intrinsic to agro-neoliberalism derives from the dialectical relationship between its *synchronic* and *diachronic* constituting factors. Corruption, as a social relation that reflects group and class inequalities, is kept alive through these very inequalities over long periods of time (this is its diachronic dimension), but proliferates synergistically across different sectors and activities whenever the mechanisms of control are weak (its synchronic dimension). Synchronic corruption is the immediate manifestation of the more persistent course of diachronic corruption. While synchronic corruption is localised in certain places, sectors or moments, diachronic corruption incorporates the legacy of past injustices and replicates them in present and future socionatural formations. Every new scandal involving public authorities in another manoeuvre to make money and maintain political alliances (the synchronic element of corruption) is also nurtured by the lasting authoritarianism of the state and persistent socioeconomic exclusion (the diachronic element of corruption). The synchronicity of corruption comprises the appropriation of public resources, manipulation of government decisions and court judgements, and attacks on the free press and independent forms of public and labour organisation. Diachronic corruption, in turn, has its basis in the maintenance of historically given relations of production, allocation and reproduction. The agribusiness sector in Brazil makes use of the appealing symbolism of triumph and modernisation to unify the interests of rural conservative groups and renovate processes of political hegemony and class domination. There is an easy discourse of food security and the need to offer customers food choices, which is employed to justify the adoption of production technologies that exploit labour and use pesticides, machinery, digital technology and genetically modified organisms in order to maximise profits for transnational corporations. Kaká Wará Jecupé, an indigenous leader and politician, convincingly argued on the TV programme *Roda Viva* (9 January 2017) that agribusiness is basically the continuation of violent socioeconomic relations introduced in Brazil in the 16th century, based on latifundia, slavery and the exploitation of nature, and constituting a sustained offensive against thousands of years of indigenous culture.

Both the synchronic and diachronic constituting factors are significant aspects of corruption as a whole and have been dynamic influences in the transformation of Brazil into an international leader of neoliberalised agribusiness (see Table 7.1). The interconnections between synchronic and diachronic corruption provide a better explanatory tool than the more common, but static, concept of 'systematic corruption' (e.g. Johnston, 1998). The theory around 'systematic corruption' typically fails to consider the important roots of corruption in national development and socio-political inequalities, focusing mainly on the spread of corruption into different areas of public administration. In contrast, the mutual reinforcement between the diachronic and synchronic dimensions reveals corruption to be a resilient and multifaceted problem. Because of its synchronic and diachronic dimensions, corruption is both a highly contextual but also a generalisable phenomenon. As a result, more relevant than trying to assess whether corruption is increasing or decreasing is a careful consideration of its

Table 7.1 Synchronic and diachronic corruption of neoliberalised agribusiness

Type of corruption	Evidence	Consequences
Synchronic corruption	Appropriation of resources and socioeconomic opportunities according to class-based relations and the balance of power; double exploitation of society and the rest of nature; manipulation of public policies and court judgements; mishandling of public funds.	Mounting socio-ecological impacts; food scarcity and farmer vulnerability; financialisation of agriculture; prejudiced privatisation of state assets and manipulated concession of public services.
Diachronic corruption	Territorial expansion based on widespread and systematic violence; displacement and privatisation of the commons; naturalisation of latifundia and commercial agriculture at the expense of subsistence and non-commercial agriculture; patrimonialism and class struggle; ideological separation between society and the rest of nature.	Land and resource grabbing; elite control of the state apparatus; social exclusion, racism and democratic deficit; agriculture production for the market rather than for nourishment; subordination of capitalist agriculture to the priorities of industrial and financial capital.

diachronic and synchronic manifestations and what these mean for the legitimisation or transformation of socioeconomic relations. Certainly, a major consequence of the corruption underpinning agribusiness in Brazil is that the sector has virtually 'hijacked' the country's economic present and future. It is claimed that Western democracy depends on carbon-based dictatorships and violence perpetrated against non-Western societies (Mitchell, 2011); similarly, Brazilian macroeconomic stability and formal democracy can be said to depend on soybean: Brazil is now, to a large extent, a 'soybean democracy'.

This reflection on the lived experience of corruption is a good illustration of the mismatch between the narrow, technocratic comprehension of corruption by national and international agencies, and the deeper social and political repercussions of the same practices. Corruption is a social relation at the interface between different scales of interaction (the sectoral, local, national and international scales) and between long-term tendencies and contemporary developments. This means that the metabolism of corruption involves spatial and temporal synergies that operate in synchronic and diachronic directions. The controversies about agribusiness encapsulate all the elements of the wider debate about the future of the public sector and the extent to which corruption is a problem with different epistemological bases and conflicting repercussions. The sector has always been a favourite locus of populism and provided an easy justification for large projects (when public funds or loans are available), which represents the diachronic pattern of corruption. Yet, rather than being a purely criminal or ethical issue, the activity of those promoting or benefiting from corruption represents a creative force for neoliberal interests and the organisation of new accumulation strategies. In recent years, agribusiness has become the locus of massive investments and spurious transactions, which have been associated from criminal activities, and large-scale projects synchronically promoted by the national government. Multiple strategies were needed to justify and implement these projects, including the manipulation of public involvement. In the end, the effort to interpret and fight the corruption ingrained in agro-neoliberalism is only one aspect of the much wider struggle to democratise the state and produce a more inclusive and egalitarian society.

Overall, overcoming the risks, inequalities and tensions of neoliberalised agribusiness means overcoming the ingrained corruption of the intense, but anti-food, type of agriculture currently being promoted in Brazil and in Mato Grosso, initially based on direct state financing and now increasingly controlled by powerful national and international business groups. One of the clearest indicators of growing inequalities is the crucial role played by agribusiness in the national trade balance, while this has also meant the declining importance of food and nourishment concerns in favour of more explicit business and elitist goals. Despite the rhetoric of food security, agribusiness is primarily about business itself and increasingly less about rural development or agri-food production, let alone questions of justice, ecological conservation and democratic rule of the state. The national state has enabled the mobilisation of agricultural resources, not for the purpose of domestic food security, but primarily for capital accumulation in transnational networks. All these factors work together to maintain a tendency towards food shortage and the eruption of agrarian- and agriculture-related protests. The trajectory of agriculture modernisation in Mato Grosso makes clear that agro-neoliberalism is especially prominent at the agriculture frontiers of Brazil because, ultimately, it is in itself an economic, ecological and ethical frontier, a disputed space where experimentation is not only possible but encouraged, even experimentation that combines elements of the hyper-modern with elements of ancient environmental history. Martins (1996), who has studied in great detail the advance of capitalist modernity in Mato Grosso and the Amazon, rightly identifies the socioeconomic and cultural frontier as the space and the time of diversity, alterity, encounter and conflict. Martins also affirms that the frontier ceases to exist when conflict disappears, when the temporality of different groups come together to form a type of collective identity.

According to this description, Mato Grosso remains an active and real-life frontier. For some other authors, the hyper-modern areas of soybean cultivation in the state are now a consolidated frontier or even a post-frontier reality, basically because of the apparent unity behind the progress and the prosperity offered by soybean-based agribusiness. However, this deceptive claim about a consolidated spatial orders cannot hide the fact that Mato Grosso remains a dramatic agricultural frontier both because the results of agribusiness are limited and transitory, and because the range of conflicts and contradictions have not ceased to increase.

These tensions continue to expand not only at the local and regional level, but are reproduced at the national and global levels. More importantly, the materiality and symbolism of the frontier persists because agribusiness demands the perennial subjugation of socionatural relations and the suppression of difference. Neoliberalised agribusiness is only the most recent expression of the dynamic and cruel frontier of Brazil's hierarchical and unequal society, offering an illusory image of prosperity and social inclusion, while in effect bringing back the worst elements of the recent and distant past built on genocide, destruction, painful social reordering and, ultimately, corruption. This means that in order to overcome the failures and impacts of agro-neoliberalism, other frontiers will have to be sought and constructed from the bottom up. One sensible option would be family-based agriculture, where rent is jointly extracted and fairly returned with no alienation of those who work the land (as indicated by Marx, 1981). Alternatives like this will have to emerge from hard work, learning from what works now, forging a transition that would require coexisting, at least for a time, with agribusiness (otherwise it would be an unrealistic proposition), but putting agriculture under the democratic control of the majority in society, producers and consumers. It will not be easy to get rid of neoliberalised agribusiness, but this book should serve to affirm that better types of agriculture are possible, viable and desirable.

Notes

1   For the general public there is a good deal of confusion, as the interests of large-scale and small-scale farmers are widely assumed to be practically the same; this misunderstanding is beneficial to the interests of agribusiness farmers, who use small-scale agriculture to legitimise their own demands.
2   Serious crimes have been exposed since 2014 by federal prosecutors and the federal police in the ongoing Operation Car Wash, which has dealt with an enormous illegal scheme involving the state-owned company Petrobras and several other branches of the government; the network of corruption seems to involve a significant proportion of national political leaders and was organised as a strategy to keep Lula's Workers' Party (PT) and its allies in power indefinitely. Month after month the scandal has continued to increase and it has, among other consequences, provided additional justification for the impeachment of President Dilma in 2016. Additional turbulence erupted in 2017 when the new president (Temer) was personally caught in an even greater corruption-related crisis.

References

Andersson, S. and Heywood, P.M. 2009. The Politics of Perception: Use and Abuse of Transparency International's Approach to Measuring Corruption. *Political Studies*, 57(4), 746–767.

Bracking, S. (ed.). 2007. *Corruption and Development: The Anti-corruption Campaigns.* Palgrave Macmillan: Houndmills.

Bracking, S. 2009. Political Economies of Corruption beyond Liberalism: An Interpretative View of Zimbabwe. *Singapore Journal of Tropical Geography*, 30(1), 35–51.

Bratsis, P. 2003. The Construction of Corruption, or Rules of Separation and Illusions of Purity in Bourgeois Societies. *Social Text 77*, 21(4), 9–33.

Brown, E. and Cloke, J. 2011. Critical Perspectives on Corruption: An Overview. *Critical Perspectives on International Business*, 7(2), 116–124.

Bukovansky, M. 2006. The Hollowness of Anti-corruption Discourse. *Review of International Political Economy*, 13(2), 181–209.

Busch, L. 2014. How Neoliberal Myths Endanger Democracy and Open New Avenues for Democratic Action. In: *The Neoliberal Regime in the Agri-food Sector: Crisis, Resilience, and Restructuring*, Wolf, S.A. and Bonanno, A. (eds). Routledge: New York, pp. 32–51.

Folha de São Paulo. 2017. Cadastro de Propriedades Rurais não Impede Desmate Ilegal na Amazônia. Available at: www1.folha.uol.com.br/ambiente/2017/01/1846064-cadastro-de-propriedades-rurais-nao-impede-desmate-ilegal-na-amazonia.shtml (published 2 January 2017).

Gephart, M. 2009. *Contextualizing Conceptions of Corruption: Challenges for the International Anti-corruption Campaign*. GIGA Working Papers no. 115. German Institute of Global and Area Studies: Hamburg.

Hardt, M. and Negri, A. 2000. *Empire*. Harvard University Press: Cambridge, MA.

Heasman, M. and Lang, T. 2004. *Food Wars: The Global Battle for Mouths, Minds and Markets*. Earthscan: London.

Huntington, S.P. 1968. *Political Order in Changing Societies*. Yale University Press: New Haven, CT.

Ioris, A.A.R. 2015. Latin America's Large-Scale Urban Challenges: Development Failures and Public Service Inequalities in Lima, Peru. *ACME: An International E-Journal for Critical Geographies*, 14(4), 1161–1186.

Ioris, R.R. and Ioris, A.A.R. 2013. Assessing Development and the Idea of Development in the 1950s in Brazil. *Brazilian Journal of Political Economy*, 33(3), 411–416.

Ivanov, K. 2007. The Limits of a Global Campaign against Corruption. In: *Corruption and Development: The Anti-corruption Campaigns*, Bracking, S. (ed.). Palgrave Macmillan: Basingstoke, pp. 28–45.

Johnston, M. 1998. Fighting Systemic Corruption: Social Foundations for Institutional Reform. *European Journal of Development Research*, 10(1), 85–104.

Klitgaard, R. 1988. *Controlling Corruption*. University of California Press: Berkley and Los Angeles, CA.

Kolstad, I. and Wiig, A. 2009. Is Transparency the Key to Reducing Corruption in Resource-rich Countries? *World Development*, 37(3), 521–532.

Lazar, S. 2005. Citizens despite the State: Everyday Corruption and Local Politics in El Alto, Bolivia. In: *Corruption: Anthropological Perspectives*, Haller, D. and Shore, C. (eds). Pluto Press: London, pp. 212–228.

Martins, J.S. 1996. O Tempo da Fronteira: Retorno à Controvérsia sobre o Tempo Histórico da Frente de Expansão e da Frente Pioneira. *Tempo Social*, 8(1), 25–70.

Marx, K. 1981 [1894]. *Capital: A Critique of Political Economy*. Vol. 3. Trans. D. Fernbach. Penguin: London.

Mitchell, T. 2011. *Carbon Democracy: Political Power in the Age of Oil*. Verso: London and New York.

Murphy, J. 2011. Capitalism and Transparency. *Critical Perspectives on International Business*, 7(2), 125–141.

Weyland, K. 1998. The Politics of Corruption in Latin America. *Journal of Democracy*, 9(2), 108 121.

World Bank. 2007. *Strengthening World Bank Group Engagement on Governance and Anticorruption*. World Bank: Washington, DC.

Index